PIETISM AND THE SACRAMENTS

 PIETIST, MORAVIAN, AND ANABAPTIST STUDIES

EDITOR

Craig D. Atwood
Director of the Center for Moravian Studies, Moravian Seminary

Volumes in the Pietist, Moravian, and Anabaptist Studies Series take multidisciplinary approaches to the history and theology of these groups and their religious and cultural influence around the globe. The series seeks to enrich the dynamic international study of post-Reformation Protestantism through original works of scholarship.

ADVISORY BOARD

Bill Leonard, *Wake Forest University*
Katherine Faull, *Bucknell University*
A. G. Roeber, *Penn State University*
Jonathan Strom, *Emory University*
Hermann Wellenreuther, *Georg-August-Universität Göttingen*
Rachel Wheeler, *Indiana University–Purdue University Indianapolis*

PETER JAMES YODER

PIETISM AND THE SACRAMENTS

The Life and Theology of August Hermann Francke

The Pennsylvania State University Press
University Park, Pennsylvania

Library of Congress Cataloging-in-Publication Data

Names: Yoder, Peter James, author.
Title: Pietism and the sacraments : the life and theology of August Hermann Francke / Peter James Yoder.
Other titles: Pietist, Moravian, and Anabaptist studies.
Description: University Park, Pennsylvania : The Pennsylvania State University Press, [2020] | Series: Pietist, Moravian, and Anabaptist studies series | Includes bibliographical references and index.
Summary: "Explores the religious life and religious thought of early modern German Lutheran August Hermann Francke from his theology of the sacraments. Provides insights into his conversion theology and the structure of his Pietist thought"—Provided by publisher.
Identifiers: LCCN 2020035754 | ISBN 9780271088006 (hardback)
Subjects: LCSH: Francke, August Hermann, 1663-1727. | Pietism—Germany—History—17th century. | Pietism—Germany—History—18th century. | Sacraments.
Classification: LCC BR1653.F7 Y63 2020 | DDC 264/.041—dc23
LC record available at https://lccn.loc.gov/2020035754

Copyright © 2021 The Pennsylvania State University
All rights reserved
Printed in the United States of America
Published by The Pennsylvania State University Press,
University Park, PA 16802–1003

The Pennsylvania State University Press is a member of the Association of University Presses.

It is the policy of The Pennsylvania State University Press to use acid-free paper. Publications on uncoated stock satisfy the minimum requirements of American National Standard for Information Sciences—Permanence of Paper for Printed Library Material, ANSI Z39.48–1992.

To Mary, Claire, and Eleanor

CONTENTS

Acknowledgments ix
Introduction 1

1 The Rise of a Pietist Pastor Theologian 11
2 Biblicism, Conversion, and Reform 36
3 From Ignorance to Oath 49
4 Baptism Grounded in Christ 71
5 The Baptismal Covenant and Rebirth 81
6 Confession 103
7 The Eucharist 118

Epilogue: The Church of the Heart 136
Notes 151
Bibliography 181
Index 199

ACKNOWLEDGMENTS

The research, writing, and revising of this work could not have been accomplished without the encouragement and help of many people. My initial interest in German Pietism came at the hands of the late Harold O. J. Brown, who introduced me to Francke and his institutes during our time in Europe. I am indebted to his wisdom and mentorship. I am also indebted to Ralph Keen, whose friendship and example as an educator have had a profound influence on me.

Several institutions and individuals were important during the research for this project. I am grateful to the Department of Religious Studies at the University of Iowa and especially Raymond Mentzer, who nudged me in the direction of Mainz. I am also grateful to the Leibniz-Institut für Europäische Geschichte (IEG), which supported my research through its doctoral fellowship program. Director of the Abteilung für Abendländische Religionsgeschichte, Irene Dingel, served as my adviser and offered invaluable insight as I worked through the dynamics of early modern German Lutheranism. I am also grateful to director Martin Mulsow at the Forschungszentrum Gotha der Universität Erfurt, where I was afforded the opportunity to complete important research in primary Pietist sources through the Herzog-Ernst-Stipendium der Fritz Thyssen Stiftung. Finally, I am extremely thankful for the help of Thomas Müller-Bahlke and Christian Soboth at the Franckeschen Stiftungen; their efforts allowed me to conduct essential archival research through a fellowship funded by the Fritz Thyssen Stiftung.

Three institutions offered me the opportunity to revise and refine the material in this book. My time as a postdoctoral fellow within Judith Becker's research group at the IEG allowed me the chance to continue wrestling with Francke's theology. I would like to thank those in the Department of Religion and Philosophy at Berry College, especially Jonathan Huggins, Michael Papazian, and Jeff Lidke, for their advice and encouragement. I am also grateful to Mark McDowell, executive director of Reformed Theological Seminary in Dallas, for affording me the opportunity to complete and make final revisions to the manuscript.

There are far too many individuals who played a role in the completion of this book to list here. But I want to especially thank the advice and friendships of Benjamin Marschke, Jonathan Strom, Dorothea Hornemann, Douglas Shantz, Paul Peucker, Calvin Lane, Jared Burkholder, and Elisabeth Orr. I am especially grateful for the patient prodding of series editor Craig Atwood and acquisitions editor Kathryn Yahner and the thorough copyediting done by Ellen Douglas. I am also indebted to Ben Rooke and the Boone Boys for their friendships and wisdom. Finally, "Danke, Francke." You have made this interesting.

While I hope this book remains a valuable contribution to the scholarly community, its worth pales in comparison to the love and grace I receive from my wife. Her prayers and constancy, and the joy of my children, have been a great source of strength, and I will never be able to repay them for their patience during this time.

ABBREVIATIONS

AFStH   Archiv der Franckeschen Stiftungen Halle, Hauptarchiv.
PuN   *Pietismus und Neuzeit: Ein Jahrbuch zur Geschichte des neueren Protestantismus*. Historische Kommission zur Erforschung des Pietismus. Göttingen: Vandenhoeck & Ruprecht, 1974–present.
TGP II.1   Francke, August Hermann. *Schriften und Predigten*. Vol. 1, *Streitschriften*. Edited by Christian Soboth. Texte zur Geschichte des Pietismus II.1. Berlin: Walter de Gruyter, 2018.
TGP II.4   Francke, August Hermann. *Schriften und Predigten*. Vol. 4, *Schriften zur Biblischen Hermeneutik I*. Edited by Erhard Peschke. Texte zur Geschichte des Pietismus II.4. Berlin: Walter de Gruyter, 2013.
TGP II.9   Francke, August Hermann. *Schriften und Predigten*. Vol. 9, *Predigten I*. Edited by Erhard Peschke. Texte zur Geschichte des Pietismus II.9. Berlin: Walter de Gruyter, 2012.
TGP II.10   Francke, August Hermann. *Schriften und Predigten*. Vol. 10, *Predigten II*. Edited by Erhard Peschke. Texte zur Geschichte des Pietismus II.10. Berlin: Walter de Gruyter, 2011.
Werke   Francke, August Hermann. *Werke in Auswahl*. Edited by Erhard Peschke. Berlin: Luther-Verlag, 1969.

INTRODUCTION

In the winter of 1914, as the "Christmas truce" was spreading among the soldiers along the Western Front, Eddi awoke in his German home to the smell of pine and incense and to the sight of a small pile of gifts stacked beside the family's Christmas tree. Tucked away among the wooden horses and toy soldiers was a book of three children's stories given to him by Frau Bufo. That evening, as he read his way through the tales of an adventurous missionary and a heroic slave emancipator, Eddi came to a small biography of the German Lutheran Pietist August Hermann Francke (1663–1727). The appearance of the biography may have come as a surprise to the boy. Francke had neither traveled to distant lands as a missionary nor risked his life freeing slaves, but the author reassured him that Francke's work was itself heroic, bringing "with it diverse and restorative fruit that reached into the furthest circles [of people]."[1] As Eddi leafed through the biography, he was told that almost 225 years earlier, in the waning winter of 1689, Francke entered the university city of Leipzig and began in earnest to seek the renewal of the Lutheran church. And much as in the previous stories in the book, Francke's efforts were initially met with derision and ridicule. Church leaders, the author claimed, bullied Francke and his followers with the newly coined pejorative name "Pietist."[2]

The biography of August Hermann Francke found in Eddi's collection of children's stories follows a tradition of ascribing the rise of Pietism as a religious reform movement to the challenges Francke encountered in Leipzig. This tradition has long been shown to offer too narrow an interpretation of Pietism, but the portrayal of Francke in the children's book serves as a reminder of his and his ministries' continued importance in defining German Lutheran Pietism in its blossomed form. The maturity that Francke brought to Pietism has led scholars to compare his work to that of Philipp Melanchthon and even the New Testament figure Saint Paul.[3] More accurately, Francke was at the center of what Ryoko Mori calls the "second wave" of German Pietism.[4] As we will see, his own ministry in Leipzig in the late 1680s began to embody and bring greater visibility and weight to Pietism, which represents one of the most important Protestant movements since the Reformation.[5]

This study recognizes Francke's importance to the history of Pietism and primarily attends to his sacramental theology as a springboard into understanding the contours of, and influences upon, his thought and life. The Protestant sacraments of baptism and the Eucharist, especially in the Lutheran tradition, provide interpretive ecclesiological categories by which we may make a historical-theological analysis of overarching dogmatic constructions and their specific development over space and time.[6] Preached and practiced in the midst of Sunday worship, the sacraments are what historian Robert Orsi calls "abundant events," heightened by religious expectations and dogmatic claims concerning divine promises.[7] Framed by the standards set forth in the Augsburg Confession (Articles 7–10), the Lutheran sacraments, as means of God's special grace "administered in conformity with the divine Word," implicitly communicate major themes of salvation.[8] As Francke articulated his views concerning baptism and the Lord's Supper, he inevitably addressed his core Pietist beliefs. Thus, this work offers a rich depiction of Francke's conversion-driven theology and how it shaped his views of the sacraments and the church.

By approaching Francke's thought from the theological perspective of the sacraments, we are also able to interpret, build upon, and extend the work of scholars like Erhard Peschke and more recently Markus Matthias, Veronika Albrecht-Birkner, and Udo Sträter, who have sought to shed light on Francke's social context and those who influenced his thought.[9] In the following, we will see that Francke's commitment to his conversion theology gave him an appreciation for controversial figures, such as the Rostock pastor Theophil Großgebauer (1627–1661), and led him to adopt Reformed-leaning theological language. Furthermore, this study interprets and extensively engages Francke's sermons and writings, breaking a relative silence in English-speaking research on the theology of Francke, who Erich Beyreuther claims offered one of "the most important and influential forms of genuine Pietism."[10]

"Ecclesiology," laments Hans Schneider, "has not been a favorite subject of research on Pietism."[11] Roland Lehmann's recent work on changing conceptions of the church in early Enlightenment thought touches on eighteenth-century Pietist formulations of church law and their relationship to the state, but there is still a relative dearth of scholarship available on Pietist ecclesiology.[12] By addressing Francke's theology of the sacraments, the following chapters not only contribute to a richer understanding of the nature of the church in his thought but also provide a case study for those who are seeking to paint a theological landscape of Lutheranism during a period in its history when some individuals and groups felt pressure to reinterpret traditional ecclesiological boundary markers.[13] In the life of the early modern church, the sacraments played a dual role in defining the boundaries of the faithful community and reorienting those communities in new theological directions.[14] Pietist figures like Francke, who relied more heavily on abstract concepts like religious conversion and rebirth to determine the identity of the Christian community, found themselves reaffirming the importance of the sacraments in the life of the church while at the same time reorienting the sacraments in a way that reflected their emphasis on a "church of the heart." In this way, a study of Francke's ecclesiology stretches James R. Gordon's claim that eighteenth-century sacramental theologies reflect an attempt to "engage" and "situate" the sacraments within modernity.[15] In Francke's sacramental theology, we find otherwise. It appears ecclesiological developments that moved in the direction of modernity were initially influenced in part by theological innovations concerning the identities of the believer and the church, which were consistently communicated in the sacraments.[16] Francke's theology of the sacraments offers a view into eighteenth-century ecclesiological developments that departed from the dogmas of the Reformation and aided and abetted the rise of evangelicalism and global Protestantism.

After Francke's conflicts in Leipzig, German Pietism became so synonymous with his activities and the "Francke Foundations" (*Franckeschen Stiftungen*)—a group of institutes or ministries originally known as the "Hallesche Waisenhaus" located just outside the city walls of Halle—that Francke functioned as both Pietism's advocate and its guardian.[17] As an advocate Francke reached out to English readers curious about Pietism during the first decade of the eighteenth century, providing an account of the founding of his institutes in a publication entitled *Pietas Hallensis*.[18] It was, among other things, Francke's attempt to offer a positive and lasting narrative of Pietism, and it quickly found a wider readership. In 1706 the Society for Promoting Christian Knowledge offered *Pietas Hallensis* to its transatlantic correspondents serving in the American colonies.[19] At other moments, we find Francke acting as guardian of the movement, attempting to, as Kelly Whitmer claims, "salvage" the name Pietist.[20] In 1714, he wrote a letter to Gottfried Wilhelm Leibniz (1646–1716), asking him to consider providing a positive word on behalf of the university in Halle so that, like the universities in Leipzig and Wittenberg, it might have access to students from eastern Europe. He assured Leibniz that "Pietism is nothing other than a name which dishonest men give to these times of the study of sacred Scriptures and true piety." These same men, Francke continues, frame Pietists as "incautious and credulous people." Francke claimed that the name Pietist arose in Leipzig, and though Leibniz may have had doubts about its associations in light of its polemical and pejorative origins, Francke reminded him of what he had seen with his own eyes during his visit to Francke's institutes. Francke insisted the students at the university were led "not only in good and solid scholarship, but also in all Christian humility and moderation."[21] They were trained to be good Pietists. Francke's desire to promote and defend Pietism at all levels of society reflects his hope that the reform movement would bring about a renewal of the individual, church, and community. In light of these renewal efforts by Francke and his "spiritual father" Philipp Jakob Spener (1635–1705), German Lutheran Pietism should be understood as having four defining characteristics: conventicles, personal Bible reading, rebirth, and chiliasm.[22]

Spener is often called the "father" or "founder" of Pietism. His most recognized work, *Pia Desideria*, which initially appeared in 1675 as an introduction to a collection of Johann Arndt's (1555–1621) sermons, was published separately later that year and quickly became the defining Pietist call to reform. Addressing the spiritual condition of the Lutheran three estates (household, church, and state), the *Pia Desideria* offers six suggestions that Spener hoped would bring renewal to a decadent church: (1) a "richer" use of Scripture in the daily lives of individuals, (2) the practice of the spiritual priesthood of all believers, (3) a renewed emphasis on the practice of Christianity, (4) a restraining from polemics within the church, (5) a reform of theological studies, and (6) a turn from verbose, theologically obtuse preaching toward a simpler form that emphasized faith and its fruits.[23] One of the key features of Spener's reform plan is its commitment to the belief that renewal, both lay and clerical, turned on the question of the nature of faith. Spener believed Lutherans who had placed importance on what Sträter describes as a "legalistic," hierarchical reform that begins with clerical renewal had missed the transformative power of true belief in the gospel, which would work from the ground up.[24]

While the *Pia Desideria* had broad public appeal, Spener's pastoral work in Frankfurt added an essential social element to the larger Pietist movement that reflected his ground-up concern for lay renewal. With the help of local lawyer Johann Jacob Schütz (1640–1690), who Andreas Deppermann argues was an "initiator and cofounder" of Pietism, Spener began holding conventicles, or private gatherings of like-minded believers, called *collegia pietatis*.[25] Conventicles constitute an important convergence in Pietism where Spener's central reform ideas were put into practice, forming what Mori calls "the most important basis of the activities of Pietists."[26] This *ecclesiola in ecclesia* ("church within the church") that formed in the context of private gatherings was to be a source of a broader reform of the household, the church, and the state—a reforming expectation that distinguished Pietism from earlier Lutheran reform plans.[27]

This is not to say that these Pietist conventicles arose purely out of Spener's innovative thought. As Frederick Herzog notes, "[Pietism] did not spring from German Lutheranism like Athena from the head of Zeus."[28] The early conventicles in Frankfurt also reflected the influence of French separatist pastor Jean de Labadie (1610–1674), whose writings Schütz and other members of Spener's conventicle had introduced.[29] Nevertheless, Wallmann rightly claims that Labadie brought something more like a "chime" than a "new melody" to Spener's efforts.[30] In his own ministry, Labadie was disposed toward separation from the institutionalized church, first from French Catholicism and then from the Dutch Reformed, due in part to the belief that introducing small group gatherings would recover what he thought was a purer, primitive church. Thus conventicles—which, Strom and Lehmann note, inherently "departed from traditional Reformation theology"—were often met with suspicion by the Lutheran church authorities.[31] Spener, mindful of this distrust, initially confined discussions in his Frankfurt conventicles to German and English devotional literature, which were common forms of edification in the Lutheran church at that time. Only as the meetings matured, did members begin to focus on interpreting specific biblical passages.[32] Despite Spener's cautiousness, Labadie's separatist influence upon Schütz and others of the Frankfurt conventicle proved too strong. Spener and Schütz eventually parted ways, the former embodying what has been labeled by some scholars as "confessional" or "churchly/ecclesial" Pietism and the latter becoming the father of "radical" Pietism.[33]

Personal Bible reading encouraged by Pietists inside and outside the context of conventicles reflected their desire to recover Luther's teaching on the priesthood of all believers. Strom and Lehmann remind us that the doctrine "disappeared almost entirely from Lutheran discourse in the later sixteenth century. A few radicals and reformers earlier in the seventeenth century suggested its revival, but Spener was the first major theologian to give it such renewed prominence."[34] Pietists like Spener wed individual, personal access to Scripture and its meaning to a common priestly access to the knowledge of God that came through faith in Christ. This "common priesthood" was bestowed on any believer, regardless of vocation, and could serve as a theological tool to dismantle ecclesiastical and social authority systems.[35] Sociological reasons for a recovery of the doctrine of the priesthood of all believers are many. The Thirty Years' War had left a trail of crises in its wake. Beyond the devastation of lives lost in the war, there were frustrations and fears associated with various economic hardships and environmental changes.[36] In one of his reform plans, Francke complained the "disorder" and "abuses" that arose from the Thirty Years' War were not appeased by the Peace of Westphalia; rather they continued to plague the German church of his day.[37] In an attempt to correct previous ecclesiastical failings, Pietism became, as Hans Schneider calls it, a "Bible movement" and enlisted laity as the priests of reform.[38]

These Pietist reformers have often been contrasted in historiography with what Francke often labeled a "decadent" church led by Lutheran Orthodoxy. Recent research has corrected this reading to show that seventeenth-century Lutheran Orthodoxy carried with it many of the reforming and devotional sensibilities of the Pietists.[39] However, Pietism went beyond common Orthodox reform ideas. Peter Schicketanz is correct in claiming Pietism grew up "in the lap of orthodoxy," but it quickly grew uncomfortable with its seat.[40] As will be seen in the case of Francke, Pietist innovations would rub against cultural and social norms. Some Pietists, meeting in small groups and affirming their place as "priests" and "children of God," would eventually call into question the accepted social hierarchy of their churches and towns. Others would find moments to challenge norms of public worship, and in doing so challenge religious practices that had shaped everyday life. The willingness of Pietists to push up against and stretch the expectations of social life can be explained in part by the influence of conventicles, personal Bible reading, and a retrieval of Luther's teaching on the priesthood of all believers, but according to Wallmann there were two other "new interests" that distinguished Pietists from their Lutheran Orthodox counterparts: rebirth and chiliasm.[41]

Johann Arndt, who should be understood as a primary Lutheran forerunner of German Pietism, provided what Strom and Lehmann call an "experiential piety" that was the melody of rebirth in the renewal movement, but we must keep in mind Pietists like Francke preached from a chorus of sources.[42] They claimed personal reading of Scripture as their primary source, and other sources, like Luther's "Preface" to the book of Romans, helped create the symphony of the doctrine of "new creation." Spener and those who followed him used Luther's "Preface" to connect the regeneration of the inner person to a new life expressed in acts of charity. To this they added themes of sanctification and experimentalism found in English devotional literature, which had been purged of Calvinistic doctrines contrary to Lutheran confessions and distributed widely in the church. In rebirth, Pietists found the perfect interplay between passivity before God and activity before the world.

New birth was so prominent in Pietist writings that Martin Schmidt claims it should be seen as the central theme and driving force of the movement.⁴³ Spener and Francke's concern for rebirth should not lead us to oversimplify Pietism and misuse Ted Campbell's phrase "religion of the heart."⁴⁴ Pietists wed to their teaching on rebirth the belief that the awakening of the laity was the key to ecclesiastical and social reform.⁴⁵

The final mark of Pietism, an eschatology labeled chiliasm, grew out of and embodied basic themes of the renewal movement, and as a theological expression, chiliasm was one of the clearest Pietist contradictions of traditional Lutheran teaching. Spener's "more moderate" chiliasm, claim Strom and Lehmann, "foresaw a future in which Christ promised an imminent better state for the church on earth."⁴⁶ In various degrees, Pietists believed the return of Christ and God's judgment of the world would not be as sudden as the Lutheran confessions had expressed. This delay in Christ's return was an eschatological hope for Pietists. Before the Parousia there would be a renewal within the church and an expansion of the gospel. Spener's language of "hope for better times" found in *Pia Desideria* would be manifested in communities of the "children of God," in the mass conversion of the Jews as interpreted from Romans 11, and in revivals (*Erweckungen*) and the global expansion of the "true" church.⁴⁷ The ministries of Francke's institutes were a concrete expression of the expectation that conversion, rebirth, and Christian faithfulness would produce a transformed society that preceded the return of Christ and consummation of creation.

August Hermann Francke, as a second-generation Pietist, not only embodied these four theological marks of Pietism, but he gave them what Carl Hinrichs calls an "active vigor" and popularized them to a broader Christian world.⁴⁸ As mentioned above, Pietism was a Bible movement, and in its confessional, Protestant character, scholars have also described it as a "preaching movement."⁴⁹ Susan Karant-Nunn observes, "In the pulpit, [early modern] clergymen, however learned they might be, were confronted with the faces of their lay charges, and in those faces their neighbor. It lay upon the clergy to communicate precisely, in simple yet unmistakable terms, what the godly person should believe and how he should behave."⁵⁰ This was true of Francke's pastoral ministry, and thus his theology should be seen as a theology from the pulpit. His fundamental mode of popularizing Pietism was through preaching, and the key to arriving at core, structural elements—not to mention innovations—of Francke's theology is primarily through his sermons.⁵¹ Francke did not set out in his lifetime to write any major systematic theological treatises and at moments complained that he lacked the time to properly address theological issues within the church.⁵² Consequently, Francke's theological "voice" is most clearly heard in his sermons. Given extemporaneously, his sermons come to us by way of his diligent students sitting at the front of the congregation copying his every preached word.[53] These sermons will be the primary sources from which we will construct Francke's theology, and to these sermons we will add his reform plans, writings on education and the pastorate, tracts and polemical writings, and correspondence. By engaging this breadth of Francke's writings we will be able to offer a historical-theological analysis of his theology that is not constrained by whether or not a sermon or letter made it to publication or by the confessional expectations often placed upon Francke's public life and language. In recognition of the centrality of sermons in Francke's theology, the following chapters are structured according to his own habit of preaching through Luther's Small Catechism.

Chapters 1 and 2 offer two avenues of introduction to Francke. Chapter 1 presents the rise of Francke to prominence as a Pietist. It follows him from childhood until his pastorate in Glaucha, where he established himself as a "pastor theologian." During his first years in Glaucha, and in those controversies surrounding his early ministry, we find Francke using the sacraments as tools to implement Pietist beliefs and practices in the life of his church. In the following chapter, we examine three important aspects of Francke's theological system (biblicism, conversion, and social reform). These three aspects form what should be understood as the core of his broader religious thought and will inform our further discussion of his theology.

The remaining chapters take the shape of early modern catechism sermons. Chapter 3 uses Francke's introductory sermon on the commonalities between the sacraments to provide a structured look at his teachings on spiritual ignorance, salvation, and the role of the sacraments as oaths in the Christian life. The sermon reveals the influence of English devotional literature on Francke's theology and his tendency to define the sacraments in terms of the human condition. The chapter also lays the groundwork for an examination of Francke's teachings on baptism and the Eucharist. Chapters 4 and 5 focus on Francke's baptismal theology, first by showing that in the midst of affirming traditional trinitarian and Christological baptismal formulations, he was willing to use the example of Christ's baptism to situate his baptismal teachings in the language of conversion and godly living. This is followed by an examination of how Francke's teaching on rebirth and baptism related to Lutheran teachings on the two sides of the baptismal covenant and how his views of baptismal rebirth reflected the influence of the controversial pastor Theophil Großgebauer. We will see that Francke walked a fine line in discussing rebirth in light of Lutheran teachings on baptismal regeneration.

Chapter 6 ushers us toward the Eucharist. In it we enter into a discussion of Francke's Pietist view of confessional practices at the end of the seventeenth century. In the midst of his attempts to reform confession, Francke critiqued the lack of "true" repentance in the communicant and the unfaithfulness in those clergy offering absolution. The improper confessional practices of parishioners and clergy undermined Francke's concern for a comfort that arises from the certainty of salvation. Chapter 7 focuses on Francke's language of individual worthiness in relation to the Lord's Supper. His recourse to various images to describe proper participation in the Eucharist offers us a platform to examine Francke's use of signs as proof of rebirth and the mystical language he adopted to describe worthy communicants.

The epilogue turns to Francke's conception of the believing community as the "church of the heart." Just as conversion and rebirth had so captivated his overarching religious thought that the sacraments were to be understood in light of them, so too the church's identity and its visible expression in worship were to reflect the centrality of being a "new creation." The conversion of individuals became the network, so to speak, which created the community of saints. Thus, the transformative religious experience that brought new life acted as the central identifier by which the church body was defined and upon which its functions were grounded. Reflecting upon Francke's view of the church, we come to see how his own theology of the sacraments provides a case study in the developing definition of the church, which in its various eighteenth-century expressions moved uncomfortably toward modernity.

By taking up August Hermann Francke's theology of the sacraments we are afforded a rich perspective into the contours of German Lutheran Pietism during a transatlantic period of influence in which Francke and other forefathers of evangelicalism, who held what W. R. Ward calls a "sense of international kinship," paved the way to the Awakenings, denominationalism, and modern Protestant theology.[54] Francke's own theology of the sacraments expresses his broader Pietist thought and, much like Jaroslav Pelikan's description of Luther, reveals "the link connecting the 'doctrine of the gospel' with the life of the Christian and of the church."[55] Luther recognized baptism and the Eucharist as, according to Robert Kolb, "the created, material means by which God gives the forgiveness of sins, life, and salvation," and this understanding remained true for Francke's confessional context.[56] Francke did not merely preach on how to reform the church. He sought ways to improve the spiritual condition of his own parishioners. As he created controversies for himself, barring some from the altar and exhorting others to bear "fruit" worthy of their calling, he also articulated a conversion theology that through his institutes would come to influence the Protestant church during a period when Christians encountered a variety of individualizing pressures. Therefore, the following study will grant insight into the relevance of Pietism in the transition from early modern to modern Christianity and help dispel previous notions that Pietism's subjectivism made it unconcerned with doctrine and learning.[57]

1

THE RISE OF A PIETIST PASTOR THEOLOGIAN

In November 1687, sitting at the dinner table of Lüneburg superintendent Heinrich Wilhelm Scharff (1653–1703), August Hermann Francke began reading the Greek New Testament in his hand. "We have a great treasure in that [Bible]," his friend Hermann von der Hardt (1660–1746) interrupted. Francke later claimed that von der Hardt's remark initially comforted him but that his own atheistic mindset immediately ripped the power of his friend's words right out of his heart. In Francke's own estimation, he was in a miserable state; he could not even attest to his own true faith. A few days later, on the Sunday after his tableside conversation with von der Hardt, Francke underwent a conversion experience, which he believed was the start of his true Christian life and laid the foundation for his Pietist motivations.[1] In the next five years Francke so energetically articulated and practiced his form of Pietism, and received such aggressive polemical outpourings against his work and thought, that the period became a turning point for him. The young man went from a virtually unknown instructor of biblical languages to a prominent theological voice in a budding Pietist movement. In this latter role, Francke embodied what Gerald Hiestand and Todd Wilson label the "pastor theologian."[2] Owen Strachan describes seventeenth-century Puritan pastor theologians contemporary to Francke as men whose "pastoral work was not an escape from theological work but the call to instantiate truth in the life of the church," and like these Puritans, it can also be said of Francke that he believed "theology cannot be anything but public."[3]

The public clash of ideologies in theological polemics gives rise to a heightened sense of the importance of ideas and their role in social formation, religious practice, and political structuring. Whether the conflict lasts a period of years, days, or hours, the justified (or justifier) codifies and frames his position against the "other," using a specific interpretation of history, one that declares the thought of his opponent as something so destructive that the well-being of an entire belief system hangs in the balance.[4] This fire-stoking nature of polemics provides a sense, though colored by the arguers and arguments themselves, of those ideas that give prominence to the event and actors in question, and it provides grounds for the overflow of literature that typically follows. Martin Luther's work between 1517 and 1521 falls into this paradigm. During this productive period Luther developed and defined key aspects of his theology in the midst of various forms of opposition.[5] The reformer's *Ninety-Five Theses* and his three treatises that appeared in 1520 express core themes of Luther's thought, and though these writings do not encompass the totality of his work, they do grant an entry point into a broader dialogue concerning his theology.[6] To understand what compelled Luther to later articulate his sacramental theology at the 1529 Marburg Colloquy, or to comprehend his critique of monastic vows, we return to this period when Luther faced tremendous opposition.

This is how the theology of Francke must be approached. We cannot properly appreciate his thought without recognizing the formative years of his life between 1687 and 1692, a span that includes his conversion experience and the ecclesiastical investigations of his theology. This period of heightened polemics against Francke's ministry forced him to move from Leipzig to Erfurt and finally to Halle. In the midst of these moves, Francke faced a number of accusations, all of which questioned the content of his theology and forced him and others to publicly defend his ministry. With Francke's 1692 installation as head pastor of St. Georgenkirche in Glaucha, he came under further scrutiny for how he applied his Pietist theological system to the regular sacramental practices of his congregation. The favorable judgment he received from the investigation that followed provided him the assurance that his Pietist program would go forward. Nevertheless, the five-year period of polemics that followed his conversion experience offers us insight into key developments in Francke's religious thought and the ways in which he applied his conversion theology to the practice of the sacraments.

Francke and Anti-Pietist Polemics: Leipzig Period (1684–1689)

Around Easter 1684 a young Francke arrived in Leipzig.[7] He had recently completed a two-month intensive study of the Hebrew language under Esdras Edzardus (1629–1708) in Hamburg, which was funded through a scholarship established by the Heinrich Schabbel (1569–1639) family in

Lübeck, and he hoped the move to Saxony would be a further step in his young academic career.[8] Upon his successful disputation over Hebrew grammar in 1685, the university awarded Francke the title "magister."[9] With this new academic status Francke began holding seminars (*collegia*) on biblical languages. The universities at this time relied heavily upon young magisters to supplement the normal course offerings with seminars on various subjects; for this reason, these gatherings were a common part of the university learning experience. For the magisters, these seminars provided another source of income and the opportunity to remain in academia. In 1686, Francke and his friend Paul Anton (1661–1730) began holding a *collegium philobiblicum* in the house of professor of philosophy Otto Mencke (1644–1707).[10] These seminars specifically focused on the grammar of Genesis and the Gospel of Matthew. Francke, equipped with years of training in Hebrew, navigated through the Old Testament text. Anton, who went on to serve as court preacher in Eisenach and then took up a theological position at the University of Halle in 1695, led the New Testament portions.[11] Though both of these magisters had come into contact with the reforming tradition in the Lutheran church—Anton having met and been impressed by Philipp Jakob Spener in 1681—their collegium philobiblicum remained primarily an academic endeavor until Anton departed to serve as Prince Friedrich August of Saxony's traveling pastor and Francke took his fateful trip to Lüneburg. In fact, Spener visited Francke and Anton's seminar in 1687, and, having noticed their tendency to keep to philological matters, advised them to seek "an edificatory treatment of the text."[12]

In May 1687, a polemical disputation occurred at the university over Quietism.[13] It appears that this particular debate reflected the spirit of the time, as Harold O. J. Brown describes it: "one's own theological position became both the presupposition and the foreordained conclusion of any debate; the only purpose of the 'disputation' was to demonstrate, at least to the satisfaction of one's partisans, the correctness of one's own theological position."[14] Francke took note of a complaint among some at the university that the original writings of one of the Quietists being debated, the Spanish mystic Miguel de Molinos (1628–1696), were unavailable, so that those debating his theology relied on partial information or excerpts from the attack on Molinos's theology by Paolo Segneri (1624–1694). In response to this, Francke translated Molinos's *Guida spirituale* and *Della communione cottidiana* from Italian into Latin; in doing so, he revealed his interest in popular mystical writings. Though Francke's decision to provide a Latin translation—instead of a German one—would at some level indicate that he intended the work for academic discussion, the accusation quickly arose that he was a follower of the Quietist. Molinos's influence on Francke notwithstanding, Francke's translations may reflect what he later privately confessed was a desire to become a "distinguished and learned man," which, ironically, Molinos warns against in his writings.[15] In light of the accusations regarding his interest in Molinos's theology, Francke made great efforts to defend his own orthodoxy, noting that those ideas that interested him in Molinos's writings were both grounded in Scripture and affirmed in Lutheran standards.

Molinos's mystical thought, though qualified and confined by Lutheran standards, had played a role in three notable areas of Francke's theology. Erhard Peschke notes that Molinos's influence strengthened Francke's understanding of the spiritual difference between the natural and converted states of the individual.[16] This belief undergirded Francke's commitment to expect visible signs in the converted person's life. Furthermore, there is a similarity in Francke's thought to the synergism presented by Molinos. Alongside the effective grace of God, both men assumed individuals played an important role in the outcome of their salvation. Finally, we find common themes regarding *Anfechtungen* (spiritual trials) in both Molinos's and Francke's theologies. With respect to Francke's sacramental theology, we will see that Molinos's influence was seemingly drowned out by other, more influential voices, and while Molinos certainly played a role in Francke's thought, it is often hard to pull him out of the shadows of more immediate influences like Johann Arndt.[17]

Further academic funding from the Schabbel family allowed Francke to leave Leipzig in the fall of 1687 to undertake studies under the watchful eye of Superintendent Kaspar Hermann Sandhagen (1639–1697), who, according to Wallmann, was the first Lutheran to have personal contact with separatist Jean de Labadie (1610–1674). As Wallmann notes, "it is interesting and noteworthy, that the man, under whose influence August Hermann Francke stood during the time of his conversion, was briefly a Labadist."[18] In the northern city of Lüneburg in Lower Saxony, Francke had an encounter with God—a conversion experience—that, as will be discussed throughout this book, interrupted his assumed course of life, shaped his theology, and eventually placed him in the middle of the Pietist movement. It was a crisis of faith that shook, if not shattered, the foundations of his beliefs. Francke's personal testimony shows that his conversion experience wove together such themes as a struggle for eternal certainty of salvation, atheism, a breakthrough of God's grace and "true" faith, rebirth, empowerment, and a critique of the spiritual state of the church and educational system.[19] Francke's conversion cannot be understood outside his encounters with Quietism and reforming Lutheran thought or his early conflicts with the Lutheran leadership in Leipzig, Erfurt, and Halle; nor can it be reduced to the recapitulation of those same influences.[20] It was a moment in which the new wine met old wineskin, and bursting forth from it came Francke's attempt to bring about what he believed to be a necessary reform of the Christian life that would have a far-reaching impact.[21]

As a "new" man, Francke left Lüneburg in February 1688 to continue studying Hebrew. He returned to Hamburg along with fellow scholarship recipient Hermann von der Hardt. There the young Pietist not only continued his academic studies but also served as a Bible tutor for the children of Johann Winckler (1642–1705), a friend of Philipp Jakob Spener and the head pastor of the popular St. Michaeliskirche.[22] Lucinda Martin notes, "both Spener and Winckler stressed that the laity has the responsibility to check the correctness of the clergy's teaching—a stance that, at least rhetorically, inverted traditional authority in questions of dogma."[23] It is possible that during this time Francke was influenced by Winckler's lay-oriented ideas. Erich Beyreuther describes this time as a "revolutionary turn" in Francke's life, during which the magister began to recognize children as a source of renewal in the church.[24] Possibly through the influence of Nicolaus Lange (1659–1720), a participant in Winckler's household community of young theological students and the older brother of Joachim Lange (1670–1744), Francke involved himself in both the intellectual growth and the spiritual formation of children.[25] Specifically, he aided in the work of Winckler's school for the poor by teaching children ages four and five, and through this experience he gained invaluable insight into the challenges and benefits of such an undertaking.[26]

While in Hamburg, Francke also befriended and participated in the conventicle of radicals Eberhard Zeller (1652–1714) and the elder Lange. Francke's Hamburg introduction to, and continued lifelong respect for, Zeller and Lange was a fertile source of evidence for later claims that Francke held dangerous, heterodox beliefs. Kramer reports that Lange, apart from his radical inclinations, was an eccentric man and that both he and Zeller, through their conventicle work and doctrinal innovations, came into direct conflict with the ministerium in Hamburg, which barred them from the Lord's Supper.[27] This conflict also led to their removal from Winckler's household, where they had also served as tutors for his children. Through Zeller's and Lange's influence and his own associations with Pietists like Johann Heinrich Horb (1645–1695), Francke entered a radical phase in his theological development. Compromising the Lutheran teaching on justification by faith, Francke incorporated a form of perfectionism into his soteriology.[28] He probably came to hold the belief, much like John Wesley's later teaching on personal holiness, that one could not only obey the law of God but could also, through some form of spiritual disposition toward God, actually live perfectly on earth.[29] Veronika Albrecht-Birkner notes that during this time he possibly held a three-tiered order of salvation "in which justification and sanctification were virtually mixed together."[30] Francke's early, radical form of perfectionism appears to have been closely tied to his notion of spiritual trials (Anfechtungen), which individuals encountered in their movement toward conversion and rebirth. These spiritual trials produced personal doubt and even depression concerning the individual's inner condition. Only after a breakthrough granted by divine grace could God's law be fulfilled by the Spirit-empowered, reborn Christian. In the case of one of Francke's early followers from Leipzig, Andreas Care, there were negative consequences to this radical form of perfectionism. Shortly before April 1693, Spener was contacted by friends seeking advice as to how they should minister to Care. They were worried that he had fallen into a deep despair related to an ongoing spiritual trial, and after reading Care's "confession" (Bekenntnis), Spener gathered that his condition was in part a result of Francke's earlier teaching on perfectionism. As Albrecht-Birkner and Udo Sträter describe, Spener saw Care's despair as a result of "uncertainty in light of his own imperfection," and Spener reached out to Francke in the spring of 1693, asking that Francke clear the air and make available his manuscript *Grace and Truth*. Spener's request reflected the desire to protect Francke from the missteps of his early followers and to correct a caricature of Pietism and perfectionism that was used often by Spener's and Francke's opponents.[31] The case of Care notwithstanding, there is a lack of substantial expressions of this radical and seemingly ephemeral view of perfectionism in Francke's own writings and preaching during this time; therefore we must walk a fine line in how we describe Francke's views.[32] Nevertheless, we must recognize that he held an early, radical view of the believer's ability to act in accordance with the law, which stretched and butted up against Lutheran views of justification.

We must also recognize that Francke's introduction to perfectionism in Hamburg should not be understood as the source of his lifelong belief in the Christian responsibility to bear the fruit of godliness. In a sermon several years later, in the winter of 1699, Francke offered a thorough defense of his views on obedience in relation to God's law. At one point he exhorts, "You believe that it is not possible to keep God's commands. So I ask you: Beloved! Have you even tried?" He goes on, "But if it is unfortunately taught one cannot keep God's commands, why wonder that people view it as a new teaching when one insists upon a true Christianity, and testifies that we must become different people with [our] heart, strength, mind, and all powers (as Luther says in his introduction to the letter to the Romans)."[33] It appears that instead of an extreme view of perfectionism, Francke's call to godly living and Christian fruitfulness was rooted in his seemingly perpetual emphasis on Jesus's command to love both God and neighbor. It marks, to some degree, the popularization within Lutheranism of the distinction between what Harold O. J. Brown describes as "works-righteousness" and the "works of the righteous."[34] Nevertheless, this brief period of radicalism during Francke's time in Hamburg would generate virulent attacks against the magister. It would later be reported in Leipzig that during a meeting in Hamburg between Francke and his former Hebrew teacher, Edzardus, the latter was shocked by the magister's articulation of Christianity and believed that Francke was possessed by the Devil.[35]

In accordance with the expectations of his scholarship, Francke left Hamburg in December 1688 and slowly journeyed back to Leipzig to continue his academic career. But he only stayed eight days there before traveling with two younger university students to Dresden for a two-month stay with Spener. The visit brought about a close friendship between Francke and his "spiritual father," a kinship that only fueled the anti-Pietist fire already burning against Spener's ministry.[36] Upon his return to Leipzig, Francke began offering lectures at the university, but this time on subjects outside his expected Old Testament exegetical studies. Beyond lecturing on the New Testament books of Philippians, Ephesians, 2 Corinthians, and Titus, Francke held lectures under the title "de impedimentis et adjumentis studii theologici."[37] He also returned to the collegium philobiblicum that he and Anton had organized three years before, and under his leadership the group took on a much different appearance. Latin, the scholarly language being used, was replaced by German, and the room was filled not only with fellow students but also with people from the city. It was not long before the popularity of Francke's lectures and meetings outstripped that of his seniors. His lectures grew to such an extent that he was forced to use auditoriums normally set aside for the theological faculty. In addition, a collection of thirty rules "for the protection of the conscience and good orderliness in conversation and social gatherings" that Francke had initially written for his own use was published in a work entitled *Schriftmäßige Lebensregeln*.[38] Both his popularity and coinciding accusations against his "unorthodox" teachings would become the grounds for the well-known investigation of Francke and his followers by the church authorities in Leipzig.

Francke's 1687 conversion experience had an immediate effect on his methodology. He began intentionally using seminars as gatherings not just for lecturing and educating but also for exhorting and evangelizing. Upon the academic responsibility to inform his students' minds, Francke placed the call to seek an awakened and living faith in the lives of those attending his lectures and seminars.[39] The repercussion of Francke's own conversion was that he saw his work as one that included both head and heart, the outward and the inward life.[40] He believed that the Leipzig theology faculty had neglected this spiritual care, so he took it upon himself to bring renewal to the church and to witness against the faculty's spiritual shortcomings. Whereas the professors maintained a social barrier between the clergy and their parishioners, the young magister sought to "honor God and seek the good of his neighbor" by enabling and encouraging the study of Scripture and the practice of godliness by all, regardless of social status.[41] The "second" or "new Reformation" striven for by Francke and other Pietists should be understood in light of this effort. They believed church reform was twofold: an awakening of clergy and congregants to new life and a cleansing of false teachers from their churches.[42]

On 4 August 1689, Johann Benedict Carpzov (1639–1699), the "soul" of the University of Leipzig's theology faculty who, like Spener, studied under Johann Schmidt in Strasbourg, began a public anti-Pietist assault on Francke and his followers.[43] In front of a church full of students mourning the sudden death of a fellow peer, Martin Born, the learned polemicist attacked Francke and those involved in his conventicles (collegia pietatis).[44] Carpzov accused the Leipzig magister of nothing less than using his conventicles to teach heterodox ideas.[45] Born, who just before his death had been preparing to preach for his homiletics training, had participated in Francke's gatherings and had wished to present his sermon in a conventicle instead of in the church. Had Born done so, claimed Carpzov, church officials would have then been forced to censure him. But the more pressing issue for Carpzov was that Born, in the footsteps of Francke, was walking down a path full of theological errors.[46] Thus the Leipzig theologian decided to use the latesummer burial sermon to warn his hearers of the dangers of Pietism.

With Born's sermon still fresh in the minds of some of those sitting in the church, Carpzov adopted the same biblical text for his sermon that Born had planned to use (2 Tim. 2:8). But instead of focusing on the passage, Carpzov set out on a harsh critique of how Pietists handle Scripture. First, the Leipzig professor claimed the Pietists failed to address the main point of the biblical text in their sermons and lecturing. They passed over the interpretive tradition of the church and the historical context of the passage and instead dealt "only with the words of the text." Moreover, these Pietists preached with too much emotion, using phrases like "O, heirs of eternal life" and "O, flowers to the Lord's praise."[47] Francke and his followers also failed to begin with and emphasize faith. Instead, they founded their piety upon a doctrine of morality (*doctrina morum*). This supposed moralism, or legalism, acted as a centerpiece in Carpzov's attacks on Francke's theology. Though these claims would arise again and again in future arguments against Francke's work, this particular sermon marks an important transition in his life. Carpzov's attack on Francke's thought is the culminating moment when his teachings were openly declared dangerous. Therefore, this was the point at which Francke the philologist became Francke the theologian. Following the late-summer burial service, Francke's theology became not only a private concern among theologians at the university but also a public discussion for all those who came to mourn the death of Born.

The theology faculty's attack on Francke quickly went beyond the pulpit. Four days after Carpzov's sermon, leaders sent materials to church officials in Dresden requesting the formation of a commission, and on 23 August, officials ordered the beginning of the official investigation into Francke's pious meetings.[48] The *Leipzig Protocol* and Carpzov's further defense in the *Doppelte Verthäidigung*, which appeared publicly after Francke's departure from Leipzig, offer several of the substantial arguments that the young Pietist faced the rest of his career as a pastor and theologian.[49] The Leipzig faculty's stated intent in the investigation was to gain an understanding of the "teaching, character, and practice" of those involved in Francke's conventicles.[50] They supposed he had gone beyond his proper role as instructor of biblical languages and had begun teaching theology, and influenced by rumors circulating at the time, the faculty feared that the Leipzig magister was using these conventicles to subvert the orthodox teachings of the church on justification and sanctification.[51]

An overview of the questions asked during the investigation reveals three major themes, which dominated the inquiry.[52] First, it was assumed by the theological faculty that Francke's conventicles propagated contempt for the ministerium and its spiritual authority. The existence of Pietist conventicles, in which attendants discussed Sunday sermons, indirectly implied that the ordained pastors preached and taught in a deficient way. What is more, the faculty believed Francke was encouraging a disdain for pastors who did not conform to his form of godliness. In their eyes, Francke was a neo-Donatist crusader, setting individuals against the Leipzig church leadership.[53] Second, these conventicles were disrupting social norms, which struck at the stability of the theological education offered by the university and at the traditional social divisions between educated elites and common citizens. For the sake of all attending conventicle meetings, the scholarly language of Latin gave way to German in these meetings. The choice not to teach in Latin was seen as an affront to the established hierarchy of the church and city. If not held in check, it was supposed unlearned townspeople would imagine themselves qualified to preach and teach, which could lead to religious separatism. This had already happened with radical Pietists in Frankfurt, and what occurred along the Main River likely echoed in the memories of the Leipzig leadership.[54] Last, in an accusation that superseded the two aforementioned themes, Francke was alleged to have taught unorthodox theological ideas. This allegation primarily arose from the belief that Francke had overstepped his role as a university lecturer; his teaching had gone beyond the bounds of biblical exegesis. With regard to his biblicism, the faculty expressed a concern that the "Bible only" methodology propagated in these conventicles denied the validity of the traditional Lutheran symbols. Francke's "new Reformation" insinuated that Luther's reformation of doctrine was insufficient or incomplete. In light of this, the faculty inquired as to whether Molinos's Quietist thought had made its way into Francke's teaching. The reference to Molinos in the protocol is proof that suspicions of mysticism in Francke's thought, which preceded his conversion experience, still lingered in the minds of the theological faculty. In addition, rumors swirled around Francke's radical associations in Hamburg. Some individuals insinuated that while in Leipzig Francke taught the same radical ideas Zeller and Lange promoted in Hamburg, and the examiners took the opportunity afforded by the investigation to imply and propagate the claim that Francke was teaching an extreme view of personal sanctification. With leading questions such as "What was the intent toward which his new teachings were actually aimed?," "How and from what place would he have come to such ideas?," and "From what you have seen, wherein lie the particularities of Francke's teachings?," the theological faculty assumed their accusations of Francke's heterodoxy were to some degree correct.[55]

These three themes reappear in Carpzov's "Vorrede" to the *Doppelte Verthäidigung*. He too saw a disrespect of the spiritual offices of the church in Francke's meetings, pointing out that there was an inherent danger in allowing such young students to teach on topics that should be handled by experienced theologians. Compounding this problem, these students were neglecting their theological studies for the study of piety (*studium pietatis*). They had replaced their systematic study of doctrine with a plain reading of the Bible, fasting, and praying, all for the hope of a spiritual reform of the church. Carpzov remarks, "All things that are new are suspicious. Nevertheless most ears itch after what is new, and people turn aside, always desiring to see and hear if there is anything good and new."[56] The Leipzig theologian saw semblances of mysticism and perfectionism in Francke's thought and as in the protocol, he reminded his readers that Francke had shown an interest in the thought of Molinos and the Hamburg radicals, going so far as to bring up

Edzardus's claim that Francke was under the influence of the Devil.[57] Perhaps W. R. Ward is right in labeling Carpzov a "theologian of formidable violence," or perhaps Carpzov worried himself over what remained hidden and unknown concerning Francke and his conventicles.[58] The distractive and "deceptive" nature of the meetings was proof enough that the Leipzig magister nurtured heterodox ideas.[59]

Though Francke did not openly admit it in the records of the investigation, his work caused a stir and commotion in and outside the university community. Francke's later mouthpiece in London, Anton Wilhelm Böhme (1673–1722), claimed that "the Clamours against these private Exercises grew more hot and violent; both the Masters and Members thereof were charged with abundance of Heretical Opinions."[60] If Francke's work was to be seen as rebellious, he believed it was in the aid of reviving a lost devotion and propriety in the church. Francke imagined himself as a stranger who had stumbled upon a group of wandering and directionless sheep and, instead of devouring them, led them back to the safety of their flock. The fault lay not in the kindness of the stranger but in the shepherds, who found local gatherings for smoking, drinking, and carousing more important than the care of their flocks.[61] And so Francke asked, Should the lack of an ecclesiastical title keep this stranger from the good work the shepherds had failed to do? Should not the shepherds be grateful?[62]

Francke provided a defense to the investigation in his "Apologia," which wedged itself chronologically between the accusations of the protocol and Carpzov's later allegations in the *Doppelte Verthäidigung*.[63] Nevertheless, the "Apologia" represents Francke's determined effort to clear his name of the various allegations. He was well aware that the church leaders had viewed his theology as questionable, but he assured those who would hear that he never sought to undercut the authority of the ministerium nor disrupt the ecclesiastical or social order in Leipzig.[64] In fact, the young magister claimed all the accusations were unfounded. The faculty had distorted his views on the Christian life and the moral obligations of a living faith, painting him as a heretic. According to Francke, he purposed merely to examine the biblical texts critically and to seek out their application in the lives of his audience, but he never overstepped and undertook theological instruction.[65] He asserted that the failure of the professors to offer seminars on exegesis and his own unwillingness to take payments from the students for his instruction—instead of the unsubstantiated charges that people took interest in his false teachings—caused the popularity and rapid growth of his seminars.[66] Francke, nevertheless, did admit to desiring a "new Reformation." It was to be a result of the traditional doctrines rightly grasped by a living faith. But this spiritual reform, claimed the young Pietist, did not include any erroneous teachings on the nature of salvation.

His written defense and the support of men such as Christian Thomasius were not enough to squelch the heated debate against Pietism and its new leader. Nearing the first Sunday of Advent, Francke traveled to Meuselwitz to visit a close friend of Spener, the Pietist sympathizer Veit Ludwig von Seckendorf (1626–1692). At this time, Seckendorf, who in 1692 would become the first chancellor of the university in Halle, had been employing his academic and political acumen to draw up in words what he labeled a "nation of Christians" (*Christenstaat*).[67] Francke then headed to Jena, where he stayed with professors Caspar Sagittarius (1643–1694) and Johann Wilhelm Baier (1647–1695). From there he visited his mother in Gotha for Christmas.[68] On 10 March 1690, the city leadership of Leipzig enacted a fine against conventicles and forbade Francke from teaching. These actions essentially brought about the end of the Pietist movement in Leipzig and the next step in Francke's career.[69] Yet the young magister's departure did not extinguish the intense flames of polemics against him that were ignited in Leipzig.

Francke and Anti-Pietist Polemics: Erfurt Period (1690–1691)

Amid his travels between Leipzig and the various homes of his newly forming network of reform-minded Lutherans, Francke accepted the invitation of his friend Joachim Justus Breithaupt (1658–1732) to preach five times to the Erfurt congregations under the latter's care.[70] Breithaupt, who along with Francke had shared in the household fellowship of Kiel professor Christian Kortholt (1633–1694), served as pastor of the Predigerkirche, senior of the Erfurt ministerium, and professor at the university.[71] Before taking up the position in Erfurt in 1687, Breithaupt spent an extended period with Spener in Frankfurt and taught homiletics at the university in Kiel.[72] These associations and influences gave the Erfurt pastor theological affinities similar to those of Francke and a similar vision and hope for the renewal of the church. These similarities are apparent in Breithaupt's first sermon as a part of the Erfurt ministerium. He preached on the dual roles of the pastor as preacher and as personal and spiritual educator (*Privatinformator*) of the congregation (the latter being one of the first of Francke's activities in Erfurt to later be banned).[73] It was no wonder, then, that both Breithaupt and others in his community took a special interest in Francke, requesting that he be received as a pastor of the nearby Augustinerkirche.[74]

Francke took the call to the Augustinerkirche seriously. He realized that by assuming the pastorate, he would forfeit a scholarship that had allowed him to take on studies and travels as he desired. At the same time, he recognized that accepting the offer would be the fulfillment of a childhood desire to preach.[75] Whether Francke's motivation to take the clerical position came from a sense of the ministry that awaited him in Erfurt, or whether Erich Beyreuther's claim is true that Francke was motivated by a dream he had during his travels between Lüneburg, Erfurt, and Leipzig, on 2 July 1690, Francke underwent and passed his examination for ordination. Six days later he preached his first sermon as a pastor of the Augustinerkirche.[76] Interestingly, he preached on 2 Corinthians 4:1–2: "This is how one should regard us, as servants of Christ and stewards of the mysteries of God. Moreover, it is required of stewards that they be found faithful." It is a passage that had implications for both the pastoral office he was assuming and the theological polemics that followed him. In Erfurt the seeds of his earlier training and religious experience began to sprout. He took up caring for the poor, educating children, and emphasizing personal biblical interpretation and application. All the while, whispers among the local leaders concerning his questionable activity in Leipzig quickly grew into shouts.

In Erfurt Francke continued what he began in Leipzig. He started a conventicle in the Augustinerkirche that mirrored the *collegium pietatis* occurring in Breithaupt's church. Alongside this, Francke began making house visits that became meetings in which he would explicate biblical passages. The gatherings may have also included singing, praying, and a shared meal, but at the center stood Francke's commitment to personal Bible reading. Consequently, the newly ordained pastor ordered inexpensive New Testaments from Lüneburg to sell at cost to those in his community.[77] Francke and those in his circles defended these gatherings as times when "true" faith was inculcated through explicating the weekly sermon, but outsiders thought otherwise. They supposed these meetings were hotbeds for radicalism. The clergymen in Erfurt who opposed Francke suspected such gatherings fomented new ideas, heterodox belief, and disrespect for God's ordained offices and means of grace, especially the preaching of the Word. They supposed he erected pulpits of subversion in house meetings that included people from the city, students at the university, and local leaders.

Interestingly, it was Francke's preaching in the Augustinerkirche that initially drew a large amount of attention. He quickly became known beyond the boundaries of Erfurt for his sermons, attracting an ever-increasing number of onlookers.[78] People even neglected their own church services to go and hear Francke explain what it meant to "truly" repent and believe. Whether their interest rested on the messenger or on the message, his draw was so wide that it crossed confessional boundaries. Catholics began attending not only Francke's sermons within the confines of the Augustinerkirche but also his meetings in various local homes.[79] Their participation, along with the mixture of university students and city residents, disquieted the broader religious community. The presence of Francke behind the pulpit became a new source of apprehension for those opposed to Pietism and a new platform for him to spread his ideas.[80]

Francke also offered lectures for university students. He spoke on a range of topics from biblical exegesis to the spiritual care of children, and just as in Leipzig, these lectures grew with each meeting.[81] A group of Leipzig students followed Francke to Erfurt, and they were joined by a handful of curious students from Jena. One of these Jena students was Johann Anastasius Freylinghausen (1670–1739), who eventually assisted Francke as pastor in Glaucha and became a director of the Stiftungen after Francke's death.[82] Describing his first experience hearing Francke speak, Freylinghausen claims, "What he said was like a new language to me and completely agreeable to hear."[83] The growth of Francke's lectures had an adverse effect on other seminars offered by notable men of the city. One of those seminars that partially emptied belonged to the pastor of the Barfüßerkirche, Augustin Friedrich Kromayer (1644–1707).[84] His frustration over Francke's rise in popularity at the university and his concerns over Francke's Pietist activities eventually compelled Kromayer to play a leading role in the second official investigation of Francke, which began in January 1691 in Erfurt.

Going beyond his work with university students, Francke began catechizing children after his ordination. Girls from the local school requested that he set aside time to explain his sermons to them, and Francke trained the younger gymnasium students in religious matters.[85] Gymnasium rector Zacharias Hogel (1637–1714) took issue with Francke's activities.[86] Francke believed that he had a responsibility to train children under his care in spiritual matters, and Hogel feared Francke was teaching his pupils that "reborn" Christians could keep the law, an accusation he adopted from earlier polemics against Francke. Breithaupt, who served on the leadership board of the gymnasium, came to Francke's defense and debated Hogel on ideas regarding perfectionism, but the conflict between these two and between the leaders of Lutheran Orthodoxy and the Pietists in Erfurt boiled over into an investigation by the ministerium of Francke's teaching and practice.[87]

Shortly after Easter 1690, the ministerium set forth a formal protest that threatened to invalidate Francke's examination for ordination if it did not receive additional written reports from a member of a theology faculty and a city leader.⁸⁸ This demand set in motion efforts to cast Francke as heterodox and push him out of the city. Erfurt, as much as Leipzig, was a place where attacks on Francke's thought culminated and forced him to clarify his theological positions. Though he continued to face opposition later in his career, by the time he reached Halle he had already gained a reputation as an innovator of the faith, a danger to the church. The Leipzig investigation had become well known throughout the region, and the polemics that originated under the watchful eye of Johann Benedict Carpzov made their way into the minds of a large number of the Erfurt churchmen.⁸⁹ We should understand the problems Francke faced in his short tenure in Erfurt in light of the ongoing codification of theological opposition to him and his work. Thus, it was no surprise that well before the ministerium formalized its protest against Francke's ordination, it contacted Carpzov and the Leipzig faculty for a report on Francke.

The letter that arrived from Leipzig several weeks before Easter 1690 recapitulated the three main themes that structured the previous investigation: Francke showed a disregard for the ministerium, for social structures, and for the orthodox faith. The faculty noted that attendance at Francke's conventicles included a mixture of students and townspeople and that the magister went so far as to meet in the houses of tradesmen. Touching on accusations of perfectionism, they claimed Francke taught "one could keep the law of God; one could become perfect in the fear of God."⁹⁰ At this point, the faculty took the liberty to connect Francke's thought to the "dangerous teachings" of the Anabaptists, Enthusiasts, Schwenckfelders, and Quakers.⁹¹ In a clarification requested by the Erfurt ministerium, professor Georg Lehmann (1616–1699) wrote that if Francke were not heterodox in his teachings concerning the law and the clergy, then he at least held dangerous and fanatical opinions.⁹² By describing Francke's thought in this way, the Leipzig faculty intentionally cast Francke in the likeness of religious groups feared and disdained by the Lutheran church, shaping the way the Erfurt investigation represented Francke's theology.

In addition to the report from Leipzig, the Erfurt leaders also requested and received a letter from Johann Friedrich Mayer (1650–1712), a well-known Hamburg theologian and pastor. Mayer had made a name for himself by attacking the work of Spener and his followers, and this reputation allowed Mayer to step into the Erfurt debate without any direct connection to the investigation.⁹³ With his entrance came a recapitulation of the rumors about the young Pietist's time in Hamburg. Mayer wrote, "But whether M. Augustus Hermann Francke is one such suspicious person (concerning which my kind, beloved brother asked me), no one can better testify thereof than his companion at the table of Edzardus, the thoroughly learned and properly pious Eberhard Anckelmann . . . , before whom Francke expressly clarified that he was involved with perfectionism, by which he meant that one could adequately perform the law and live without sin."[94] Mayer went on to reiterate the testimony Edzardus gave during the Leipzig investigation that Francke expressed "horrible errors" in Edzardus's seminars and during his exams. Mayer also targeted Francke with leftover arrows from his battle with Spener, associating the work of the mentor with the mentee. Thus, just as with Spener, Francke's understanding of justification came into question. Mayer could not imagine that someone with a theology like Francke's would be able to remain true to Lutheran standards, especially in a city filled with Catholics.[95] The unsubstantiated accusations were enough, in Mayer's opinion, to keep him from serving the church.

With reports from Leipzig and Hamburg and their own claims of unrest in the city, the Erfurt leadership had enough suspicion and circumstantial evidence to begin a formal inquisition at the beginning of 1691. Led by a coalition of clergy and city leaders, the commission in charge of the investigation accused Francke of the same three thematic faults laid out by the Leipzig investigation: Francke's work produced theological errors and social and ecclesiastical discord. On its very first day, the commission enacted a prohibition against Francke's conventicle meetings and his other Pietist activities. At points, it appeared that many of their arguments merely repeated the allegations of Mayer in Hamburg and of the faculty in Leipzig. The commission claimed Breithaupt, Francke, and their followers were a "Quaker-like, adventuresome sect" who held "house churches" for townspeople. They claimed that in these meetings Pietists poisoned both women and children with their ideas. The leadership went so far as to draw upon such historical examples as the Arian heresy that plagued the early church and the 1525 Peasants' Revolt in order to convince their Catholic and Protestant audience of the dangers of Pietism.[96] Elsewhere, the conventicles were purported to have had a political orientation, cultivating dissension toward civil leaders.[97] These fears and allegations led not only to the prohibition of Francke's conventicle work but also to a ban on his lectures at the university. As the tensions peaked in the summer of 1691, Jena professor Caspar Sagittarius offered one of the first major defenses of Francke and Pietism.[98]

Starting in July, Sagittarius published three works on Pietism.[99] The first two laid out the Pietist agenda and the allegations against Pietism, and the third provided a clarification and defense of both Pietism and Francke's theological positions in answer to the ministerium's accusations. Defending against associations with Quakerism and legalism, Sagittarius went from one claim of heterodoxy to another, attempting to dispel notions that the Pietists failed to follow the teachings of the Lutheran church. Activities within conventicles, and the benefits thereof, received the majority of Sagittarius's attention. They were places where not only the educated but also women and children could study the Bible. All "true Christians," just like those men, women, and children of the early church, had a "spiritual anointing [that] taught them all."[100] The Pietists, claimed Sagittarius, confirmed and built up their faith in conventicles, which excluded even the hint of questionable activity: "That pious Christians (Pietists) suspiciously meet in all kinds of corners and houses is an unproven—in fact, if I should speak the truth—quite devilish impression."[101] Sagittarius asserted the great glory of the work occurring in Erfurt was to the shame of the trained professors. Francke's discussions of sermons and private instruction in houses and his catechizing and examining of children in schools was establishing a treasure where "no thieves can dig it up and steal it, and also where rust and moths cannot consume it."[102] Saggittarius would have his readers believe that Francke was one of the few working to build up the true church.

Francke's own defense against the charges of the ministerium and the city leadership came shortly after Sagittarius's works. In a nine-point treatise Francke exculpated himself from the serious allegations of heterodoxy and misconduct. After addressing the reports from Hamburg and Leipzig and dismissing them as misinformed or incomplete, Francke boldly writes, "Someone show or prove to me where I deviated in any one point from Lutheran doctrine or from one church ordinance and ministerial instruction." While claiming to stand solidly within orthodox teachings, Francke did find it necessary to address his views on sanctification. He reiterated that he did not believe one could become perfect in this life, but that by means of rebirth, sin no longer reigned in the true Christian's heart. It was not enough for some just to say that they were Christians because they experienced a battle between the spirit and flesh: "For all that is born of God overcomes the world, and our faith is the victory, which has conquered the world, and I stand by this." Francke also fended off claims that his *Schriftmäßige Lebensregeln*, the publication of which was used against him in Leipzig, was a "political" tool in his subversive conventicle work.[103] He was not seeking to establish a new sect, undo the authority structures of the ministerium, or forge a new faith. Nevertheless Francke's words, which ironically were held to be dangerously persuasive by so many, had no power over the investigators.

Even the pleas of his congregants could not sway the Erfurt commission. Church and civil leaders authored a decree in September 1691 that called for Francke to leave his post at the Augustinerkirche.[104] They quickly barred him from the pulpit. Francke responded by leaving Erfurt for Gotha, where he found the support of his family and the duke. But the events of Erfurt only confirmed that Francke had gone from a lecturer in biblical languages to a divisive pastor theologian. It now could be expected that everything Francke undertook, whether with the pen or in the public square, would face the scrutiny of his antagonists.

Francke and Anti-Pietist Polemics: Halle (Saale) and Glaucha (1692)

Gotha became the haven Francke needed as he contemplated his next step. He spent close to three weeks in the company of his family, preaching in both the duke's chapel and a town church, also named Augustinerkirche. Groups and individuals disappointed by his dismissal from Erfurt traveled the short distance to hear the young pastor speak. In addition to his preaching, Francke also led a *collegium exegeticum* over 1 Timothy.[105] The nobility in both Gotha and nearby Weimar expressed interest in having Francke serve in their respective communities, but Francke avoided committing to either offer and began an extended trip to Berlin, where Spener awaited. He tarried in Quedlinburg a few weeks and carried himself in much the same way he did in Gotha, preaching and teaching to committed or curious onlookers.

In the middle of November 1691 Francke arrived in Berlin, and he immediately found himself in the society of important politicians and notable figures of the state. By way of the network already established by Spener, he associated with nobility from Denmark and Sweden and befriended influential state leaders, including chamber councilor (*Hofkammerrat*) Christian Friedrich von Kraut (d. 1714), *Premierminister* Eberhard von Danckelmann (1643–1722), privy council to the king (*Geheimrat*) Franz Meinders (1630–1695), and minister of education Paul von Fuchs (1640–1704).[106] These connections would prove to be invaluable as Francke faced a further round of polemical attacks.[107] Spener's network also allowed Francke to be considered for positions in Berlin (Neukölln) and Coburg.[108] Of greatest interest, though, was the offer of head pastorate at St. Georgenkirche in Glaucha, a small, working-class community that butted up against Halle's city wall.[109] With the church office came the position of professor of Greek and Hebrew in the philosophy department of the newly founded university in Halle.[110] Marianne Taatz-Jacobi has shown that the academic position was offered to Francke with more reservation than earlier biographers would lead readers to believe. He was the only first-generation professor at the university who was ordered to travel to Berlin and who had his abilities and personal disposition examined.¹¹¹ Nevertheless, the encouragement and behind-the-scenes orchestration of Spener, the presence of his friend Breithaupt (who had left Erfurt for a position at the university), the uncertainty he felt about the other positions, and his desire to "follow God's will" all led Francke to accept the Glaucha offer.¹¹²

"7 January I arrived in Halle with the mail coach. I was immediately led to Dr. Breithaupt's, whom I met while in a private lesson, and I found good friends from Erfurt and Jena there with him. . . . It was reported to me that nearly 40 persons attended his (Dr. Breithaupt's) Collegia publica and somewhere around 30 attended his [Collegia] privata." Francke found himself instantly in community with several like-minded Christians, and in this context he took up those activities expected of a newly installed minister. He met with various leaders and townspeople in the area and with parishioners from St. Georgenkirche and churches in Halle, allowing those who held lingering uncertainties or expectant excitement to inquire as to the young pastor's intentions. Beyond these visits, Francke held company with visitors from Gotha, Jena, Leipzig, and Erfurt, who reported on the condition of those communities Francke had served.¹¹³

Francke faced immediate opposition from those in Halle and Glaucha, with attacks coming from three directions: Pastor Albrecht Christian Roth (1651–1701), the consistory in Halle led by Johann Christian Olearius (1646–1699), and Francke's own congregants.¹¹⁴ As these three groups coalesced against Francke and his thought and work, important developments occurred in Francke's theology. In his first year in Glaucha, Francke took concerted steps to implement his Pietist schema of the Christian life in the administration of the sacraments. Thus, the polemics of this period not only reflect the three themes that followed him from his Leipzig investigation but also the attempts of Francke to apply his Pietist views to the practice of baptism and the Eucharist. Had Francke not had the benefit of standing outside the reach of the Halle consistory and under the protection of influential figures like Seckendorf, his early years in Glaucha most certainly would have had an outcome much like that of Leipzig and Erfurt. As biographer Gustav Kramer notes,

> The city of Glaucha, to which pastor Francke was called, did not belong at that time—in spite of its direct proximity—to the city of Halle as it does today. Instead it was an independent civil community, which had its own administration. . . . Concerning the ecclesiastical relationship, it was at that time a leading factor of the highest level of importance that the naming of a pastor was dependent upon the government, and

not, as it was with the church positions of Halle, dependent on the magistrate. Thus through the conferment of his office, Francke was promised critical protection. It was also important that he, at least for the moment, stood as the sole pastor of his church, and he did not have to fear counteraction from another clergyman within the church.[115]

The polemics Francke faced during his first few years in Glaucha reflected the previous arguments made against his theology, new accusations of radicalism, and Francke's own attempt to make the sacraments a place of true piety. The opposition against Francke no longer saw him as an outside danger to the church, causing ruptures to Christ's body through private conventicles, but now as an inside divider of the church through the administration of his office.

Before Francke set foot in Glaucha, Albrecht Christian Roth, the head pastor of St. Ulrichskirche in Halle, wrote the first substantial anti-Pietist work of the time, *Imago Pietismi*.[116] Roth's reactionary writing arose primarily from the calling of Christian Thomasius and J. J. Breithaupt to positions at the newly forming university in Halle. Whether or not the leaders were seeking to establish a distinctly Pietist university is questionable, but it is clear that the Lutheran Orthodox leaders in the Halle consistory saw the arrival of several persons sympathetic to Pietism as a threat.[117] Though Roth's work preceded the publication of the Leipzig investigation, it reiterated those major allegations attached to Francke and his followers. Among his complaints, he mentioned the troubling manner in which these Pietist meetings included women (who were allowed to teach) and that those in these gatherings addressed each other as "brother and sister."[118] These Pietists, so claimed Roth, "suppose that . . . neither prayer, nor the Lord's Supper, nor other practices of godliness are necessary."[119] To these social and ecclesiastical charges, Roth added the accusation that they follow heterodox ideas concerning the role of justification, the perfectibility of man, and the thousand-year reign of Christ (chiliasm).[120] But what may be most telling about Roth's work is that it was published anonymously. Thus, when questioned by Johann Christian Olearius concerning Roth's claims, Francke used the anonymity of *Imago Pietismi* as ammunition against its validity.[121]

Olearius, the inspector of the consistory, showed more caution in his approach to Francke. He met with Francke the day after the latter's arrival and revealed in his questions the underlying theological and practical apprehensions held by the ministerium. The inspector had already encountered a man in his own congregation who evidenced a discontent with Francke and his preaching, and he voiced concern that something like that which occurred in Leipzig might happen in Halle. Francke answered that he had no "intention to establish new dogmas or overthrow old, commendable church ordinances."[122] Olearius sought Francke's assurance that "Pietists" did not hold a low view of the ordained minister or of practices such as confession, to which Francke answered that though he could not speak for the "whole world," he could reassure him that those who were being called Pietists in Erfurt and Leipzig did not hold such low views. In their second meeting, a little less than a month later, Olearius focused more directly on Francke's conventicle practices. While again seeking Francke's assurance that he would not depart from church ordinances and ecclesiastical authority, the inspector directed him to conduct his university seminars without the inclusion of townspeople and to receive approval beforehand if he were to conduct conventicle meetings with residents. More interestingly, in their second meeting Olearius questioned Francke concerning his confessional practices. Olearius desired to know why Francke was unwilling to accept the usual offering given to pastors during confession. Francke recounted this in his journal but omitted much of the substance of the conversation, leaving readers with the idea that he had simply told Olearius how he had handled such situations in the past.[123] Francke's silence proved ominous. The day after meeting with Olearius, Francke held confession. The controversy that grew out of his administration of the sacraments would become an invaluable example of how his Pietist emphasis on the Christian life could affect early modern Lutheran articulations of sacramental theology.

Although Francke had faced innumerable questions about his theology in the preceding three years, when goldsmith and judge Jacob Vogler and innkeeper Elias Naumann approached the Halle consistory in the summer of 1692 with their complaints about their new pastor's practice of confession at St. Georgenkirche, it became clear that Francke's Pietist spiritual program could not be carried out without it directly affecting the sacramental practices of his congregation.[124] In the few years before Francke took up the head pastorate, the St. Georgenkirche congregation had already seen its share of hardship. In 1682 a plague struck Glaucha and Halle, killing between fifty and sixty persons per day.[125] Albrecht-Birkner estimates that about two-thirds of Glaucha's population died during this time.[126] The passing of such a large number of citizens directly struck worker productivity and hindered the local economy. Francke held the opinion that Glaucha was also hindered by a long tradition of alcohol consumption. Though we have good reason to question his claim that when he entered Glaucha in 1692 thirty-seven of the approximately two hundred houses were inns and taverns, Albrecht-Birkner appropriately notes that in comparison to the other, wealthier cities where

Francke had lived, Glaucha's weak economic and social condition made a poor impression on him.[127] Furthermore, Francke's predecessor at St. Georgenkirche, Johann Richter, was removed from his pastoral office on 26 September 1691 in part by his own parishioners.[128] Some claimed Richter had gained a reputation in Glaucha as a "carouser" and accused him of sexual misconduct.[129] In this social and moral context Vogler and Naumann came to Francke for confession on 18 June 1692. They offered their new pastor a form of penance that had been confirmed with the hands of absolution time and time again. But to their surprise, Francke did not consider them properly repentant and barred them from the Supper. The activity that brought about this harsh judgment was Vogler's and Naumann's distribution and consumption of alcohol on Sundays.[130] For Francke, they were living in sinful revelry, failing to find comfort in God's grace.[131]

With a strong difference of opinion concerning their spiritual state and a desire to mend damaged self-images, on 22 June 1692 Vogler and Naumann lodged a formal complaint to the consistory against Francke. Couching their critiques in Matthew 7:15 ("Look out for false prophets, who come to you in sheep's clothing, but on the inside are ravenous wolves"), they sought to persuade the Halle consistory that Francke was in fact teaching heterodox ideas and acting improperly.

> We do not desire to lay out what we above all else must experience here and there from him and his behavior; that in each place we willingly indulge [him in] his proclivities . . . , which are so many that a book would not permit us enough room to describe. We also do not desire to make known in particular those heterodox things that are often presented in public meetings, of which he seeks to impress upon the people. [For example] that they must first be rightly afflicted in a proper and melancholic way or else they would not feel the inner drive and power of the Holy Spirit.[132]

Their attempt at diplomatic language could not cover over the harshness of their accusations. Francke's heterodox ideas had spilled over into every sphere of his ministry. He treated the pastor's house like an inn, restricted visitors to those who had the appearance of piety, held "prayer meetings" that included "many young, beautiful women" and strange visitors, and most important, permitted people from foreign, outlying places to take part in the Lord's Supper.[133] Nevertheless, their main complaint was that Francke did not grant them absolution for what they felt were truly repentant acts of confession, and without this absolution they were held back from the altar. For Francke, these men continued to involve themselves in activities that were not representative of truly remorseful Christians; their confession was not reflected in their lives. Thus they were barred from celebrating the very Supper in which they claimed even outsiders participated.

This controversy needs to be understood in light of two important factors. First, even in Leipzig Francke expressed a disdain for what he called "drinking" and "smoking" meetings. Francke sarcastically asked his Leipzig investigators, "The drinking gatherings [collegia] on holy Sunday are too many to be counted. How many meetings are held in beer and wine houses during the sermon?"[134] It could be said that beginning with his work in Leipzig, Francke openly challenged activities considered *adiaphora* by the church. His view of the true Christian life conflicted with some of the community's daily comforts. Francke noted in his journal the differences between his sermons and the sermons of his peers during his first weeks in Glaucha: "In Dr. Breithaupt's *exercito Sabbathico* I spoke on faith, how it is born, nurtured, and perfected in the cross alone. Dr. Olearius preached that one must set aside money in order that he might have something when he becomes older. Pastor Stießer preached that games are by all means not forbidden, but rather are an admissible pleasure."[135] Second, it is important to recognize that Vogler and Naumann's complaint arose almost six months after Francke's arrival in Glaucha. Francke and these men had had sufficient time to evaluate one another, so the complaints sent to the consistory that summer reflected an escalating conflict between the two parties. We can assume that Francke had already taken issue with their lifestyles. In his journal, he mentions that he preached against abuses like theirs and, furthermore, that he barred Vogler and Naumann from the table not only because of their actions but also because of their unwillingness to better their lives.[136]

Vogler and Naumann, on the other hand, saw Francke and his teaching as heterodox and rigid. He had gone beyond his assumed role. Albrecht-Birkner points out that on 9 July 1692 Spener wrote Francke to "politely but explicitly critique Francke's practice of church discipline."[137] In the eight years leading up to this conflict, Spener repeatedly affirmed in his writings and letters that while individual pastors may withhold absolution from unrepentant parishioners, these pastors may not act autonomously and bar those who disagreed with them over the sinfulness of their acts.[138] By withholding the bread and wine from Vogler and Naumann, Francke had acted contrary to the common experience of his parishioners and the opinion of his spiritual mentor. Francke's sacramental practices, the fears of Vogler and Naumann, and the appearance of the two townsmen's wives before the Halle consistory at the end of June to request another confessor factored into the forming of a commission to investigate Francke.

This time, though, the investigation would be led by university chancellor and Pietist sympathizer Veit Ludwig von Seckendorf. The accusations against Francke arose from the clergy and laity alike. Albrecht Christian Roth and Christoph Schrader, both of whom were by this time serving as pastors (in Leipzig and Dresden, respectively), attempted to turn the investigators' attention to Francke's recent associations with female ecstatics.[139] An unauthorized publication of letters sent to Francke and Breithaupt by women who claimed various visions and new revelations offered Francke's adversaries fertile ground on which to stand.[140] Alongside these letters, the commission considered the various complaints against Francke's ministry in Glaucha and Halle. The investigation officially opened 18 November 1692 and concluded nine days later. While encouraging both Breithaupt and Francke to make changes to their seminars and conventicles, they concluded,

> After diligent investigation it was not found that Dr. Breithaupt or Magister Francke conveyed one error in their teaching or one false thing in their doctrine. Thus both of these professors have been done injustice and harm by those who have attributed to them false teachings and attached the name "Pietists" and other improper and maliciously contrived and applied abusive language, or by the few who have implied even worse in this regard. No one from the ministerium, however, could testify that they had done such things. Rather each and every one of its members recognized through the oral and written clarification and attestation of both men that they were free of, and unblemished by, heterodox ideas.[141]

With the findings of the commission, Francke gained a greater sense of security in his ministry. Regarding his foregoing ministerial and sacramental practices, he rejoiced to Spener that he was especially glad he could continue meeting with congregants before confession, for "it eased the burdened conscience concerning the confessional."[142] The investigation and Francke's reaction to it reveal that he had developed a plan to further individual piety, and the sacraments played a central role. Now Francke required a visit with congregants in the days leading up to their confession, an indicator that he now subordinated the sacraments to his plan to awaken the church.

Though Francke was directed to make concessions in his conventicle work, the 1692 investigation provided him official confirmation that he stood within the bounds of orthodoxy. Throughout Francke's life, he would continue to face opposition from certain leaders in the Lutheran church concerning his beliefs, but he now had the open backing of Berlin. The official opening of the university on 1 July 1694 and his transition from the philosophy faculty to the theology faculty in 1698 only solidified the investigation's findings.[143] With his call to the pastorate of Halle's St. Ulrichskirche in 1714, Francke's place of prominence in the city became indisputable.[144] What his first year in Glaucha evidenced most pointedly was that his Pietist program did not devalue the sacraments but rather used them as a tool to inculcate a Pietist spirituality in the lives of his congregants. He wrote in his journal, "God also gave the grace that through my earnestness, which I showed in confession, and through the often frequent reminder from the pulpit, a greater reverence for the sacrament was awakened in the people."[145] Thus as his theological program moved forward, baptism and the Lord's Supper played a crucial role in supporting Francke's Pietist theology.

2

BIBLICISM, CONVERSION, AND REFORM

Though the 1692 Halle investigation absolved Francke of accusations against his ministry, the process revealed that Francke's form of Pietism had crept into every area of his theology. This is especially true of his interpretation of the sacraments, which had become tools at Francke's disposal for erecting the "true" Christian life. His application of the sacraments arose from a complex theological system that does not immediately lend itself to systematization. In many ways Francke followed in the footsteps of his forefather Luther, who, according to Carter Lindberg, emphasized "that the exegesis of the Bible is the task which makes theology theology."[1] For Francke, theology not only arose from an encounter with Scripture but also from an empowering experience of God, and such a theology should result in the transformation of the individual and the reformation of church and society. Thus the theological task was inherently pietistic for Francke, and he could exhort his students, "The study of theology is the cultivation of the heart."[2]

It is nevertheless possible to see three dominant themes that define the core of Francke's theology: biblicism, conversion, and individual and social reform.[3] These represent a doorway into Francke's broader system of thought and therefore serve as reference points for contextualizing peculiarities of his theology. For the sake of clarity, this chapter orders these themes according to an assumed chronology of Francke's life. His early interest in Scripture and biblical languages—Francke took up the study of Greek while a schoolboy in Gotha—places biblicism at the front of these three themes, but his emphasis on piety caused an inevitable comingling of biblicism, conversion, and reform.[4] It is hard to encounter one of these themes in Francke's writings without being drawn by him into a discussion of the others. Even his *Lebenslauf* reflects this interdependence of the three themes. He believed the education in biblical languages that he pursued into adulthood was to some degree "redeemed" and put into its proper place as a result of his 1687 Lüneburg conversion experience. Francke claims, "From then on it became easy for me to deny ungodliness and worldly lusts and to live [a] disciplined, righteous and pious [life] in this world. Since then, I have steadfastly adhered to God, disregarding [my own] advancement, glory and esteem by the world, wealth and good days, and outward, worldly gratification. And though before I had made an idol for myself of learning, now I saw that faith, like a mustard seed, is worth more than a hundred sacks full of learning."[5] At first glance it might appear that Francke was dismissing education as an important means of reform, and yet Thomas Albert Howard appropriately notes, "It would be wrong . . . to judge Francke as anti-intellectual."[6] Instead we should interpret Francke's words as a reorientation. Education in the hands of converted persons could be a means to worldwide reform. The establishment and growth of Francke's institutes in the 1690s reflect Francke's belief that the learning of Scripture by a converted heart would bring about ecclesiastical and social reform. He held that a worldwide reform, consisting of personal and social improvement, would be a visible proclamation of God's glory by faithful, fruitful followers of Christ. So like a stool, Francke's theology rested upon the three load-bearing legs of biblicism, conversion, and improvement, each one dependent on the other.

Biblicism

Though the doctrinal reverberations of "sola Scriptura" and the subsequent Lutheran tradition that built upon this cry of the Reformation found resonance in Francke's theology, his biblicism focused primarily on personal reading and interpretation of Scripture. Francke's biblical hermeneutics of personal interpretation reflects a "new" distinctive in Lutheranism that Johannes Wallmann attributes to the slogan "tota scriptura" found throughout Pietism.[7] At the center of Francke's hermeneutics stood a concern for individual understanding, which Markus Matthias frames as a question over the "assuredness of the truth of the biblical Word."[8] In his preaching and writings, Francke does not seem to see the need to reaffirm confessional understandings about the nature of God's revelation.[9] Such claims about the infallibility and authority of Scripture were assumed in his language on the role of the Bible in the life of the Christian.[10] In Scripture, he notes, "God has revealed himself according to his being, according to his attributes, according to his majesty and glory, according to his work and according to his will. Thus when we have the longing to rightly know the name of God, ... we must seek and search with diligence in Scripture."[11] Francke did not evidence a concern for convincing his students and parishioners that Scripture was divinely inspired and authoritative as the source of the knowledge of God and salvation; rather, he was challenged with persuading them that there was a proper and faithful way to engage Scripture. Francke's effort to promote individual reading and understanding of the Bible provides us with his articulation of a distinctively Pietist hermeneutic, a biblicism of the heart.

Three years after his arrival in Halle, the new professor published his first work for students of theology, entitled *Timotheus zum Fürbilde allen Theologiae Studiosis dargestellet*. The text reflects Francke's desire to reform theological training in universities, and it offers early insight into the main concerns Francke held for the life of the theologian. "I am not trying here to make you learned but rather pious (and thus lay the foundation upon which a true learnedness of God could be built)—of course not I, but rather the grace of God which is in me."[12] Francke took hold of the New Testament person of Timothy to exemplify the proper way to study theology. His students were to imitate all aspects of Timothy's life, especially in their reading and application of Scripture. Thus to the degree that Francke claimed Timothy represented the true theologian, the New Testament claims concerning Timothy became a support system for Francke's biblical hermeneutic.

"*Timothy knew the Holy Scriptures from childhood*, 2 Timothy 3:15. This has meaning for every person, but foremost for you who are studying theology."[13] At the very heart of Francke's critique of theological education was the disconnect between studying the Scriptures and the pious life. He believed that students neglected the revelation of God by either not reading the Bible or not studying it with eyes of faith. Without such eyes, the core of the gospel would be obscured by trivial questioning and rabbit trails: "It is certainly also the backwards way of men that they more often apply themselves to useless questions or mysteries in the Holy Scripture instead of first laying a proper foundation in repentance and faith."[14] Francke formed an inseparable connection between revelation, salvation, and sanctification. Scripture existed as a means to eternal salvation and as a means to sanctifying each individual life.[15] Instructing on the proper way to read Scripture, he summarizes, "If you take up the reading of the Holy Scripture, it must be your single-hearted goal that you want to become a believing and pious Christian and not according to appearances but rather in true power."[16] For Francke, it was not just that the reading of the Bible led Timothy to belief but that Timothy's godliness arose from his faith-filled attention to the biblical text. It was the first and overarching characteristic Timothy exemplified. From childhood on, he knew Scripture. Consequently, Francke's own theological schema emphasized a faithful, personal reading and interpreting of Scripture.[17] He reflected his time and tradition, affirming the supernatural nature and authority of Scripture, and he affirmed the supernatural role that Scripture played in generating individual faith and cultivating a godly life.[18] Nevertheless, for the Bible to have its full effect, it must be engaged by believing individuals.

Francke's emphasis on the spiritual condition of the reader resulted in a biblicism of the heart. This biblicism laid out by Francke was not simply limited to theology students. Timothy was a pattern for every person, and by using such inclusive language, Francke (like his spiritual father Spener) coupled personal Bible study with Luther's doctrine of the priesthood of all believers.[19] All those who were justified by the blood of Christ were not just priests before God but also interpreters of God's revelation. Thus believers were to enter into the reading and application of Scripture with the interpretive aid of the regenerated heart. They should possess a "simple heart, that is a sincere and unfeigned longing," which allows them to be instructed by the Scriptures unto salvation. The corrupted condition of the church—in both the pulpits and the pews—arose from contemptuousness toward the revelation of God, in which the Bible was treated as a book among books. The scribes and Pharisees of Jesus's time read the Scriptures, claims Francke, but their lives were not bettered. The "Pharisees" of Francke's time also did not rightly approach the text—with eyes set upon the cross—but instead looked toward earthly things.[20] Faithful readers of Scripture were to approach the text correctly, with the threefold key of "heartfelt prayer," "holy desires," and the light of a love for Christ. Through prayer they addressed God with mouth and heart and approached him with a childlike spirit and contemplative heart: "The love for Christ will change your mind, and cause you to participate in his mind so that you become like him."[21] By acting in this way, according to Francke, believers were given the opportunity to taste the power of the Bible through the grace of God.

Furthermore, Francke believed that Christians who properly took up and applied the Scriptures found confirmation of their personal hermeneutics in spiritual trials (Anfechtungen).[22] Francke's belief that spiritual trials were a means toward properly understanding the Bible led him to claim that the "beloved cross is now the powerful means to understanding the Holy Scripture, and even more to tasting and perceiving it." Thus taking up the cross of Christ, and the spiritual trials inherent in this act of self-denial, became a form of both aiding and reaffirming one's interpretation of Scripture. "How your understanding of [Scripture] will be that much more deepened under the cross as it was before the cross! Finally know that to the degree that you will die to the world, you will see and understand in the Holy Scripture."[23] But Francke cautions, "Listen to and read the letters a thousand years, and if you do not bow your neck to this yoke [of the cross], you will remain as dumb and unknowing as you were before."[24]

To his theological students, Francke offered a biblical hermeneutic consisting of seven *lectiones* ("readings"), which he divided according to a "husk-kernel" schema specific to the study of the Bible. The "husk" consists of three readings: historical (*lectio historica*), grammatical (*lectio grammatica*), and logical or analytical (*lectio logica*). These lectiones are concerned with the historical understanding, the linguistic sense of the passage, and the structure and inner coherence of Scripture, respectively.[25] According to Markus Matthias, Francke's "husk" lectiones seek the "historical determinations of the biblical text," while the "kernel" lectiones are concerned with the "suprahistorical message of the biblical text."[26] The "kernel" in Francke's hermeneutic is made up of four readings: exegetical (*lectio exegetica*), dogmatic (*lectio dogmatica*), deductive (*lectio porismatica*), and practical (*lectio practica*). Erhard Peschke notes that those following Francke's exegetical reading would "identify the *sensus litteralis*, the sense of the word and topic [intended by the Holy Spirit], which is differentiated from the purely grammatical *sensus litterae* [the meaning of the words]."[27] *Lectio dogmatica* is concerned with determining the spiritual teachings of the passage, in how they are directly or indirectly portrayed by the text. The deductive and practical readings seek to develop the edificatory and practical applications of the text. Francke believed a proper balance of the husk and kernel of Scripture provided students insight into the divinely intended meaning of the passage.

The husk-kernel schema, though important in its affirmation of the salvific message found throughout Scripture, was to be the prelude to Francke's more pressing concern: whether the "kernel of the whole Scripture"—Jesus Christ—was being encountered by hearts that were regenerate. The Lutheran law-gospel division of Scripture was also made subservient to this concern. "The Old Testament is not alone law," Francke confirms, "nor is the New Testament alone gospel. Rather both law and gospel are found in the Old and also in the New Testament."[28] But both law and gospel served to bring "Christ the kernel" into sharp focus. Thus the study and application of Scripture needed to be made profitable through true faith coupled with the belief that all of Scripture spoke of Christ. Francke claims, "Finding Christ in Scripture is costly, but it is even more costly to find him in [one's] heart." It was not enough to determine the meaning of passages using the various lectiones within the husk-kernel schema. One must use the "higher and more glorious way to seek and find Christ in the Scripture."[29]

The deeper question Francke posed was whether the individual encountering the Scriptures, and applying Francke's method of study, was a "child of God" or a "child of the world." Were their understandings "natural" and "darkened," or "spiritual" and enlightened by love?[30] For Francke, claims Peschke, "It is not enough to know theoretically that Christ is the kernel of Scripture. One must seek, eat, and taste this kernel."[31] For individuals to have this type of access to a true understanding of the Bible, they must be a new creation and dwelling place for the Spirit. Here Francke draws on the idea of mystical participation in Christ (*Christum mysticum*). The way Christ dwells with his bride, the church, through the Holy Spirit serves as an analogy for how he is to be encountered in all of Scripture: "How the process of Christ from the beginning is portrayed in his members is also how Christ is to be searched for in the whole of Holy Scripture. [He is to be searched] not merely in his own Person and in how he is the Head, but also in how he, through his Spirit, enlivens all his members. [How] in them [he] lives, works, struggles, suffers, and overcomes the world."[32] Thus, Francke's biblicism of the heart—his hermeneutic of spiritual understanding—was grounded in the reborn individual's participation in the Spirit. According to Ulrike Witt, it was an "enthusiastic hermeneutic," in which Francke believed the individual's inner experience of scriptural truth was a display of the Spirit's work.[33] Without the Spirit's inner activity, one could, claims Francke, "read a chapter out of the Bible and meanwhile [her] heart could remain" in sin.[34] In light of this, Lindberg's claim that Spener "subordinates Luther's *fides ex auditu*," implying in his language "that the Word may not be effective without the *additional* power of the Holy Spirit," was also true for Francke.[35] Francke believed the individual's affective participation in the Spirit would be evidenced in her earnest approach to the Bible through acts of prayer and devotion.

It is also helpful to understand Francke's biblicism in light of his own broad philological training. Erich Beyreuther's claim that Francke decided during his conversion period in Lüneburg to make biblical studies the center of theological study needs be interpreted in light of the influence of Francke's preconversion academic work and thought.[36] As early as 1666, Francke began receiving private tutoring in biblical languages, and this childhood education certainly factored into his early self-proclaimed love for Scripture.[37] At every stage of his academic career that followed, he built upon a growing expertise in Hebrew and Greek, which was informed by voices beyond his own Lutheran tradition. It is likely that while studying with Superintendent Sandhagen in Lüneburg, Francke came to appreciate the philological and theological writings of Reformed theologian Johannes Coccejus (1603–1669).[38] In addition, his preconversion seminar work with Paul Anton at the university in Leipzig, which Spener visited in 1687 and critiqued for its lack of application, factored into Francke's developing biblicism.

Francke's conventicles in Leipzig, Erfurt, Gotha, and Halle, which emphasized personal interpretation of Scripture, not only reveal the centrality of biblicism in the early period of Francke's ministry but also point to the influence his academic study of biblical languages had on his theology and on his attempts at reforming theological studies—a reform he believed had broader social implications.[39] This emphasis on personal interpretation and "awakened" study of Scripture played a major role in his efforts to distribute inexpensive copies of the Bible, beginning in Erfurt and culminating in the Canstein Bible Institute in 1710, which was established at Francke's Stiftungen in cooperation with Baron Carl Hildebrand von Canstein (1667–1719).[40] Nine years earlier, in 1701, celebrating the growing accessibility of Scripture, Francke exclaims, "Now one can have a hand Bible, which he buys for 10 Groschen and children can take it to school. Look how useful it is! He can also use it in his house."[41] It was hoped that these printed copies of Scripture would have their effect: aiding in the conversion of many souls and bringing about a worldwide reform.

Conversion

Erhard Peschke writes, "The experience of his conversion in 1687 sits at the beginning of August Hermann Francke's theology."[42] Peschke represents the standard assumption concerning the character of Francke's theology, but as momentous as Francke's conversion experience might have been and as central as it was for his subsequent theological expressions, it would be a mistake to see it as the starting point of his theology or, as Jonathan Strom points out, to make it the paradigm of Pietist conversion experiences.[43] Markus Matthias has more properly noted that Francke made conversion (*Bekehrung*) the "middle point of the religious life."[44] The Lüneburg event Francke described in his autobiographical *Lebenslauf* paints a dramatic picture of spiritual transformation, where his "dead" religious habits were exchanged for a new, living faith. One of the results of this life-changing experience was that conversion became the goal of his theology. Though he did not expect it to occur the same way in the lives of others as it had in his own, a desire to see the conversion of those around him became the driving force of much that Francke said and did. His preaching, teaching, educating, and facilitating all had the goal of converting or reconverting souls.[45] Since the following chapters explore the way Francke's Pietism shaped his sacramental theology, this consideration of Francke's theology of conversion seeks only to set the groundwork for a richer description of his thought.

Many of the core elements of Francke's theology of conversion are encountered in his *Lebenslauf*. The fact that Francke's conversion narrative is a "retrospective account"—he had not finished writing it when he wrote Spener in the spring of 1692—gives further evidence that he had time to process the various dynamics of his experience.[46] Matthias argues that the core elements of conversion in Francke's *Lebenslauf* reflect the influence of Johannes Musaeus (1613–1681), whose notes on systematic theology Francke claims to have had "in hand" during his Lüneburg experience.[47] Musaeus presents conversion from "transitive" (theological/divine) and "intransitive" (psychological/human) perspectives, the latter mirroring the elements of the former. As Eric-Oliver Mader explains, "Early modern Lutheran dogma distinguished two ways to process a conversion: 'transitive' and 'intransitive.' While the transitive 'conversio' of a sinner was understood as a conversion effected directly by God and performed suddenly, the intransitive type was conceptualized as a process."[48] In a 1649 disputation, Musaeus distinguishes between the two, stating that "transitively" God grants the individual a "sound mind," while "intransitively" individuals "convert themselves, that is, they return to their senses"; nevertheless both "note the very same thing."[49] More specifically, Musaeus's construction of transitive conversion found in his systematic theology notes included (1) a knowledge of sin and a contrition of the heart through the law, (2) an enflaming of "the light of faith" in one's understanding and an enflaming of "trust in Christ" in one's will through the gospel, and (3) an accompanying attention to bettering one's life. The coinciding experiential elements of intransitive conversion, according to these same notes, are seen in a personal fear of God's wrath and sorrow over sin.[50] The law-gospel hermeneutic that undergirds Lutheran soteriology clearly stands out in this construction of transitive and intransitive conversion. God convinces the individual of her sin through the law, and her emotions of repentant fear and sorrow reflect this encounter. The gospel is coupled with faith, which results in corresponding joy and love. This close relationship between the law-gospel hermeneutic and conversion allowed Lutheran conceptions of conversion to be connected to traditional categories of repentance and faith.[51]

In Francke's conversion theology, repentance necessarily preceded faith.[52] "The Lord Jesus bound both together: repentance and faith in the gospel. Thus the one who does not lay repentance as the foundation must have no faith."[53] Before they could properly take hold of the merits of Christ by faith, unbelievers were to first become aware of their corrupted estate. At every turn in Francke's writings he urged individuals to take their condition seriously. Sin had invaded all of life and brought the church to such a deplorable state that even those within its walls could not be trusted to hold a living faith. Francke believed his task was to lead his parishioners to repentance and facilitate an awakening to matters of the heart. Once sin was properly recognized and rejected, Francke encouraged his congregants to apply faith to the taking hold of God's promises and to the confirming of their heartfelt repentance.

The spiritual transformation anticipated by Francke in conversion cannot be confined to the doctrine of forensic justification. To traditional teachings on repentance, faith, and righteousness Francke added an experiential empowerment unto Christian faithfulness. It is in this point that Francke found Musaeus's twofold construction of conversion insufficient. As Matthias describes,

> The account concerning his spiritual struggle *before* the actual conversion to faith shows how much he allowed himself to be led by Musaeus's theological parameters. [Nevertheless] he could not find an answer in Musaeus for the last scene of his conversion. There was nothing more left for him to do except wait upon a supernatural intervention from God, which deeply stirred and overwhelmed his will and revealed itself as a work of the God who speaks in Scripture. Or to say it another way: a singular stirring, which leads to a fundamental change of life, could and must be traced back to God as the author. And in fact, this befalls Francke in his conversion.[54]

The outworking of conversion included a struggle against worldly entrapments and an empowerment to produce the fruit of godliness. To the degree this is true, Francke's theology of conversion encompassed the repentance struggle (*Bußkampf*), which speaks to the recognition and despair of oppressive sin, and rebirth (*Wiedergeburt*), in which the individual is transformed into a "new creation."[55] While the relationship between conversion and godliness may be traced back to Philipp Melanchthon, Francke's own thought is directly connected to the tension between faith and faithfulness he experienced.[56] Francke took note of the disconnect between the faith proclaimed in Scripture and the Christian lives he witnessed, including his own. In his view, the church pews were filled with those who confessed belief in the justifying work of Christ but failed to act in accordance with their religious confessions. The decidedly converted person would not merely rest in the merits of Christ but would naturally perform those activities expected of a transformed life. As Matthias notes, this belief is derived directly from

Francke's own conversion, in which he experienced "as a power, the resolve to direct his own will toward a God-pleasing life, which can only come from God—through the biblical promise."[57]

This led Francke to emphasize self-awareness in his theology of conversion. Believers, though not necessarily aware of the exact time or date of their conversion, were to be able to acknowledge a specific point in their lives when they made a distinctive break with worldliness. A child of God could not live as a child of the world, and if asked when their conversion occurred, claimed Francke, those who were truly reborn would at least be able to point to a specific year.[58] By experiencing a rift between heavenly and earthly realms in their hearts, believers could have certainty of their spiritual state. Thus, Francke wrapped the comfort of salvation up with the individual's conversion experience and the ongoing implications of a converted life. One who saw the Christ of Scripture with the eyes of true faith and had experienced the new birth should naturally live a life that glorifies God.

Individual and Social Reform

To the degree that Francke's biblicism expressed Scripture as the means to "true" Christianity and his theology of conversion described the transitional act that placed one in a right spiritual relation to God, his theology of individual and social reform served as the visible outworking of his theological program, which sought God's glory as its end. This third theme arose organically out of the first two, and as such it is anticipated by his biblicism and conversionism.[59] The call to social improvement, nevertheless, was not uncommon during Francke's time. As Kelly Whitmer notes, "Before [the] founding [of Francke's institutes] there had been no shortage of utopian, reform-minded plans for improvement in virtually every corner of Europe and among Protestants and Catholics alike."[60] So Francke's 1704 *Der Große Aufsatz*, a reform plan he worked on as early as 1700, did not so much fill a void caused by an absence of exhortations to spiritual and social improvement as provide suggestions for how, in Francke's words, "a common improvement at every level, not only in German lands and Europe, but also in the remaining parts of the world" could occur.[61] *Der Große Aufsatz* laid out both Francke's theological motivations behind his reform plan and his suggestions as to how to cultivate such a worldwide improvement. At its conceptual center were three doctrines: (1) the degenerate state of individuals and communities, (2) the great commandment to love one's neighbor, and (3) the universal call of the gospel. Francke built from these three beliefs a theology of reform that sought to make education the platform through which social and spiritual reform could occur.

The degenerate state of civil authorities, households, and educators formed the starting point of Francke's beliefs on reform.[62] In drawing attention to human sinfulness, he affirmed traditional constructions of fallen human nature, but his stress on the way sin was strangling the life of the church invigorated his warnings against remaining an unregenerate churchgoer. He believed that an ongoing complicity with sin was preventing real reform: "Those whose eyes God has opened just a bit may quite easily recognize that not only everything in the world but also everything in Christianity and in the Lutheran church lay in a cursed condition and in appalling corruption." Francke supported this claim by referencing the earlier reforming works of Johann Arndt, Theophil Großgebauer, and Spener, all of whom pointed to humanity's tragic spiritual state.[63] In response to this overarching human problem, Francke made conversion and transformation the precondition to reform.[64] Only through rebirth could individuals bring about change in their spheres of influence.

By 1689, Francke had already incorporated the responsibility of Christians to serve their neighbor into his teaching. Individual interpretation of Scripture and the various meetings that Francke promoted in Leipzig were, in his view, to result in a visible love for neighbor. Francke saw a considerable lack of this spiritual fruit in the Leipzig church leadership, which he believed was a reflection of a much broader spiritual epidemic.[65] If there were to be true Christians within the church, then there must be believers exhibiting love toward their neighbor, regardless of their religion.[66] There was a great battle to be won by serving one's neighbor. The desire to, in Francke's words, "bring down the reign of Satan in the world in order that only God's will may occur" motivated Francke's own concern for neighborly love toward all, and he often laid this responsibility upon the shoulders of kings and nobility, preachers and teachers.[67] As Lindberg notes, "His energetic efforts on behalf of the poor and marginalized expressed his understanding of who the neighbor is and how to love him or her."[68] We notice nevertheless that Francke did not understand neighborly love as mere outward forms of kindness. Rather, it required the support of conversion and a biblical hermeneutic of the heart. The foremost expressions of love were the reading and teaching of the Bible and the conversion of souls. Only after these could individuals rightfully address the earthly conditions of others.

For Francke true conversion led to true charitableness, and consequently his commitment to the doctrine of a universal call to salvation reflected his theology of improvement.[69] Predestination and doctrines that undermined

God's desire to offer salvation to all individuals usurped the human ability to bring about reform on earth. One could argue that the free call of the gospel in Francke's theology formed the basis for his belief that education and training would usher in individual and social reform.[70] A universal call of the gospel assumed that each person had the ability to discern and decide something essential not only for salvation but also for social change. Educational reforms that Francke believed would lead to a broader social and spiritual reform required the innate ability of individuals to discern—that is, to apply an acquired knowledge—in order that they might implement reform. Thus, it is not strange that he turned to the pedagogical reform ideas of men like Johann Amos Comenius (1592–1670), Ehrenfried Walther von Tschirnhaus (1651–1708), and Gottfried Wilhelm Leibniz (1646–1716) to help construct at his institutes what Whitmer calls a "scientific community" based on eclecticism, in which experience played an important role in the process of learning. There are moments in which it seems Francke hinted at a reciprocity between experiential learning and spiritual awakening.[71] Francke's affirmation of the doctrine of God's universal call to salvation, therefore, indirectly affirmed his broader beliefs in the human capabilities of discernment and the acquisition of knowledge. If individuals could act upon the gospel, they could by the same capacities grow in such knowledge that would bring about large-scale reforms in the world.

Still, the effectiveness of education and training relied upon a proper use of the Bible by truly converted Christians. Thus Francke's theology of improvement carried the train of the wedding gown in his marriage between biblicism and conversion. Francke had not "camouflaged skillfully" what W. R. Ward assumes was a paradox between new birth and education.[72] Individual and social reform was the culmination of his thought concerning the application of divine revelation and the regeneration of the soul. As such, it acted as the third major aspect of his theological system. In the end, Francke believed all things were to bring God glory, and a worldwide spiritual and social reform would be the visible evidence of the church's heartfelt turning toward God. As Lindberg notes, "Materially speaking, Pietism set about to continue the Reformation as the transformation of the world through the transformation of persons."[73]

The growth of Francke's institutes in Glaucha should be understood as a "material" consequence of his theology of reform. He wished to address the spiritually corrupt state of the church by catechizing children and their parents and by reforming pastoral training. The former would lead to the founding and growth of the various schools included in his institutes. The latter would lead to his attempts to advance theological education through new systems of training and application. These were only a few of the activities in which his institutes were involved. With the support of the electoral privilege granted in 1698 and under Francke's watchful eye, a body of ministries developed, which were expressed in various branches of the institutes—its schools, hospital, mission work, agricultural and manufacturing activities, and publishing efforts. All of these branches were to work together as agents of social transformation. Some individuals, like exiled Lutheran pastor and church critic Friedrich Breckling (1629–1711), joined their chiliastic hopes to Francke's institutes. Breckling believed that Francke's ministries contributed to the bringing about of a "New Jerusalem," and consequently for some Pietists the institutes embodied the eschatological "hope for better times."[74]

Biblicism, conversion, and reform held together Francke's theological structure, but without the polemics that preceded his installation as pastor of St. Georgenkirche and the conflicts between Francke and his Glaucha parishioners, he would likely have remained in the periphery of late seventeenth-century reform idealists. His self-proclaimed 1687 Lüneburg conversion experience and conflict with church leadership in Leipzig shortly thereafter gave Francke notoriety beyond the confines of the university city. In the eyes of his adversaries, he was promoting a disregard for church and civil hierarchies. Francke's ministry, they claimed, manifested itself in "Quakerism" and "Schwermerey."[75] Nevertheless, these Lutheran defenders of the faith found something even more dangerous in Francke: heretical ideas. He had become a mouthpiece for unorthodox theology and a disrupter of the faithful, and they could point to his handling of Scripture and his emphasis on conversion and obedience.

Francke, on the other hand, presented himself not as a destroyer but a rescuer of the church. In all the trials and investigations concerning his beliefs and practices, he continued to maintain that he merely practiced what Luther had preached: his conventicles and private meetings in which sermons were repeated only furthered individual piety and devotion toward the Word of God. Francke believed that personal interpretation of the Bible and conventicles, which encouraged a denial of the world, posed no danger to the church. They did, nevertheless, pose a danger to the dead faith of his fellow clergymen. The disruption he caused, alleged Francke, was to the benefit of the church, and Glaucha and Halle became the ground from which Francke sought to challenge the church and further build his Pietist program of renewal. Thus it comes as no surprise that Francke's initial work in Glaucha included inculcating a Pietist understanding of the sacraments in his congregants.

3

FROM IGNORANCE TO OATH

When Francke stood before his congregation in winter 1694 and preached *Von Sacramenten insgemein*, he had only been pastor of St. Georgenkirche in Glaucha one month short of three years.[1] Francke had hoped that in Erfurt he would find a place to anchor himself, ministering alongside his friend Joachim Justus Breithaupt, but the swell of controversies that arose in Leipzig over his teachings and conventicle practices drove him in 1691 out of the city divided by the Gera River and led him to the Glaucha community of Halle, nestled against the Saale River.[2] What biographer Armin Stein called a series of "open doors" that led him to Glaucha appears to have been more like a series of intense whitewater rapids.[3] Not surprisingly, within the first year of pastoring in Glaucha, Francke had again embroiled himself in controversy. He attempted to use sacramental practices of the church to instill key theological tenets of his Pietism in his parishioners' hearts and minds.

Those sitting in the pews of St. Georgenkirche that winter morning had already heard Francke preach through the first three articles of the catechism. This second Advent sermon on common characteristics of the sacraments was to serve as an introduction in preparation for more detailed sermons on baptism and the Lord's Supper.[4] Beginning with a reading from Romans 2:28–29, Francke then turned his attention to what he called the "misunderstanding and abuse" of the means of grace by the Jews. But Jewish abuses of God's provision were not the pastor's main concern. Francke was troubled by his congregation's ignorance and misuse of the sacraments. He laments, "For it is often found, that one meets people who are seventy or eighty years old and have never known what the sacraments are! . . . Sure, we say 'amen,' 'hallelujah,' 'Kyrie eleison,' and [yet] have not paid attention to understanding [the articles of faith]."[5] This ignorance Francke claimed to see in his parishioners was symptomatic of what he believed to be a broader spiritual ignorance that plagued the church.

Francke used *Von Sacramenten insgemein* as a platform for addressing this issue of ignorance. In his estimation, ignorance regarding the sacraments did not reflect merely a misunderstanding of God's gifts to the church but a misunderstanding of one's own standing before God. And without a true knowledge of their Savior and their salvation, individuals would abuse the sacraments. Francke assumes a close relationship between epistemology (*Erkenntnistheorie*), salvation, and the sacraments, and this presumption serves as a valuable entrance into a consideration of Francke's theology of the sacraments.[6] Thus the following discussion will draw from Francke's catechism sermon introducing common features of the sacraments in order to address the relationship he builds between the ignorant state of the unregenerate, the conscience as the means to a true knowledge of God, and the sacraments as oaths of commitment to God. Along the way, we will consider influences of reforming Lutheran and Puritan thought on Francke's theology.

The Sacraments and the Knowledge of God

Francke's epistemology connected true knowledge with faith and correct involvement in the sacraments with participants' true understanding of both their fallen condition and God's redemptive work on their behalf. His theology reflects the pastoral and pedagogical responsibilities he held in Leipzig, Erfurt, and Halle, and his desire to see his congregants recognize their own spiritual state played a part in how these ministerial responsibilities took shape. From his perspective, a vast majority of the church avoided a self-reflective recognition of personal sin, and he approached the sacraments with this epistemological concern.

The very form Francke's writings took exemplifies how his concern for proper knowledge of God pervaded all of his work. Though Francke eventually held a theological position at the University of Halle, he maintained Spener's concern for theological perspicuity. In *Pia Desideria*, Spener reacted against a normative practice in theological debates: writing in Latin. "On the whole, however, it would be desirable . . . that disputations be held in the schools in the German language so that students may learn to use the terminology which is suited to this purpose, for it will be difficult for them in the ministry when they wish to mention something about a controversy from the pulpit and must speak to the congregation in German, although they have never had any practice in this."[7] Francke took Spener's recommendation to heart, primarily using German in his teaching and writing. During the early Pietist unrest in Leipzig, church leaders accused Francke of being willing to transition from instruction in Latin to German when those in his conventicle meeting did not understand his teaching.[8] This egalitarian practice allowed a more diverse audience to have a higher level of accessibility to Francke's ideas.

Furthermore, his concern for spiritual understanding irrespective of social status and education compelled Francke to present his complex theological concerns in lucid, emotive, and responsive ways. Instead of attempting to speak to lofty doctrines on the nature of God, which he believed the Lutheran confessions and their interpreters adequately addressed, he presented his concern for the knowledge of God through seemingly simple questions, such as "What does Christ mean to you?" and, even more so, "Is Christ essential to you in your daily life?"[9] His style of preaching and instruction was inspired by the desire to draw his audience away from what he imagined were the entrapments of the world and compel them toward a daily experience of God.

Consequently, Francke poses a question in *Von Sacramenten insgemein* that reflects his pastoral concern for true spiritual knowledge. He began by asking: "What are sacraments?" For Francke, a proper knowledge of the means of grace was essential in a true relationship with God, but he recognizes a problem: "In this area [one] finds a such a great ignorance among people, in that they do not know what sacraments are, what their proper use is, and how they should be applied." Though his parishioners may have believed they actually understood the essential doctrines of the sacraments, Francke assumed the neglect of baptism and the Eucharist in the church was rooted in a lack of true knowledge, and therefore a lack of true conversion. Without such knowledge, parishioners were unable to honor God in worship and further their own spiritual blessedness.[10] By rejecting the ignorance of worldliness and turning to the true knowledge of the sacraments rooted in repentance, faith, and holiness, individuals became worthy participants in the sacraments.

The Ignorance of a Worldly Life

Attempting to explicate the central theme of the biblical passage Romans 2:28–29, Francke began *Von Sacramenten insgemein* by pointing out what he felt were his congregation's spiritual shortcomings. Francke believed that his parishioners habitually entered the doors of his church, worshipped together, and celebrated the sacraments, but they lived in a dangerous ignorance of the true meaning and use of the sacraments. Their ignorance revealed a much deeper epistemological problem, a problem that is echoed in Francke's critiques of baptismal, confessional, and Eucharistic practices. His parishioners lacked the true spiritual understanding that arose from a daily experience of God and resulted in a life of suffering according to Christ's example.[11]

Francke's teaching on the epistemological state of unregenerate humanity arose in part from his study of Luther.[12] While in Leipzig, Francke led a seminar on Luther's Genesis lectures, and this study influenced his later articulation of the fallen human condition.[13] According to Francke, the fall of humanity—its loss of reverence for God, its lack of faith, and its concupiscence—was wrapped up in the idea of unbelief.[14] Repeating the core of Luther's Augustinian conception, Francke understood the unregenerate to be trapped in a state of ignorance and inability.[15] Unbelievers did not know God; nor did they obey God's commands. In such a state they could be nothing else but at enmity with God. In order to express this disposition, Francke applied terms like "thief" and "murderer" broadly to unregenerate individuals. In his catechism sermon on the seventh commandment against theft, Francke claims, "[Man] is from nature a thief in the eyes of God. As so it is in all the rest of the Commandments."[16]

While maintaining a traditional position on the fall, Francke nevertheless expressed the condition of unregenerate humanity in a way particular to his own Pietist concerns. In his 1712 catechism sermon on the seventh commandment, Francke remarks, "But also the unbelief, in which we are conceived and born, is to be fittingly regarded as *the main cause and root of all sins*. And thus we are by nature also transgressors of all God's commandments. By nature we are atheists and idolaters. By nature we are all despisers of God's name and his honor and glory. By nature we are all unholy [people] to whom his Word, like God himself, is a distaste and annoyance. By nature we are all disobedient, murderers, adulterers, thieves, false witnesses, and so on."[17] It is particularly important in this discussion to recognize how Francke described the unbeliever's epistemological state. Fallen humans were atheists and idolaters. Idolatry is a misappropriation of the knowledge of God, while atheism is a denial of the knowledge of God through a denial of God's existence. Thus "atheism" is significant in understanding the epistemological dilemma Francke believed existed in the sacramental practices of his church.[18] As atheists, unbelievers lacked any true knowledge of God or his will and instead sought worldly forms of understanding. Though Francke justified his own interpretation of the human condition with traditional articulations, we will see that his use of "atheist" to describe unbelief reflects a common application of the term in seventeenth-century thought, his own conversion experience, and his emphasis on the human experience.[19] Moreover, Francke's use of atheism reveals his underlying concern for epistemological awareness in his congregation's understanding of God and the established means of grace.

Atheism

According to Francke, atheism appropriately described the spiritual condition of those separated from Christ through unbelief. By applying the term to the unregenerate state of humanity, Francke stressed not only that individuals, in their natural understanding, were completely devoid of any relational knowledge of God but also that such "atheists" were able to openly claim true knowledge of God while living a "godless" life. In doing so, he revealed a layered early modern concept of "atheist."

The *Philosophisches Lexicon* by Lutheran philosopher Johann Georg Walch (1693–1775), published in 1726 in Leipzig, provides insight into the late seventeenth-century sense of the word "atheism." Walch divided atheism into two realms: the theoretical and the practical. Theoretical atheists dismissed God's existence through philosophical systems. Whether by such means as a naturalistic philosophy or a denial of the supernatural, this form of atheism maintained that a belief in the existence of God was unnecessary.[20] Practical atheists were individuals who did not deny God's existence through words or a philosophical system but by their actions.[21] It was therefore possible, in this second construction, to be a professing Christian and also a practical atheist.

Nevertheless, in Walch's twofold description of atheism, he reveals that Lutheran academics at the time had their doubts that anyone could *actually be* a theoretical atheist. It was often the case that disbelief in the existence of God was not a dismissal of the existence of a god; rather, it was seen as a denial of the Christian, triune God. Walch's use of Baruch Spinoza and Aristotle as examples of theoretical atheism expresses this. One could argue, therefore, that atheists of this type merely exchanged one deity for another, which Francke would have considered idolatry.[22] Walch states, "No one can tear from their hearts the inner perception and natural disposition to the idea that there is a God. If one says [that God does not exist] with his mouth, he feels otherwise."[23] While Francke briefly discussed theoretical atheism in his writings, the majority of his references to atheism are allusions to its practical, "pharisaical" form, including his use of the term in his own conversion experience.[24]

Upon receiving the Schabbel scholarship a second time in the fall of 1687, Francke headed to Lüneburg, where he was to further his studies in the

Hebrew language under Superintendent Sandhagen.²⁵ Once he arrived in the northern city, Francke was asked to preach at Johanniskirche on the text John 20:31. As he meditated on the text, Francke realized that he did not possess the very faith he was to exhort from the pulpit. He went on to claim,

> I took in my hand a manuscript of Johannes Musaeus's *collegium Systematicum* [seminar on systematic theology].... But I had to lay it aside and could not find anything on which I could speak. I thought I could surely speak on the Holy Scripture, but the idea quickly came to me, who knows whether the Holy Scripture is God's Word? The Turks [Muslims] offer their Quran and the Jews their Talmud as such. Who will then say which of these is right? Such questions quickly spread until I finally had not the least remaining faith in my heart towards all those things which I learned my entire life, especially my theological studies on God and his revealed nature and will that I pursued for over eight years. For I no longer believed in a God in heaven. And with this everything was gone, so that I could cling neither to God's Word nor to the word of man. I found at that time as little power in one as I did in the other.²⁶

Describing his mindset following this inner epistemological conflict, Francke writes, "At the same time it seemed that through [Scripture spoken to me by a friend] a hidden comfort sank in my heart, but my atheistic mindset quickly used my corrupted reason as its tool to again rip out of my heart the power of the divine Word." This internal struggle of doubt, in which Francke claimed he lost his faith in God and his certainty of truth, brought with it a brief period of atheism.

Francke's reference to atheism should be understood in light of his early, radical incorporation of spiritual trials (Anfechtungen) in his broader conception of the process of conversion. Becoming "atheistic" in mind embodied intense questioning of an assumed knowledge of God and despairing over one's spiritual state.²⁷ In a March 1692 letter to Spener, to which he attached a portion of his *Lebenslauf* for Spener's consideration, Francke mentions a correspondence he received about a person who experienced an "unascertainable atheism." He claims that as a consequence of the role of atheism in conversion, "reason submits itself to faith, so that the person does not possess the glory that he himself has run [well], but rather that God has mercy upon all [Rom 9:16]."²⁸ Spener wrote to Francke a few days later: "As for unascertainable atheism, it would be dear to me to receive [your conversion narrative], and I shall handle it with consideration and gentleness. And I hope that God shall not leave it, along with what will further be written about it, unblessed."[29] Though Helmut Obst argues Spener also experienced a similar atheistic spiritual trial while a student in Strasbourg, it appears that Spener's desire to hear more from Francke shows a level of unfamiliarity with Francke's application of atheism.[30] This unfamiliarity may reflect the distance Spener had with some of Francke's earlier radical beliefs, especially perfectionism.[31] In the spring of 1693, Spener wrote to Francke about one of the latter's former Leipzig followers, Andreas Care. Care had sought help from Spener, requesting prayer regarding an ongoing spiritual trial that had left him with thoughts of "eternal darkness." Spener suspected that Care's depression reflected a form of perfectionism taught by Francke and his Leipzig associates, Heinrich Westphal and Heinrich Julius Elers.[32] It appears that the spiritual trials experienced by Care arose from a specific understanding of Christian perfection, which led him to despair over the "eternal" implications of ongoing sin and imperfection in his own life. Francke's language of atheism, as it pointed to a similar despair over the knowledge of God, expressed his early views of spiritual trials that may have influenced Care. The fact that one of Francke's other friends from Leipzig, Johann Caspar Schade (1666–1698), seems to have had a similar wrestling with atheism during his conversion strengthens the claim that this form of an atheistic spiritual trial has its origins in Francke's early ministry in Leipzig.[33]

Francke's self-proclaimed atheistic condition should not, on the other hand, be understood as a "theoretical" denial of God's existence. Francke clarified that a desire to reject God had not led him to his moment of unbelief. Rather, he remarks, "How I would have loved to have believed it all, but I could not."[34] His bout with atheism did not result from a lack of effort but instead from the futility of his efforts. Throughout his account, Francke reiterates that he did all within his power to maintain a devout Christian life. In fact, he hoped the opportunity to preach in Lüneburg would cultivate personal righteousness. Nevertheless, despite his attempts to construct an appearance of lived Christianity, whether through theological training or various forms of devotional activity, he could not bring about his own conversion, and this was due in part to the powerlessness inherent in his spiritual ignorance.

Further proof that Francke applied practical atheism in his conversion account is found in the moments directly following his self-professed denial of God. Upon claiming that he "no longer believed in a God in heaven," Francke abruptly transitioned to describing a moment where, as if he were in a tower overlooking a city, he was able to consider the sinfulness of his entire life—what he had done, said, and thought.[35] It was only in this state of complete doubt that Francke was able to see his utter sinfulness. Still, this moment of self-reflection was predicated on a continued belief in God's existence and future judgment. As Obst observes, "These words are a witness of very fierce atheistic spiritual trials [doubt], but are not a witness of an existential atheistic disposition. For Francke, the possibility of the nonexistence of God, in contrast to many philosophical atheists, was not freeing, comforting, or redeeming. Rather it plunged him into unrest and fear."[36] Francke, in his brief period of atheism, denied the existence of God as it related to his possession of a personal knowledge of God—an empowering knowledge that led to godliness, and having not *lived* as one who was in God's presence, he lost the certainty of God's presence and the security of the very faith he was called to preach.

This practical atheism shaped Francke's later description of the state of unredeemed humanity as atheistic. He was not declaring that humanity had no sense of the existence of God. Instead, his congregants—like Francke before his own conversion experience—were living as if God did not exist, and as a result they could not be certain of their knowledge of God or whether they were properly participating in the means of grace established by God. Their everyday life did not appear to depend on the daily experience of God in Christ. Francke wrote his 1693 *Glauchisches Gedenck-Büchlein* in part to counter this perceived lack of concern for spiritual matters in his local community. He exhorted his audience to serve God out of a "true repentance and with genuine earnestness." Francke critiqued open drunkenness on the streets and apparent disinterest in spiritual things while also encouraging his parishioners to prepare beforehand for sermons and read at home devotional works like Johann Arndt's *Wahren Christentum*. At one point in the text, Francke associated participating in the Word and sacraments with participating in a marriage ceremony with Christ.[37] The sacraments are the blood of Christ and the wedding gown of the church, and they are to be understood in light of the inward relationship of individuals with God and their proper preparation for worship. Were congregants truly ignorant of the realities of the sacraments, they would correspondingly be ignorant of the reality of their eternal union with Christ, their groom.

Rostock pastor and reformer Theophil Großgebauer was likely one of the main influences on Francke's views of practical atheism. Shortly after beginning his university studies at Erfurt in 1679, Francke received his first scholarship from the Schabbel family that allowed him to undergo three years of theological training in Kiel. This period would become very important for Francke's later thought. While living within the household fellowship of Kiel theologian Christian Kortholt, Francke met fellow student Joachim Justus

Breithaupt.[38] Beyreuther claims the community Francke engaged in Kiel "read and loved" the writings of reform-oriented Rostock theologians, to whom Großgebauer belonged and from whom he stood out.[39] Francke held Großgebauer's work, in particular his *Wächterstimme Auß dem verwüsteten Zion*, in high regard. Not only did he find Großgebauer's *Wächterstimme* important to his own pastoral ministry, but Anton Wilhelm Böhme, Francke's spokesperson in London, promoted it as a book that opened the eyes of Spener.[40] Included in the original publication of *Wächterstimme* was Großgebauer's work against atheism entitled *Praeservatif wieder die Pest der heutigen Atheisten*. In it he claims, "For what are they for fellows, who deny the power of the Holy Scripture? Unspiritual people, who love lusts more than God, who have muzzled and shriveled their consciences with a branding iron, and have ceased to feel the persuading words of God. They are our atheists."[41] In much the same way Francke linked his atheism to doubt in relation to Scripture, Großgebauer linked atheism to a rejection of the authority and power of God's Word. Furthermore, both theologians also traced a relationship between atheism and the individual conscience—something important to Francke's construction of true knowledge of God. Francke, like Großgebauer, insisted the revelatory function of the human conscience aided in eliminating practical atheism and ignorance of God.

The Conscience and the Knowledge of True Life

How does someone ignorant of the meaning and proper use of the sacraments become genuinely knowledgeable in spiritual matters? For Francke, epistemology was wrapped up in salvation, and true faith was essential to true knowledge: "Thus it must and can and will be different with us, if we first see the main reason of corruption, and come to recognize the horror of original sin in us. For no improvement can follow if this is not addressed, that one must first feel and sense his deep and foul-smelling misery. Nothing else can be of help to us."[42] The first step in this process was a personal recognition of sin. It was not merely a recognition of the problem—that sin had come between God and man—but a personal conviction of one's own state of damnation. For Francke, coming to terms with disobedience toward God was at the heart of the salvation process.

While seventeenth-century Lutheran divines' language of salvation reflected their attempts to differentiate God's application of grace (*gratia applicatrix*), Francke's own conversion experience led him to articulate the process of salvation from the visage of man.[43] He emphasized the individual's inward experience of God's love, which brought enlightenment and empowerment to every area of the person. In this transformative experience, the ignorance of the past life was replaced with a true knowledge granted in rebirth. As a consequence of beginning with the experience of man, Francke emphasized the human conscience as the bridge between ignorance and enlightenment. In doing so he presaged later existentialist articulations of the role of the conscience in the life of the believer.[44] Through a struggle of the conscience one could achieve faith and knowledge of salvation, and the conscience would help provide an ongoing sense of certainty within the heart of the individual. Francke's conception of the psychological role of the conscience in conversion and the Christian life is important in understanding his epistemology in relation to the sacraments. The conscience, according to Francke, served a primary function not only in the process of salvation but also in the believer's preparation for sacramental celebrations. The ever-present problem of humanity's atheistic condition was resolved, in part, through the individual's interaction with the conscience. Therefore in seeking to understand the relationship between Francke's epistemology and his sacramental theology, it is helpful to consider how he articulated the functions of the conscience, specifically in transmitting divine knowledge to the individual, and how his articulation expresses the influence of Puritan devotional writings.[45]

In his famous attack on the clergy's spiritual condition entitled *Von den falschen Propheten*, Francke remarks, "Although if [the clergy's] consciences were correctly examined, it would be found, that one entered his office through terrible ways, as *a thief and murderer has climbed into the sheep stall at a wrong door* [John 10:1]."[46] As "thieves" and "murderers"—and as atheists—those who improperly held ecclesial offices ought to turn to their consciences as sources of knowledge regarding their spiritual condition. This role of the conscience was not relegated to the clergy alone. According to Francke, the conscience functioned first as a means of revelation. It acted as a mediator of knowledge, revealing the divine law in the hearts of humanity. "In repentance you will experience how God puts to death through his law and strikes your conscience through its power."[47] The process of coming into a true relationship with God was contingent on the conscience bearing the Mosaic commands upon the hearts and minds of individuals. As individuals felt the weight of God's law, they were exposed to the secrets of their hearts.[48] Thus the conscience held a twofold function. It revealed the law, and it shed light on one's spiritual condition. Francke claims individuals whose consciences are "awakened concerning [their] sin" feel "as if God looked upon [their] sin alone."[49] Admonished by the preached Word, individuals were aided by their consciences, which set, according to Francke, "their corruption and misery before their eyes."[50]

While the conscience acted as a revelator of both the law and sin, it also served as an accuser of the soul, and like the previous twofold function of the conscience, Francke divided its accusatory role into two activities. First, it testified against the individual as a sinner. The consciences of both unbelievers and believers provided them with a sense of their sinful condition and a recognition of the disobedient life they had lived.[51] By directing attention to personal sinfulness and inappropriate lifestyles, the consciences of individuals aided in generating heartfelt concern for the inner life. Second, the accusatorial function of consciences also awakened individuals to God's impending judgment of their souls. Francke claimed that exalted in his heavenly courtroom God would mete out his justice upon those who ignored the accusations of their consciences. "The soul has a terrifying witness in itself, namely a bad conscience. It would like to suppress [the conscience], but it cannot control or bridle the constant accusations. And these continual accusations provide [the soul] with a witness of a day of judgment, which is in the future. From this comes the fear and terror of death. For, [the soul] does not like to think about the fact that it shall die."[52] Thus the conscience not only revealed sin but also accused and sought to generate a reaction within the individual heart regarding one's spiritual condition and the divine punishment to come. In its accusatorial function, the conscience is often labeled "bad." In Francke's conception, a bad conscience was not dysfunctional; rather, it opposed the individual's worldly desires, actions, and pride.

Nevertheless, Francke claimed the conscience also functioned in a positive, nonoppositional manner. Beyond witnessing to the imminent and eternal danger of individuals, consciences also comforted those who heeded their warnings. In this positive, comforting function, consciences depended on the response of individuals to God's inner revelation. Those who ignored and avoided the work of their consciences would remain in their "atheism" and continue toward eternal judgment. The likelihood that some would reject the messages of their consciences in order to remain in an undisturbed worldly life of false comfort greatly concerned Francke. He remarks, "Thus one does not fight as the world fights, which only conceals the magnitude of its sins, desires only to kill off the memory [of its sins], and would like to have them hidden from other people. It does this in order to avoid being unsettled by its conscience and to act pious before other people."[53] Francke's theological anthropology allows for the unbeliever to seek out a comfort apart from salvation and the inner testimony of the conscience. This worldly comfort, however, provided a false sense of security, which in the end could not withstand the onslaught of inner accusations.[54] Repentance and faith provided the only way to heed the call of the conscience. Francke believed that only with the assistance of these two spiritual tools could individuals experience the benefits of a good conscience, one that affirmed their spiritual condition.

Throughout his descriptions of the major functions of the conscience, Francke consistently grounded its work in God's grace. The inner stirring of God was necessary in awakening the human conscience: "But look, if the Lord God awakens the conscience in a man, then all of his sins are at once presented to him as if spread out on a table. There he sees the evil of his heart that began in his adolescence. It is as if he stood at the top of a tower and could look upon all his sins that he committed from childhood on."[55] God not only awakened individuals to the call of the conscience, but he also intensified its work upon their hearts. Therefore, whether individuals acted in good or bad faith, the activity of their consciences as revealers of God's law and as accusers of sin originated from God's activity in each person's life. The Spirit of God enabled individuals to examine their hearts and contemplate their spiritual condition.[56]

At the same time that the conscience depended on God to be awakened and active, individuals could impinge upon the effectiveness of their consciences. Like Spener, Francke believed that individuals, by ignoring the inner conviction of their sin, could hurt or disable their consciences.[57] Thus it was the responsibility of individuals not to disparage but to search their consciences. Martin Schmidt, discussing Francke's exposition of Psalm 139, notes, "Francke understood the contents [of the Psalm] as a challenge to continuously search his conscience," and like the biblical figure of Job, to "again ask (for he must ask) whether he had done something wrong, always mindful that God was right and that those perceived to be pious were not allowed to argue with him."[58] Believers were to question and test their own personal actions and inclinations against the testimony of their consciences. Thus when Francke challenged his congregation in 1695 to consider in their hearts whether or not they were reborn, he specifically addressed his parishioners *and* their consciences.[59]

It is in the context of human responsibility in relation to the conscience that Schmidt claimed Pietists, and Francke as a primary figure, adopted English Puritan ideas about the conscience.[60] Udo Sträter has shown the influence on Pietism of a variety of late seventeenth-century Puritan devotional writings, which had been translated and published in German Lutheran regions. He divides this period of Puritan influence into three distinct phases before the turn of the eighteenth century. The first phase (1593–1630) was dominated by the works of William Perkins. The second (1630–1660) was dominated by the writings of Emanuel Sonthom, Lewis Bayly, and Daniel Dyke, and the third phase (1660–1690) brought with it a wave of translations, which included works from Richard Baxter, Thomas Goodwin, and Joseph Hall.[61] Francke's interaction with these Puritan writings, especially Sonthom and Dyke, can be seen as early as 1687.[62] Jeremy Dyke wrote *Good Conscience* in 1632, which in its German translation became a popular late seventeenth-century source for spiritual edification in the Lutheran church. The archive of the Franckeschen Stiftungen holds two seventeenth-century copies of *Good Conscience*, leading to the likelihood that Francke was familiar with many of its themes.[63] For Dyke, the conscience was a mediator of God's truth, proclaiming the will of God to the souls of individuals. It was also an accuser of the actions of individuals and therefore bore witness to their transgressions of God's commands. Individuals, according to Dyke, could maintain good or bad consciences, depending on how they reacted to its inner work.[64] These correlations between Francke's and Dyke's descriptions of the conscience speak to the role Puritan devotional writing may have played in the development of Francke's theology.

Nevertheless, there are clear differences between the Calvinistic-leaning works of seventeenth-century Puritans and that of Francke. Research exploring broader influences on Francke's theology has sought to associate his ideas on the Christian life more directly with these Puritan writers than with the Lutheran tradition in which he stood.[65] Though an influence of one upon the other exists, we must always keep in mind that Francke was a devout Lutheran, seeking reform in Lutheran churches. At moments he evidenced an animosity to the Reformed faith and wrote against some of its major doctrines.[66] With regard to influences upon Francke's theology of the conscience, especially in his description of the movement from ignorance to knowledge, a rich tradition of Lutheran writings existed alongside the translations of Puritan devotional literature. It could be argued that both Puritan and Lutheran works on conscience have their origins in the work of Luther. Luther's own conversion has long been understood as a struggle of the conscience, and Karl Holl goes so far as to call Luther's faith a religion of the conscience.[67] Following in the footsteps of Luther and the Book of Concord, early works on the conscience by Friedrich Balduinus (*De casibus conscientiae*, 1628) and Johannes Stolterfoth (*Bericht vom Gewissen*, 1654) had an important place in seventeenth-century theological training, especially as sources of practical theology on the conscience.[68] The tradition of Lutheran work on the conscience was not silent during and after the influx of Puritan writings on the topic, and consequently Francke's construction of the "inner witness" should not be seen solely through the lenses of Puritan devotional writings.

One major difference of note between Francke's theology of the conscience and the Puritans' is its role in sanctification. Puritan theology, reflecting the influence of Calvinism, leaned heavily on the law of God as a representation of God's character. While Luther had proposed two major uses of the law, one as a means of constraining social evils and the other as a "tutor" leading sinners to the gospel, John Calvin and his successors claimed a third use. For the Reformed, the law expresses God's character and will.[69] It is out of this third use that Jeremy Dyke writes, "When [the conscience] doth incite and urge us to doe good, and doth stay and hinder from evill. It is uprightly good when it spurs to good, and bridles from evill."[70] For the Puritans, the conscience played an active role in the believer's sanctification. As it "incites" and "spurs," the conscience not only witnesses to the law and the condition of the individual but also aids in bringing about a godly life.[71] Francke, on the other hand, maintained traditional Lutheran law-gospel dichotomies. Though the conscience could accuse and witness against the person's condition and actions, it functions only as a mirror (tutor) and not as a prod. A perfect example of this distinction in Francke's thought occurs in his *Schriftmäßige Lebensregeln*, a short text of thirty rules that reads in some ways like the casuistry of William Perkins and his theological heirs. In his opening, Francke states, "Society provides ample opportunity to sin. If you desire to preserve your conscience, then (1) imagine that the great and majestic God in omnipresence is the foremost in society. One should be in awe before the presence of so great a Lord."[72] From this starting point, in which Francke appeals to the reader's desire for a peaceful conscience, he goes on to exhort them toward proper conversations and social activities. Francke mentions the conscience in two other rules (21, 24), but in both instances the conscience is presented as the means of revealing sin and convicting the individual. At no point does he address the conscience as source of stirring godliness. Godly living, claimed Francke, was seated in faith, and he framed the role of the conscience within the constraints of the first and second uses of the law. The conscience either reveals sinfulness or witnesses to the need of individuals to turn toward God through repentance and faith.

While it may be said that Francke situated salvation in the heart, he rooted the communication of divine knowledge concerning the law of God and the condition of man in the mediating role of the conscience. At every step in the transition from spiritual ignorance to true knowledge of God and his means of grace, the conscience played a key role. It was the inner voice that informed believers of their spiritual state, whether or not they approached the sacraments as converted individuals. Consequently, Francke's emphasis on the conscience is important to understanding how he believed Christians should prepare for participation in baptism and the Lord's Supper. Just as Francke used atheism to describe the epistemological deficiencies of unregenerate individuals, he used the idea of a good conscience to describe the inner witness that confirmed the worthiness of individuals to approach the means of grace. The epistemological dichotomy we find in the language of having a good or bad conscience meets us at the doors to Francke's sacramental theology. For believers who claimed a certainty of their good conscience, the sacraments became personal, visible declarations of their commitment to God.

"Oaths" of Commitment

The various dimensions of Francke's answer to the question "What are sacraments?" in his 1694 catechism sermon show that he expected a visible sacramental expression from those who now responded in faith to the witness of their consciences. Instead of strictly following the themes set out in formal Lutheran confessions, Francke used *Von Sacramenten insgemein* as an opportunity to frame baptism and the Lord's Supper in terms of ignorance, knowledge, and experience. The latter was often expected to evidence itself through personal discipline. As Harold O. J. Brown notes, "[Pietism] began by trying to get individuals to take their official religious commitments as deeply binding, personal obligations."[73] The Christian experience was closely related to the Christian's obligation. Therefore, the sacraments as means of God's grace did not take center stage; rather, Francke inverted traditional sacramental theology, beginning with human experience and ending with God's redemptive activity. This is poignantly seen in his signifying of baptism and the Lord's Supper as human "oaths" (*Eide*).[74] By offering a definition of the sacraments grounded in individual expressions of commitment to God, Francke differed not only from standard Lutheran teaching but also from Spener, who emphasized God's redeeming work in his definition of the sacraments. As will see, Francke's inverted theological articulation of the sacraments as oaths drew to some degree from Puritan Lewis Bayly's *The Practice of Piety*. Oath also served another purpose for Francke. He possibly incorporated oath into his theological language in order to ward off early accusations that he was teaching Quaker ideas. This application of oath to the sacraments reveals an aspect of Francke's theology in which he adopted controversial Lutheran language to refute accusations that he was promoting controversial Quaker ideas.

Comparing Spener and Francke

Spener and Francke followed the tradition of seventeenth-century Lutheranism and preached through the Small Catechism.[75] Following the structure of the catechism, both pastors had the opportunity to address the sacraments as a whole before explicating the features of baptism and the Lord's Supper. In his *Kurtze Catechismuspredigten* (1689), Spener included a sermon very similar in theme to that of Francke's *Von Sacramenten insgemein*. Like Francke, Spener began his sermon *Was die sacramenten seyen und was sie nutzen?* by expressing concern for correctly understanding the sacraments. "A very necessary part of our Christian faith, next to the knowledge of God and of the salvation to which God has called us, is to understand the means of grace."[76] And as with Francke, this concern for true knowledge directed Spener's further explication of the sacraments.

From this shared epistemological foundation, Spener adopted the categories of the catechism. He addresses the origin, existence, features, administration, and benefits of the sacraments as set forth by the confession. Furthermore, in each of these points Spener grounded his theology of the sacraments in the work of God. Though consecrated by the pastor, the sacraments were established and made beneficial to believers through the work of God. The grace and strengthening power of the sacraments, when taken by faith, were contingent on the promise of God. Only in closing did Spener describe the benefits of the sacraments for believers: "The foremost use of the sacraments is the awakening and sealing of faith."[77] Even in this point, though, Spener noted the preparatory work of the Spirit in the participation of believers. Thus, Spener throughout his catechism sermon sought to root his audience's understanding of the sacraments in God's work and promise.

Francke's own structuring of his 1694 catechism sermon on the common features of the sacraments does not appear much different from his mentor's. He divided his exhortation into three sections: (1) the meaning of the sacraments, (2) their use and benefit, and (3) the proper number of sacraments in the practice of the church. Yet closer examination reveals that Francke did not strictly follow the structure of the catechism. Instead of explicating Luther's instruction, Francke defined *sacramentum* for his audience and expounded upon the Scripture text (Rom. 2:28–29). This led Francke to interact primarily with Pauline and Old Testament passages and approach key doctrines referenced in the catechism through the exposition of Scripture.[78] The centrality of Scripture—over and not against the catechism—in Francke's sermon expressed his twofold desire (1) to give Scripture the primary position in the hearts of the worshipers and (2) to provide a reference point for personal contemplation, devotion, and later discussion within the household.[79] The presupposition that church leaders had neglected God's Word and indirectly discouraged parishioners from personal reading of Scripture stood in the background of Francke's two desires.[80]

Moreover, by avoiding direct references to the catechism, Francke created space in which he introduced doctrinal themes important to his theological schema. It was in this space that Francke turned his attention to the obligation and experience of believers. Whereas Spener introduced the sacraments in his catechism sermon by describing their origins in God's Word, Francke began by explaining the political meaning and application of "sacrament" in its Roman context: "The meaning of the word is actually taken from the Latin language. Namely, 'Sacramentum' as a Latin word [used] by the Romans does not mean anything other than *oath*." This philological turn allowed Francke to construct the sacraments as human declarations to God. Individuals in their preparation and participation were to approach the sacraments as oaths to Christ—expressions of their faithfulness and obedience. He went so far as to describe a prototypical oath for his own parishioners: "Thus it would be no different than as if he stretched out his finger at the altar to the living God and said: As truly God is my help! and as truly [this] is the body and blood of Christ! So I truly promise to be faithful and obedient to him, and I truly intend from now on to improve my life."[81] In Francke's theology of baptism and the Supper, God did provide a special grace, but it was the follower of Christ, with hand outstretched, who took center stage.

Francke claimed the early church lifted the word out of its social context without leaving behind its original meaning and appropriated it to the Christian practices of baptism and the Eucharist. He maintained that in Roman society, men taking up the call to military service would swear themselves to the symbols of the state and thus commit themselves completely to their authority figures.[82] Although later theological developments surrounding the means of grace would cause "sacrament" to take on various nuances, the word continued to retain its original meaning. At this point he seems to be reflecting the thought of Johann Gerhard. David P. Scaer notes, "Gerhard took this original meaning [of *sacramentum*] into his own definition so that sacraments are believers' promises to God to carry out faith's obligations and satisfy the sacraments' requirements. [He] saw the sacraments as mutual obligations between God and man."[83] For Francke, individuals who participated in the sacraments were doing nothing less than declaring their faithfulness to God and obligating themselves to follow Christ. Just as Luther desired believers to continually be reminded of the baptismal waters of their initiation into the church, so Francke desired believers to continually renew their oath, or allegiance, to God.[84] Francke exhorts, "Since we then call Holy Baptism a sacrament or a taking of an oath, and do the same thing with the Holy Eucharist, then we also have the opportunity to remember several good [things concerning our oaths]. For in truth it is conducted in such a way that we make a covenant with God in baptism, and do the same thing in the Holy Eucharist."[85] Francke would have his audience understand these covenanting acts as bodily oaths (*Cörperliche Eide*), which were to help remind believers of the implications of their commitment to God. These bodily oaths entailed a life that kept the sacraments "holy" and, therefore, kept the individual in God's grace. If participants were to misuse or mistreat the sacraments by continuing in their sinful lusts and desires, they broke their covenant commitments and stood to receive the anger and wrath of God.

The goal of these sacramental oaths was twofold. First and foremost, the believer's sacramental commitment was to lead to improved lifestyles. As an oath, the sacrament directly shaped the daily activity of individuals, and by pledging themselves to God, believers pledged themselves to sanctification measured by a growth in holiness. Second, the sacrament as an oath was to result in a personal resolve to fight against worldliness. Francke believed that a consistent meditation on one's baptism would lead the individual to recall, "There! There at the flag I swore myself to Christ! There I agreed to be loyal, faithful, and obedient to him; that I would struggle against the Devil, the world, and my own flesh and blood."[86] Francke often repeated this idea of struggling against worldly evil in his sermons, and he believed sacramental oaths were a vital means by which believers oriented themselves in the spiritual battle.

By incorporating the idea of oath into his sacramental theology, Francke was not immediately negating central Lutheran doctrines on the sacraments. At the same time that he clarified the importance of baptism and the Lord's Supper by drawing upon the Latin meaning of "sacrament," he also affirmed that they were real instruments of God's grace. The oath rested upon the assumption that the Lord's Supper involved the true body and blood of Christ. Thus Francke's theology of the sacraments as human oaths was not a sharp turn toward memorialism. Rather, Francke adopted and adapted earlier seventeenth-century Puritan thought into his theology without replacing traditional Lutheran doctrine.

The Oath, Francke, and Lewis Bayly

Almost two hundred years before Francke, Swiss theologian Huldrych Zwingli (1484–1531) used "oath" to describe the Christian's pledge to God in the sacrament. Zwingli's "shift in accent from God to man," notes W. P. Stephens, "coincides with a movement away from seeing the sacraments as an assurance of forgiveness and a strengthening of faith."[87] Though we may find similarities between Zwingli's and Francke's language of the sacrament as oath, there is no evidence that Francke took an interest in Zwingli's thought or was influenced by it. Rather, Francke's application of the term "oath" to the sacraments most likely represents a point of intersection between his theology and the work of the early seventeenth-century English Puritan Lewis Bayly. Likely born in the late 1580s or early 1590s, Bayly eventually rose to the position of bishop of Bangor and chaplain to King James I.[88] He used his prominent position to speak out against what he considered to be England's moral shortcomings. His critiques led to persecution and imprisonment in the decades preceding his death in 1631. As chaplain to the king, Bayly expressed contempt toward James's publication of *Book of Sports* and his amiable disposition toward Spain. Even after James's death, Bayly's Puritan ideals put him at odds with Bishop William Laud. Carl Trueman remarks, "While Bayly's biography indicates a man whose life was shaped by a series of controversies relating to the nature of the reformation of the Church of England, his principal claim to fame is his work, *The Practice of Piety*."[89] Bayly's *The Practice of Piety* not only became a popular source of piety in the cities and countryside of England but also shaped seventeenth-century German devotionalism and Francke's sacramental theology.

In 1628, Bayly's popular book was translated into German and published in Basel under the title *Praxis Pietatis*, and three years later, the Stern brothers produced a version in Lüneburg edited for Lutheran audiences.[90] Wallmann claims that Großgebauer integrated Bayly's ideas into his theology, and during Spener's time in Rappotsweiler, Spener became familiar with the Puritan classic.[91] Whether Francke first learned about Bayly's sacramental theology through Großgebauer's writings, through his relationship with Spener, or by way of his own family, it is clear that he was not only familiar with *Praxis Pietatis* but returned to it throughout his life. Francke's son, Gotthilf August, revealed in his autobiographical work that his father as a young boy used Bayly's writing in preparation for the Lord's Supper.[92] Thus at a young age, August Hermann encountered the language of oath making in Bayly's *Praxis Pietatis*, the same language that would appear almost two decades later in Francke's catechism sermon on the common characteristics of the sacraments.

In *Praxis Pietatis*, Bayly approached the concept of oath in its relationship to the sacrament while discussing the "ends," or goals, of the Lord's Supper. The bishop noted the sacrament was to "bind all Christians, as it were by an oath of fidelity, to serve the only true God; . . . and so to remain for ever a public mark of profession, to distinguish christians [sic] from all sects of false religions." Reflecting the same concern for personal commitment as Francke, Bayly stated that the Christian should "lay aside all earthly thoughts and cogitations, that thou mayest wholly contemplate Christ, and offer up thy soul into him."[93] Believers not only received the fortification of grace in the Supper but they also offered themselves up to God through an oath. Participation in the sacrament, according to Bayly, was a declaration of solidarity with the will and glory of God.

There is, nevertheless, a distinction between Bayly's and Francke's use of the oath in relation to the sacraments. First, the Lord's Supper as an oath is offered by Bayly as the last of seven *"Ends for which this holy Sacrament was ordained."* Though the sacrament as an oath found its place in his theology, it arose only after Bayly gave six theocentric ends. In each of the preceding six, God's work and grace are central. Thus, Bayly overtly grounded the human responsibility of participating in the sacraments on the foregoing work of God. Second, Bayly directly related the sacrament as an oath to anti-Catholic polemics. Not only did Christians make an oath to God, according to the Puritan, but they made an oath against the doctrine of transubstantiation. Francke, on the other hand, remained entirely focused on the believer's piety inherent in a faithful commitment to Christ. Where the oath for Bayly was against "false" doctrine, the oath for Francke was against a false trust in worldly things. Last, it should be noted that Francke applied oath to both baptism and the Lord's Supper, and Bayly does not. Thus, while Francke may have incorporated Bayly's use of oath in relation to the sacraments, he molded its meaning to fit his own desires and intentions.

The Oath, Francke, and Separatism

One of Francke's intentions, especially early in his Glaucha ministry, was to distance himself from various forms of separatism, which often claimed origins in early Pietism or were being associated with his ministry.[94] In the realm of education, Kelly Whitmer notes that even the form of pedagogy encouraged by Francke at his institutes "was part of his effort to set his community apart from those of religious enthusiasts or *Schwärmer.*"[95] Francke used the publication of his *Fußstampfen* in the English language not only to promote his ministry in Glaucha but also to define Pietism in contrast to what he believed were false associations. One of the common accusations against Pietists was that they held Quaker beliefs, and as Francke rose in prominence, he faced the same charge.[96] Francke's use of oath in relation to the sacraments can be seen as a form of distancing himself from the anti-oath sentiment found in English Quakerism and those separatist groups it influenced in German regions.

Even before the appearance of *Fußstampfen* in England, Francke defended himself against claims that he was following in the footsteps of George Fox and the Quakers. In his 1689 "Apologia," which he presented as a defense during his Leipzig trial, Francke wrote about his own conventicle work: "One describes it as a shameful innovation. [He] describes it as a reformation, criticizing it as Quakerism and Radicalism, [and he] will not rest until he exterminates this new sect, as he calls it."[97] Using sixteenth-century Anabaptism and seventeenth-century separatism in England as forms of "false religion," the leadership in Leipzig sought to nullify Francke's work as heretical and therefore unacceptable. By introducing the oath into his theological discussion of the sacraments, Francke positioned himself against such accusations.

While George Fox, in his *A Small Treatise concerning Swearing* (1675), recognized an "Oath of the Lord" in Old Testament Judaism, he believed that Christ's redemptive work superseded the law of the Israelites and, therefore, reduced the tradition of oath making to a simple "yea or nay" in the "time of the gospel." It was not just that the Christian should make an oath *only* to God, but that it was forbidden to make *any* oath at all. Fox was certain to delineate the extent of Christ's new command against oaths: while Israelites could make oaths to God (but "not an Oath by the Book, or by any Creature"), Christians were to make no oath at all.[98] By the 1650s, this strict anti-oath doctrine led to heavy persecution of the Quakers in England.[99]

Using oath as a central theme in sacramental participation, Francke's theology opposed the label "Quaker" in two ways: he affirmed the role of a visible oath in the church, and he presented an earthly context for the oath. For Francke, the sacraments were declarations of commitment made not only to God but also to those witnessing the event. For this reason, Francke could speak of participating in the sacraments as swearing an oath.[100] Second, the oath not only involved a verbal commitment but also tangible elements. While Fox claimed that the Old Testament Israelites were not to make oaths using earthly objects, Francke readily combined material realities with sacramental oaths. According to Francke, individuals not only felt the water of baptism and tasted the bread and wine of the Supper but also made "bodily oaths" through their participation in the sacraments. Thus, as Francke drew on Bayly's language to emphasize the centrality of commitment in practicing the sacraments, he naturally distanced himself from accusations that he held Quaker or separatist beliefs.

In his 1694 sermon *Von Sacramenten insgemein*, Francke did not fail to acknowledge at length those doctrines central to Lutheran sacramental theology. Before closing with an explanation of the proper number of sacraments, he discussed baptism and the Lord's Supper in terms of the ordering of God, as special sources of strengthening and grace, and as testimonies of God's promises.[101] Nevertheless, the influence of Pietism on his theology is unmistakable. His underlying commitment to conversion led him to introduce the sacraments using epistemological and anthropocentric elements. Francke believed many of his parishioners remained in the spiritual ignorance of their unconverted hearts. They had not truly come to know God as he is revealed in Scripture, and they remained atheists, blinded by their worldly entrapments. Were they to know and properly participate in the sacraments, they must first come to know their fallen spiritual state and find their salvation in converting to Christ. Granted a certainty of salvation by their consciences, believers were to turn to the sacraments as oaths of their allegiance to God.

4

BAPTISM GROUNDED IN CHRIST

When Francke stood before his Glaucha congregation on 8 January 1702, his nearby institutes were already over five years old. Begun with the simple desire to care for and educate children living in a working-class community outside the city walls of Halle, his ministry had grown exponentially. Perhaps it was his Pietist-leaning focus on children as agents of reforming the church that led him that wintry Sunday to preach directly on the meaning and value of baptism. He had watched, and claimed to have experienced in his own heart, the intellectual consequence of misinterpreting the sacrament of water, and he had seen the outward ritual have priority over the inward realities connected to baptism. Exhorting his parishioners to reconsider their own baptism, Francke divided his Epiphany sermon, *Von der H. Taufe Würde und Bedeutung*, into two major sections: first, a discussion of those things that give baptism its intrinsic value, followed by a clarification of these values in relation to the believing community. He organized the first section into seven values, which increase in importance and are connected to teachings on the Trinity and Christ's redeeming, mediatorial work. As a clarification of these values, the second section is attentive to how they give baptism its importance. The sermon played such an important role in articulating Francke's thought that, after its initial publication in 1702, it found its way into a popular collection of Francke's sermons entitled *Sonn- Fest- und Apostel-Tags-Predigten*, first published in 1704.

Francke's values of baptism set forth in *Von der H. Taufe Würde und Bedeutung* are useful in understanding preliminary elements of his baptismal theology. They reveal both his underlying Lutheran commitments while also pointing to ideas and themes in Francke's theology that are distinctly Pietist. Francke displays commonly held trinitarian and Christocentric structures of the sacrament. Nevertheless his husk-kernel biblical hermeneutic allowed him to use accounts of Christ's baptism at the waters of the Jordan as a pattern for the faithful experiences of believers.[1] For Francke, Christ's baptism finds its importance in how it revealed a set of expectations that awaited the true believer and the true church.

Baptism and the Trinity

To the question "What is baptism?" Luther responded in his Small Catechism: "Baptism is not simply plain water. Instead it is water enclosed in God's command and connected with God's Word."[2] In his sermon on the value of baptism, Francke affirmed Luther's teaching. Using the practice of John the Baptist in the wilderness as one of two proof-texts for the sacrament, Francke claims, "and with this we were shown, that he [John] acted *according to God's command*, and thus his baptism was not a work of man. Rather, it arose from the command and establishing of God."[3] Since baptism arose from the establishing or ordaining command of God, it ought to be practiced wholeheartedly in the church. Francke's theological constructions on baptism, though corresponding to the Lutheran confessions, reflected his own philological training and the influence of men like Philipp Jakob Spener. Francke took his cues from the narrative provided in the biblical text; his exegesis took preeminence and allowed him to affirm what he believed to be the true meaning or "heart" of the confessions.[4] Consequently, baptism—as it functioned in the Christian life—found its worth both in the "establishing" command given to John the Baptist and in the trinitarian commission Jesus gave to his disciples (Matt. 22:19).

Jesus's commissioning of his disciples to baptize "in the name of the Father, Son, and Holy Spirit" gave the sacrament its significant worth. Baptism as an expression of the Trinity, claimed Francke, bridged the gap between God's transcendence and creation's finiteness. Quoting Luther's hymn "Christ our Lord came to the Jordan" (*Christ, unser Herr, zum Jordan kam*), Francke writes that, "we should not doubt if we are baptized. For all three Persons have baptized [us], and therefore are devoted to live with us on the earth."[5] This bridging of worlds through the hope of trinitarian faithfulness brought with it a confidence in the efficacy of baptism. Believers could be assured of the grace of baptism because the sacrament was rooted in the triune God, who lived with them.

Also rooted in the Trinity, according to Francke, was the baptismal hope of rebirth: "With this it was signified to us that it is the whole Trinity to whom we have ascribed new birth, and from it we have received a new constitution and nature. For this reason we also were baptized in *the name of the Father, Son, and Holy Spirit*."[6] Through the bath of rebirth the baptized was simultaneously accepted into the family of God (and thus received membership in the church) and clothed with Christ's righteousness. The trinitarian formulation, as it directed the hearer's mind to the economic roles of the Father, Son, and Spirit in redemption, was the ground for new life. God's work of redemption was a work that brought the dead to life. Thus the baptized and reborn entered into the community of God through the Spirit, enjoying the benefits of the righteousness and blessedness of Christ.

According to Francke, the grace of God stands between and connects the trinitarian baptismal formula and the bath of rebirth: "There, there God the Father, Son, and Holy Spirit granted and gave us all his grace, which is in Christ Jesus. There, there we received the bath of rebirth, as it is named in Titus 3:5."[7] Baptism was to be understood as a source of divine grace, wherein all the benefits of salvation were given.[8] Participating by faith in a baptism set upon the promise of God and confirmed by the trinitarian formulation, the baptized received the forgiveness of sin, the merits of Christ, and the hope of new life: "We are now baptized Christians, and in Holy Baptism we received the forgiveness of sins and were washed of all our sins. Contrary [to our sin], we have entered into a covenant with God, and he has taken us on and in as his children. We have been made partakers in the righteousness of his son, Jesus Christ, and thus also his fatherly favor and grace."[9] In his preaching, Francke offered much, if not all, of the central Lutheran teachings on baptism.[10] Baptism was established by God's command and seen in light of the redemptive work of Father, Son, and Spirit. Springing from the trinitarian work of God and individual faith, the reborn experienced the justifying and adopting work of God.

Christ as the Baptized and the Pattern

"Behold, everything is portrayed and patterned in Christ's baptism."[11] In Francke's biblical theology, the Old Testament serves as a pattern of Jesus, and Jesus's earthly life, in its fulfillment of Old Testament prophecy, serves as the pattern of the church.[12] Thus, Jesus's baptism by the hands of John in the Jordan assumed special significance in Francke's sacramental theology. In this Jewish ritual, Jesus took steps toward fulfilling "all righteous," while also signifying the "fulfilling" of his redemptive work.[13] For Francke, Jesus's baptism maintained a twofold meaning for the church. First, it was a divine declaration of historical significance. Second, it patterned the experience of the church. Though these two interpretations of Christ's baptism remained distinct, their common biblical origin (Matt. 3:13–17) and Francke's willingness to fluidly transition between the historical and spiritual interpretations indicates that the two interpretations of Christ's sacramental event were contingent upon each other. If Jesus had not been baptized, the sacrament would not serve as a pattern for the church. And if Jesus's baptism held no spiritual significance for the present-day church, the historical event would lose its own importance.

Francke assumed that Jesus's baptism was in itself inherently of the same quality as the sacramental practice of the church. This allowed the New Testament event to ground the ecclesiastical practice. He remarks, "For much was laid out to us here so that we may recognize Christ Jesus not only as the one who established baptism, but also as the one who himself would be baptized and who consecrated our baptism with his baptism."[14] The command of God in the commissioning word of Christ, as the grounds for the sacrament, was only one half of the equation. Christ's actual baptism also served to establish the ritual as a means of grace.[15] Thus for Francke, baptism—like the Lord's Supper—had its origins in both physical and verbal acts; Christ was baptized and he commissioned his disciples to baptize. Rooted in both word and deed, Christ's baptism allowed for and supported the continuing existence of the practice in the church.

Jesus the Baptized

In a sermon given in Glaucha in January 1715, Francke preached on the special significance of the Father's declaration "This is my beloved Son, in whom I am well pleased." According to the biblical text, Jesus came to John at the Jordan River in order to receive the same baptism John was offering the Israelite community. With hesitation, John baptized Jesus. As Jesus came up out of the water, the Spirit of God in the form of a dove descended upon him, and the voice of God was heard declaring Jesus to be his "beloved Son." Focusing on this divine declaration, Francke writes, "Let us consider the following phrase: this is. It was not spoken from a past or future time but rather from the present. To this one who stood presently in the Jordan and allowed himself to be baptized by John, it is said, 'This one is.'"[16] Francke saw in Jesus's baptism, where this divine declaration from heaven was mingled with the descending of the Holy Spirit, a trinitarian declaration. Christ exists just as the Father and the Spirit exist. He is. Yet going beyond the actual words of the biblical text, Francke also believed the divine "this is" was a declaration of

Christ's messianic role. "You stand there in the Jordan and the voice said: This one is. Therefore you and you alone are and remain my Jesus through whom I am helped. I have redemption in your blood, namely the forgiveness of sins."[17] Francke freely associated blood sacrifice, spiritual redemption, and forgiveness of sins to the seemingly unassuming act of Jesus's baptism. In fact, this redemptive interpretation of Jesus's baptism appears to take precedence in Francke's understanding. The Father's declaration toward his Son was a statement of love, and embedded in these paternal words was the crucifixion of Jesus.

Nevertheless, it was of equal importance for Francke to describe the actual baptism of Jesus as an ongoing source of contemplation for believers. "Listen you, O soul, concerning the one of whom it is said: This one is. He is just as present to you now as he was present with John that time in the Jordan. He is as near to you as you are to yourself. He desires to live in your heart through faith."[18] The Father's declaration of Jesus's divinity at his baptism provided Francke with grounds to claim that Jesus was as present in the hearts of his believing parishioners as he had been at his own baptism. The historical reality of Christ's sacramental practice had a spiritual significance for the church, and as they dwelt upon the biblical narrative, Francke desired his listeners to associate the waters of the Jordan with the blood of Jesus. "I went into the bath in faith in the same way as you were covered and your body washed with Jordan's water. Thus in your pure and tender love you have washed me from all my sins with the precious flow of your red blood."[19] The realities of Christ's baptism—that his own body felt the waters of baptism—shaped the redemptive hopes of the church. Faithful believers were to reflect on the baptism of Jesus at the Jordan and on their own baptism. The baptism of Jesus stood as the source of ecclesiastical practice, and the significance of the individual's baptism arose directly from the waters of the Jordan.

From this central aspect of the sacramental practice of baptism—that is, it arose from the historical baptism of Christ and thus had ongoing inner significance for believers—Francke not only made the water of Christ's baptism a significant source of personal reflection but he also, out of Christ's baptism, developed a pattern for the church. Francke's belief that the Christian faith and life was to be understood in "steps" led him to construct the historical event of Christ's baptism into a chronological account of redemption.[20]

Jesus the Pattern

Within Lutheranism there was already precedence for making baptism a pattern of the believer's participation in Christ's Passion. In the fourth question of the Small Catechism, Luther claimed that baptism "signifies" the death of the individual's former self and a resurrection into the life of godliness.[21] Following Luther's exegesis, Romans 6:1–11 became the primary text used by later theologians and pastors to explain the soteriological significance of the water sacrament. In *Kurtze Catechismuspredigten*, Spener writes, "Thus we find in Paul's words a double treasure, which is met in baptism and of which baptism is also a pattern."[22] Baptism, for Spener and his contemporaries, was a pattern for the believer's death and resurrection with Christ. All who were baptized in faith partook in the death of Jesus and enjoyed the benefits of his resurrected life. Thus baptism served as a pattern for personal spiritual transformation: the death of the old self and a rebirth to new life. Francke extended this tradition of patterning the sacrament to include the baptism of Jesus. Building upon his belief that Jesus's baptism offered biblical grounds for the ecclesiastical practice, Francke interpreted the Jordan baptism as both a foreshadowing pattern of Christ's sacrifice and an expectant pattern for the church. He divided Christ's baptism experience into five moments of significance: the literal baptism (application of water), his exiting from the Jordan River, the opening of heaven, the Spirit's descent as a dove, and the Father's verbal declaration.

Of the five divisions, Francke's initial discussion of Jesus's actual baptism in the Jordan received the majority of his attention. Drawing from 1 Corinthians 15:45, Francke began by appropriating to Jesus the role of redemptive representative of humanity.[23] Christ, in his incarnation and earthly life, assumed the humble position of "a child of the second Adam," and by doing so he became the substitutionary representative for humanity. In this position, where his divine glory was clothed in humanness, Christ as God was humiliated. To communicate this doctrine Francke claimed that before entering the Jordan Christ undressed himself to the point of nakedness.[24] Humbled and with nothing to hide behind, Jesus declared himself to be the sacrificial representative and incarnate God.

Francke's assertion that Jesus was naked during his baptism held a second meaning. It foreshadowed Christ's crucifixion. Just as Christ received his baptism naked in the Jordan, he would receive a baptism of blood on the cross: "That he allows himself to be immersed must represent how he would be baptized with the *cross-* and blood-*baptism* and how he would then be undressed and stripped naked." Francke supported his interpretation by using the traditional form for baptismal immersion: Christ was "dipped" by John into the water. Building upon this immersion, Francke used the waters of the Jordan to represent the sufferings of Christ. No less than the "water of tribulations" flowed down his skin.[25] Thus in the act of baptism, Christ entered naked into the water and underwent baptismal immersion to declare his substitutionary role and to foretell his Passion.

Applying the baptism of Jesus to circumstances surrounding his own congregation, Francke saw the various moments as patterns for the true church. Just as Jesus's baptism spoke of his forthcoming suffering and crucifixion, so also the church, especially in "the last days," was to expect being dipped into a time of collective suffering and tribulation. Following eschatological themes present in Luther's theology of baptism, Francke imagined that the baptismal uniting of the believing community to Christ's suffering and death would only increase as judgment and consummation drew near. In this vein, baptism not only signified inner suffering and death but also an external dying that presumably led to the resurrection life. Individuals were to grow in the realization of their death to sin through their physical suffering and death. Francke called this the "baptism of the cross," and presumably the more diligently the church continued in Christian suffering, the more they identified with John's baptism of Jesus.[26] For, when John dipped Jesus in the Jordan, the daily baptismal death of the church was proclaimed.

The baptism of Jesus patterned a further eschatological hope for the church. According to biblical accounts, after Jesus entered the water, the Holy Spirit in the form of a dove came to rest on him. Francke did not primarily describe this event as a declaration of united, divine ministry of Christ and the Spirit, but rather as a representation of the Day of Pentecost, during which the apostles received their spiritual empowerment. At Pentecost, the Spirit filled Christ's disciples and empowered them to lead the New Testament church. Francke writes, "Luke's goal and intention in the description of Acts comes in part from the beginning of his gospel (when seen in connection with Acts 1:1). Namely, that he continues the gospel narrative, and then further describes in an orderly fashion how it was promulgated after Jesus Christ's ascension and how the Christian church was planted through the Lord's Apostles, whose teaching God strengthened with signs and with the distribution of the Holy Spirit according to his will."[27] The dove that rested on Jesus at his baptism was, for Francke, a foreshadowing of the outpouring of the Spirit upon the church, which enabled believers to live in the power of God. Yet the Spirit-as-dove also patterned the hope that awaited those who underwent their own baptism of death. "He desires secondly that the *Holy Spirit*, which is a *Spirit of glory and of the Lord, rests on him*, and that he would live and reign there eternally with Christ."[28] Those who were baptized into Christ's sufferings were also identified with his heavenly reign. The dove represented this hope of a meaningful suffering. For, according to Francke, just as the church would rise out of the waters of suffering, so too the heavenly Jerusalem would descend—like a dove—ushering in Christ's reign.

Francke bridged the waters of death and the dove of a heavenly hope by incorporating the Ascension into his interpretation of Jesus's baptism. "Furthermore, the opening of heaven meant that if he were to rise from the dead, he would also ascend to heaven, and be seated at the right [hand] of majesty in heaven."[29] The baptized was to see the opening of heaven as a proclamation of the Christ's heavenly reign, which was the basis of the Spirit's empowering work. In Francke's view, the Spirit's replication of the Christian life in the hearts of believers rested upon Jesus's reign at the right hand of God the Father. Thus the witness and miracles of the apostles and the true life of the believer were contingent on Christ's ascension.[30] By making this connection, Francke drew a link between Jesus's resurrection and the fruitful life of the true church.

Just as important for Francke, the Ascension, as the bridge between Christ's actual resurrection and the Spirit's empowering of believers, became a basis for his division between the earthly and heavenly life. Discussing Colossians 3:1–4, Francke writes, "For we understand from such words, that it is this power of Jesus Christ's resurrection by which man does not strive after the things on earth anymore. Rather he *strives after that which is above, where Christ is sitting at the right [hand] of God.*"[31] These verses, with which Francke connected Jesus's resurrection and reign in the same way that he did in his interpretation of Jesus's baptism, are situated just before a prominent passage on baptism and are followed by a discussion of themes also found in Romans 6. In fact, Francke stated a second theme of Colossians is the "instruction concerning Christian behavior, [that is] *how it is to be led with diligence unto sanctification.*"[32] He noted that the process of sanctification, discussed in Colossians 3:7–14, flowed from the individual's taking off of the "old man" and putting on the "new."[33] Thus the death of the old Adam (the waters poured over Christ and the removal of the old man) and the life of the new Adam (the dove resting on Christ's head and the putting on of the new man) depended upon the ascension of Jesus to his heavenly throne. Through Francke's interpretation of the Ascension, the reign of Christ in heaven became the grounds for the suffering reign of the church on earth.

Last, Francke draws on the Father's verbal declaration "*this is my beloved son, in whom I am well pleased,*" not as a confirmation of Jesus's divinity, as he would do in his 1715 exposition of the same passage, but rather to emphasize Christ's commissioning of his disciples to proclaim the gospel "to all the world" (Matt. 28:19–20).[34] The earnestness with which Francke held to his own interpretation can be seen in the reforming work of the Stiftungen. As

Francke presented this sermon on baptism in 1702, he had already established reforming efforts that reached far beyond surrounding regions.[35] Through a relationship with Heinrich Wilhelm Ludolf (1655–1712), who had diplomatic connections to England, Russia, and East Asia, Francke was able to initiate contact with Russian communities.[36] Though his original hope was to conduct missions in China, Francke eventually developed a strong relationship with Peter the Great, which allowed him to educate Russian expatriates and send Halle-trained theologians east. These educators, pastors, and theologians trained in the confines of the Stiftungen carried with them Francke's books and his pedagogical disposition to see spiritual awakening united to the empirical acquisition of knowledge. Ludolf also provided Francke the opportunity to enhance the influence of his institutes in England. It was through his relationship with Ludolf that Francke sent Böhme to England, and just as in Russia, the ecumenical impulse to establish a "universal church" expressed itself through education, social work, and book printing.[37] Francke's influence in England also allowed him to send missionaries to India.[38] In cooperation with the Danish colony in the Indian town of Tranquebar, Halle-trained missionaries established a church and translated the New Testament into the native language. Francke's work in eastern Europe, England, and India was motivated by the same desires that led him to incorporate the call to worldwide evangelization into his interpretation of Christ's baptism.

Francke based his theology of baptism not only on the command of God but also on the biblical testimony of Jesus's baptism. The symbolism of that which occurred in the Jordan held the seeds of Christ's impending Passion and the earthly life of believers. Francke held that the waters of Christ's baptism were of inestimable value in patterning the earthly trials and heavenly hope of the believing community. Just as Christ went under the waters of the Jordan, believers were to expect undergoing a baptism of suffering, and just as the dove came to rest on Christ, they were to find hope in the empowering of the Spirit. These images, derived from Jesus's own life, were to be a comfort to true Christians, as they battled the temptations of worldly attractions. The emphasis Francke put on this spiritual interpretation of Christ's baptism had the effect of elevating his spiritual interpretation to the same status as the literal, historical interpretation of the text.[39]

Francke's patterning of Christ's life demonstrates his broader biblical hermeneutic. Scripture held both a literal/husk (*sensus literalis*) and an applied/kernel (*sensus litterae*) interpretation. Individuals holding a true faith in Christ were to find the Bible useful as it presented the reader with a meaning that could only be grasped by faith. The simple, historical knowledge derived from the text was insufficient for salvation. By faith, individuals were to seek out the Christ-centered kernel of the passage. Interpreting Francke's biblicism for his readers, Peschke claims, "Whoever would wish to break the husk with an excessive scholarly apparatus, in doing so only proves that he does not desire the kernel enough."[40] By applying this hermeneutical formula to Christ's baptism, Francke drew out of the biblical text a call to conversion and a godly life. In doing so, he made the historical event subservient to the spiritual application he derived from the event.

This speaks to the thrust of his sacramental theology. A recognizable (or "mature") conversion and a godly life form the core of Francke's baptismal theology. As a result, he gives teachings that help convey these important aspects a prominent place in his preaching and writings. Traditional, grounding values of baptism now felt the weight of Francke's biblicism of the heart, pushing them to speak of a faith formed by Pietism.

5

THE BAPTISMAL COVENANT AND REBIRTH

In early July 1714, Francke traveled to preach in Könnern, a town just north of Halle. The local Lutheran inspector, Christian Stürmer, had made arrangements so that Francke would hold a sermon during the celebration of the visitation of Mary.[1] By this time, Francke had established almost all the functioning arms of his institutes. The year 1706 saw the arrival of two Halle missionaries in Tranquebar, India, signaling the beginning of modern Protestant mission work, and four years later Francke helped to found what would become known as the Canstein Bible Institute. The institutes had taken on what Thomas Müller-Bahlke calls an "international character."[2] Francke himself had also transitioned. In 1714, he left his position at his church in Glaucha to become head pastor of the prominent St. Ulrichskirche inside the city walls of Halle. It was a move that signaled not only a rise in Francke's fame but also a growing acceptance of Pietism as a form of religious expression.[3] In Könnern, Francke preached a sermon entitled *Alles und in allen Christus*, an exhortation that exemplified his Christocentric style of preaching. The biblical narrative of the visitation of Mary became an opportunity to challenge the spiritual lives of his congregants and enjoin them to convert to the Lord. His final application of the liturgical text, though, cut straight to a major problem in the church: a false trust in baptism. Though his hearers had been made partakers in Christ's righteousness through the baptismal washing of rebirth, they had embraced the ways of the world and found themselves in a "horrific deception." They were like soldiers who failed to hold their oath to the flag to which they had sworn.[4] They needed a true conversion to God.

One of those in attendance was his son, Gotthilf August. Having turned eighteen a few months earlier, Gotthilf August had begun his theological studies at the university in Halle in May. Though he would go on to become the director of the foundations, playing a large role in furthering the global presence of the institutes, that summer day became the turning point in his life. Johann Georg Knapp, who published Gotthilf August's *Lebenslauf*, claims,

> [Gotthilf August] received such a deep impression from hearing and writing down [his father's] sermon that he sought from that time on to obtain a living confidence in the forgiveness of sins in Christ, and to count all else loss in light of the surpassing knowledge of Christ Jesus, his Lord, in order to gain Christ and be found in him [Phil. 3:7–9]. And on the same Fest day he attended a private gathering, which the local inspector [Christian] Stürmer arranged in his house after public worship. [Gotthilf August] was even more powerfully moved through his father's evangelical presentation on, among other things, the love and joyfulness of Christ. In such grace he also hereafter remained faithful, although not without a constant struggle against spiritual dullness.[5]

For Knapp, this signaled a "powerful awakening" in Gotthilf August's life; it marked his conversion experience. What is not to be overlooked, though, is that Gotthilf August does not appear to have led a wayward Christian life before that day in Könnern. Shortly after his birth, he was baptized and so taken into the "covenant of grace of the Triune God," and as a child, his Pietist parents prayed and watched over him. Knapp informs his reader, "Although this boy sought to walk before the world in a way that avoided punishment . . . conducting himself in a still, orderly, respectable, and outwardly-virtuous way, so that he could be presented to many others as an example; yet God still made himself known to him."[6] Preceding his conversion, Gotthilf August became aware of his deep, wretched sinfulness and longed for the certainty of God's grace in Christ. According to Knapp, he experienced these so that he might be counted among the children of God. It was only through the spiritual "breakthrough" offered by means of August Hermann's words that Francke the younger would come to stand in the certainty of the true Christian life.

Not overlooking questions of the historicity of his account, Knapp provides a late eighteenth-century glimpse into what had become a version of the expected Pietist steps leading to the true Christian life. Though a child be baptized, she would nevertheless require a thoroughgoing experience of her sinfulness that would find resolution in the "breakthrough" of God's grace and the forgiveness found in Christ. This would result in her becoming a "new creature," born into the family of God. These steps reflect major themes in Francke's conversion theology. Nevertheless, by emphasizing conversion in his preaching and teaching, he inevitably weakened traditional teachings on baptismal regeneration. It was in some ways a balancing act for him. He derived his baptismal theology from a human-centered view of the baptismal covenant, and while he attempted to maintain adherence to Lutheran doctrine on baptism, he undermined that doctrine at the same time with his consistent insistence upon a self-reflective, mature conversion experience.

The *Taufbund*

Lutheranism, as a theological system, was not the target of Francke's arrows. Instead, he aimed his rebukes and exhortations at what he assumed was a lack of true faith in the midst of true doctrine, and in light of this, Francke's theology of baptism should be understood as reactionary. Though the church was to imitate Christ in his baptism, a baptism that patterned future suffering, death, and empowerment of the believing community, Francke was concerned that churchgoers had made the sacrament into something far different from what he imagined Luther had intended. This concern and critique at the center of Francke's sacramental theology was signified in the idea of *Taufbund*, or baptismal covenant.

Luther to Francke: The Two Sides of the Baptismal Covenant

In accord with the broader Christian tradition, Lutheran theologians rooted baptism in the Old Testament covenantal practice of circumcision. Just as God established circumcision as a sign of his grace toward the Israelites, so too baptism signified God's salvific work on behalf of the church. Consequently, theologians like Francke had no problem giving circumcision the label of sacrament.[7] Lutherans associated many of the themes inherent in the practice of circumcision with baptism, including the idea that both served as signs of God's covenant with the community of faith. In 1519, Luther himself attached the words *tauffbund* to the covenant between God and the individual in baptism.[8] Though it was quite normal for Luther to refer to the covenant as a declaration of God's promise and also a pledge of the believer toward God, according to Bryan Spinks, the "covenant is explained as God's promise to be present in the sacraments which are signs of justification. The human response is to trust that the covenant is indeed unilateral." Luther believed

God conferred grace in baptism, and the baptized was to respond to this sacramental gift by daily turning to God in repentance and faith. Although Luther does not appear to emphasize what some later theologians would call the "two sides" of baptism, Spinks notes that as early as Philipp Melanchthon, we find a human responsibility toward God incorporated into the baptism covenant.[9] This inclusion of the individual will into baptismal language signified a tendency by some Lutheran theologians to see a bilateral covenant in the sacrament.

Martin Chemnitz (1522–1586) confirmed this two-sided aspect of the sacrament. In a 1572 sermon on baptism, he entered into a discussion of the baptismal covenant by describing the promises of God invested in the sacrament: "Through Holy Baptism God the Father promises, and pledges himself to us just as in a covenant because in baptism he gives and unites us to the merits of Christ's death and resurrection, that we should see ourselves as having him as our graceful Father of all grace, the forgiveness of sins, and eternal life."[10] Toward the end of the sermon, Chemnitz addressed the human side of baptism: "For this is what water baptism means. Namely, that it might be a reminder that we should not wrongly understand the covenant of grace of Holy Baptism as if it were a *priuilegium turpitudinis* [privilege to indecency] that we freely made to the Devil instead of to God, without a fear or dread of sin, and [as if] God must consider us no less than his children and inheritance. Instead, we are obligated and bound before God to put sin to death and to strive against the Devil because through baptism we were redeemed from his reign."[11] Chemnitz, in discussing the *Gnadenbund* (covenant of grace) of baptism, acknowledged the same two-sided nature of baptism that Luther mentioned. Not only does God act on behalf of man in the covenant of baptism, but man is to remain in the covenant through repentance and faith. It is of great importance, though, to note that Gnadenbund and Taufbund in Luther's and Chemnitz's theology refer to the same idea. There does not appear to be a clear distinction between the two terms. In baptism, God makes a covenant with his church that has divine and human dimensions.

The early seventeenth-century Lutheran divine Johann Gerhard (1582–1637) constructed the baptismal covenant in a similar way. Gerhard, like Luther and Chemnitz, referenced both the Gnadenbund and the *Bund der Tauffe* but does not appear to make a distinction between the two. Gerhard did, though, make a clear distinction between the two sides of the covenant. In responding to the charge that repentance would not be necessary if the baptismal covenant were eternal, he remarks, "On our side we can freely transgress God's covenant and forfeit the benefits of this covenant, but on God's side it remains intact; for he does not deny himself."[12] Thus by the early seventeenth century, Lutheran theology directly distinguished a dichotomy in the baptismal covenant that was only vaguely discussed in sixteenth-century descriptions of the sacrament. The *Bund* of baptism consisted of a "God side," which remained unbreakable under the protection of God's faithfulness, and a "human side," which stood or fell according to whether the believer remained in God's grace.

This articulation of the sides of the covenant continued into the second half of the seventeenth century. Spener picked up this phrasing in his catechism sermons: "Although the enacted baptismal covenant has been broken on the side of man, and he has thus fallen from salvation, on God's side the baptismal covenant has in no small way firmly remained."[13] Just as with his predecessors, Spener used Gnadenbund and Taufbund to refer to the baptismal covenant. Thus from Melanchthon to Spener, theologians recognized a two-sided covenant attached to the sacrament of baptism and rooted in God's grace toward man. When these men spoke of the human responsibility toward the baptismal covenant, it was consistently in the context of the foregoing redemptive activity of God on the part of humanity.

Francke continued in this theological development that gave sides to the baptismal covenant, but he so closely connected his emphasis of the sacramental oath to the baptismal covenant that the term Taufbund primarily came to represent the human commitment to God. Since Francke's starting point in his baptismal theology was the believer's responsibility, he expressed all other elements of baptism in light of the covenant between the individual and God. Even when Francke addressed the divine side of the baptismal covenant, he did so primarily to caution against rebaptism.[14]

> But when people do not keep their baptismal covenant, but rather serve and remain beholden to the sins which they denied in baptism, allowing them to rule over [their lives], it follows that they break their baptismal covenant. Since the covenant on God's side remains firm, they are surely not permitted to be rebaptized. For the order prescribed from God is that true repentance and a thoroughgoing conversion procure the renewal of the baptismal covenant on the side of man. Faith is again kindled in the heart through the gospel, and in such form the grace of God will be offered through faith.[15]

While Chemnitz and Gerhard addressed the human responsibility connected to baptism (that believers were to daily remember their baptismal waters) as something that flowed from the divine act, Francke made the human act of primary concern, and the Taufbund—as a symbol of the individual's commitment to God—became the overarching theological concept in Francke's articulation of the sacrament.[16]

Breaking, Renewal, and Maintaining

"One may also say: baptism is of use if you hold to the baptismal covenant and worthily go about in Jesus Christ's teaching. If you do not do this, but rather turn your back to God . . . and live in unrighteousness, greed, hate, enmity, drunkenness and other works of the flesh, then in your baptism you have not improved before God and cannot in this sinful and unchristian condition be comforted by his grace, forgiveness of sins, and eternal life."[17] Francke's inverted formulation of Taufbund naturally led him to set out and stress the covenant-keeping responsibilities of believers, but his pessimistic outlook on the spiritual state of the church caused Francke to believe that very few, if any, remained in their baptismal covenant. He was not shy about making this known in his preaching: "For this and other reasons it is to be found, sadly, that few children keep their baptismal covenant."[18] Francke's own personal experience sheds light on his pessimism. Though he begins his *Lebenslauf* by mentioning his own baptism, he describes his life as one that strayed from the baptismal covenant. He had come to trust a form of outward religiousness, and the practices that embodied this form of Christianity became abhorrent to Francke after his conversion experience.[19] Just as he had trusted in the spiritual benefit of mere outward practices in his youth, straying from true faith, so too he believed the majority of those baptized no longer honored their covenant. Since Francke claimed that such a large portion of his congregants had fallen from their covenantal commitment, he set out to awaken what he believed were lost souls and exhort his listeners to the renewal and maintenance of their childhood pledge.

Francke turned the Old Testament tradition of the covenantal relationship between God and his people into an occasion for this exhortation. Building off the common theological association of circumcision with baptism, he paralleled the covenantal unfaithfulness of the Israelites to the unfaithfulness of his present day congregants, who neglected their Taufbund: "These days our so-called Christians do a terrible job holding their baptismal covenant just as the Jews did back then with the covenant of circumcision."[20] According to Francke, the Israelites became comfortable in the mere outward ritual of circumcision, and that was their downfall: "For such words give the impression that the Jews acted like present-day Christians. They believed that since they were circumcised they must necessarily enter into heaven, where Abraham would be because he was circumcised. But they did not look at the heart!" This neglect of internal things on the part of the Israelites led to God's judgment upon them, and those in Francke's generation who forsook the "baptism of the heart," which their Taufbund represented, were to expect the same consequence.[21] Standing outside the grace of God, a grace likened to that experienced by the Israelites, parishioners had strayed from their baptismal covenant with God, and now acted with hearts "like a plot of land unkempt and full of the weeds of unbelief."[22]

In light of this sacramental problem in the church, Francke made Taufbund renewal an important feature in his articulation of the sacrament. True believers must return to a right standing in the baptismal waters of their youth. To initiate the process of renewal, Francke directed individuals to seek the testimony of their consciences. "Now then, he whose conscience testifies that indeed up until that point he had been comforted by God's grace though he had still not concerned himself with an honest conversion to God, must allow himself to be moved [to show] through this appointed examination that he truly has arrived at the grace of God."[23] Following 1 Peter 3:21, Francke believed baptism granted faithful participants a good conscience, but once they forsook their Taufbund their consciences became accusers of the condition of their heart.[24] As a revealer of such unfaithfulness, the conscience waited upon to individual to convert back to God through the expected means of repentance and faith or conversion before it again became "good."[25]

Once the conscience had directed individuals toward their mistreatment of the Taufbund, Francke believed that certain acts must follow in accordance with the renewal of their baptism: "You must come in the proper order. There must not be any falsehood or hypocrisy in your hearts. For, who would not like to be comforted by eternal salvation? But only a few want to bite the sour apple, to properly recognize their sins, to heartily regret them and avoid them, and thus renew their baptismal covenant, that, just as they earlier renounced the Devil and all his work and all that has to do with him, in these the baptismal covenant would be renewed by them and on their side."[26] Individuals repented of a spiritually tangible object. Falsehood and hypocrisy—Francke's representations of sin—were to have no place in the hearts of believers. Repentance and converting to God, a process summoned by the conscience, involved a concerted stand against unfaithfulness. Thus Francke made the personal pledge against the Devil and his work the foremost act of renewal. In this sense, Francke's theology of Taufbund rested on the believer's constant revisiting of the baptismal oath.

As the seat of true conversion, the heart was a vital spiritual organ in Francke's thought.[27] In denying the Taufbund, the heart, which was the dwelling (*Wohnung*) of the Holy Spirit, was given over to the Devil.[28] He made it his abode, and with each passing day that individuals lived in opposition to God's Word, their hearts grew hardened in the ways of the world.[29] Satan turned and directed the heart in accordance with his evil plans. Either the Devil or God directed the heart; either Satan or Christ made it his abode.[30] Believers were not passive in this. It was their responsibility to turn their hearts toward God and away from worldly attachments by concentrating on the Word of God set in their hearts by the Holy Spirit. Francke used heart-centered language to make known his desire to move beyond the forensic understanding of justification to the holiness that should proceed from it.

> It is not enough to boast of Christ with their mouth, and to confess with words only, that they trust in the merits of Christ, for we see, when these Mouth Christians, come to any one, lying on his sick bed, and in the agonies of death, just on the brink of Eternity, who, I pray, are more ready than these sort of hypocrites, to ask the question, Have you Jesus Christ in your Hearts, now a man would think, that they not only barely knew, that Christ was dead for them, but more that he must be in them, and live and dwell in their very hearts if ever they intend, the felicity they seek in him, shall have sure ground, and be founded according to truth.[31]

Since spurning the Taufbund was a rejection of God's grace and an invitation for Satan to reign in the individual's heart, Francke described Taufbund renewal as a drawing near to God with the heart.[32] Even more dramatically, Francke stressed the volitional act of giving the heart over to God. A return to God and the baptismal covenant required the person to relinquish the seat of human activity to the power of the Holy Spirit. Scripting a proper renewal, Francke remarks, "Thus I renounce once again the Devil and all his work and all that has to do with him, and I give you, O Lord Jesus, my heart all over again. Behold, you have saved me because you died and rose again for me. You have given me this salvation in Holy Baptism. Therefore I come to you once again upon your Word, and I give you my heart all over again."[33]

Francke's method of maintaining the Taufbund required believers to establish habits rooted in those elements expressed by baptismal renewal. Inherent in Francke's call to "hold" or "remain in" the Taufbund was the exhortation to continue in faith and be obedient.[34] Individuals accomplished this through biblically centered means, the foremost being self-examination.

He often turned to the biblical narrative to support the need for self-examination. Francke claims, "Jesus's disciples give us an example from which we should learn to examine ourselves as to whether we have remained in the covenant of Holy Baptism from our childhood up until this very hour."[35] Believers were to take every thought and action captive and test them as to whether they conformed to God's promise. Aspects of maintaining the baptismal covenant were incorporated into self-examination, which required a sincere interaction with the Word of God. Believers were to ask themselves whether they had truly "heard" the Word or merely listened to it with a peripheral concern.[36] Francke added prayer alongside the role of God's Word in maintaining the Taufbund. Individuals were to approach the Lord in prayer, praising him for the grace given in baptism.[37] Last, Francke made the individual's struggle against the Devil and the lusts of the flesh an essential part of maintaining the Taufbund. Guilt, a key feature of Lutheran discussions of justification, now hid behind Francke's calls to stand against the power of the world. Such a formidable force could only be overcome by God's grace, which Francke, like other Pietists, often represented with the term "power." Believers stood against the power of sin and the Devil through the empowerment of God's grace.[38] "Therefore it would be the least that parents could do if they diligently reminded their children from their youth on what they have for a covenant with God in Holy Baptism, and how they are to lead their entire lives in the denial of ungodliness and worldly lusts with its power, and [how they are to] bow their own way of thinking under the cross of Christ. For what is said at Holy Baptism? Do you renounce the Devil? Yes. And all his work? Yes. And all that has to do with him? Yes."[39] The maintenance of the baptismal covenant, like its renewal, placed heavy emphasis on the faithfulness of believers. Christians acted in accordance with the baptismal pledge when they took hold of every moment to examine their lives: Have I been attentive to the Word of God? Do I pray? Have I taken up the call to battle against the power of Satan and the world?

Comfort

> For he sees how distanced he was from the life that comes from God; the horrible darkness in which he was stuck; how he had become like livestock; how he carried the mask of Satan instead of the image of God; how his heart was a hell in which unclean spirits danced, coming and going as they wished; how he was like a cursed plot of land that had not been weeded of its thorns and thistles. And nevertheless he

comforted himself that he was a baptized Christian. O how such a fleshly comfort sickened him no differently than if it were like lukewarm water, which one spits out of his mouth![40]

Taufbund offered believers the benefit of spiritual comfort. In a life that presented a myriad of temptations and trials, Francke claimed individuals could find no better source of eternal comfort than in holding to the baptismal covenant.[41] Much of Francke's exhortation and critique sprang from the belief that salvation was truly wrapped up in the sacrament of baptism, but this belief also led him to carefully instruct his congregation on the difference between finding comfort in baptism through faithfulness to the Taufbund and building a false comfort upon an outward reliance on baptism.

The Christocentric and soteriological signification of baptism framed Francke's discussion of the comfort-benefit of the Taufbund. In the first place, individuals who lived upon repentance and faith—signified in their baptismal waters—continued *in* Christ. Baptism was the putting on of Christ; the blood of Christ, his merit, and the benefits of his sacrifice became the Christian's garment of justification.[42] Being rescued from the sin of Adam, from death and all ungodliness, believers found the comfort of Christ's righteousness in their Taufbund. Second, the Taufbund signified the reception of power to rule over sin, the Devil, hell, and the world. It was not, for Francke, that baptism held in itself such empowerment, but that believers received power through the outpouring of the Spirit into their hearts. This outpouring was contingent upon true faith and brought with it comfort to a sickened conscience.[43] Thus the faithfulness of individuals to the Taufbund comforted and emboldened them. Last, the Taufbund signified the comfort of God's continued faithfulness to his own, that in the midst of tribulation God would rescue believers from evil.[44] This rescue was not to be seen as a hope that believers would be taken out of trials, but that the Lord would not allow them to fall into desolation.

The comfort Francke tied to the Taufbund closely mirrored Johann Arndt's teaching in *Wahren Christenthum*. Arndt initially related comfort to the promise of God and to the Christian response of repentance. The merits of Christ and the forgiveness of sin granted believers spiritual comfort. Baptism confirmed God's promise that he would view believers in light of Christ's redemptive work: "Therefore you can comfort yourself with this eternal covenant [which Christ confirmed with his death], in which God has included you. For he particularly repeated with you, and confirmed it to you once again in Holy Baptism."[45] As a ritual that arose from God's covenant of grace, baptism was to be a source of comfort for believers. It declared them to be God's children through repentance and faith.[46]

Nevertheless, Arndt spent four chapters of the second book in *Wahren Christenthum* discussing the relationship between spiritual trials (Anfechtungen) and comfort. The nature, source, reason, and benefit of spiritual trials constituted an important part of Arndt's theology, and comfort played a central role in what he called the "school" of trials. For the worried Christian, who struggled with doubt and unbelief, Arndt pointed to the comfort found in Christ's indwelling. Comfort, for Arndt, counteracted the barrage of temptations and trials Christians faced. Amid great distress and turmoil, believers were to remember and be comforted by the eternal life granted in Christ. These trials were the means to a certainty in the eternal comfort found solely in God.[47] Arndt expected that trials would cause believers to fear eternal damnation and lead them to a spiritual comfort of the soul.[48] Thus comfort stood in direct relation to the individual's faith. Arndt juxtaposed the hope of comfort to the fears, worries, and doubts of the heart, and believers could only enjoy the peace of eternal life by passing from the latter to the former through the transforming power of the gospel.

The Arndtian connection between spiritual trials and eternal comfort can be seen as the foundation upon which Francke built his attack against misuse of the Taufbund as a source of comfort. Francke believed that his congregants used baptism as a means by which they avoided the conviction of sin. He claims, "Holy Baptism falsely comforts the one who is not dead to sin [and] who does not earnestly struggle with the goal that sin is dead to him."[49] Most parishioners of the church, in Francke's opinion, sought a comfortable life instead of the spiritual comfort of a faithful life. They avoided the whispers of their consciences and ignored the leading of the Holy Spirit, thus failing to examine their hearts. They sought what Francke called a fleshly or false comfort. Where Arndt spoke of the person without comfort, Francke spoke of the one with false comfort. He rooted this error not only in the individual's heart but also in biblical history. Francke reminded his audience that the Jewish people during the time of John the Baptist's ministry made the same mistake. They trusted in their circumcision—in a religious heritage that traced back to Abraham—and did not search their hearts to see if they had faith.[50] The error of certain Jews during the time of Jesus and of Christians contemporary to Francke arose from their earthly understanding of an outward act. Such empty rituals could not offer eternal security in the hearts of individuals.

This abuse of baptism created a tension for Francke in his approach to discussing the sacrament. He wanted to extol the value of baptism but also avoid making it an end in itself. Francke began his catechism sermon published in 1726 by claiming baptism was to be a place of salvation in the life of the church. "Now, the word which Jesus spoke stands: Whoever would believe and be baptized, that one would be saved."[51] Nevertheless, it was not to be understood as the source of salvation, *ex opere operato*: "Do not be so bold as to imagine that you are baptized, and now have obtained such blessedness."[52] Francke did not want his congregants to be misled and comforted by the mere outward practice of the sacrament. The longer people lived in the world, the more likely that they would be led astray by the lusts of the world, embracing the Devil and his work. Such an individual, who found comfort in the act of baptism and not in repentance and faith, followed "his own understanding and his flesh and blood."[53] For the faithless, claimed Francke, the Taufbund was not to be a spring of comfort but rather a well of guilt. They had broken their contract with God, they had not honored their side of the sacrament, and they lacked true peace without first seeking the renewal of their baptismal covenant. Yet, these unfaithful Christians had assumed the great benefit of baptism: rebirth. Here we see the underlying tension that Francke held in his theology. He affirmed baptismal regeneration, but his conversion-centered theology compelled him to articulate a relationship between baptism and rebirth that stretched traditional Lutheran doctrine. Though baptism brought with it new life, Francke saw himself in the midst of a fallen church, which had neglected its Taufbund. Baptism could offer no comfort unless the individual was "truly" reborn.

Rebirth and Baptism

The late scholar Martin Schmidt, and those who followed his lead, claimed that rebirth played a central role in Pietist thought.[54] In spite of Johannes Wallmann's effort to frame Spener's theology as one focused on renewal, Spener's stress on rebirth—notably seen in his major collection of rebirth sermons published in 1696—and the constant exhortation to rebirth by those spiritual leaders following in the train of Spener's thought reinforce the thesis that this theological point played a prominent role in Pietism.[55] Francke was no exception to this. By 1697, he had also published a sermon on the subject, giving rebirth a crucial place in the order of salvation. He claims, "No doctrine is more necessary in Christianity than the doctrine of rebirth. For it is the foundation upon which the rest of Christianity exists."[56] It is no wonder, then, that Markus Matthias writes, "Conversion and rebirth as the change from 'only' baptized to a 'decided' Christian moved for Francke into the foreground of his pastoral and paranetic work. [Unlike] Philipp Jakob Spener, Francke laid value upon the expectation that conversion or (second) rebirth inaugurates a lasting new condition."[57] The very need that Francke saw in a "second rebirth" speaks to the line Francke sought to walk between traditional Lutheran beliefs about baptism and Pietist concerns for new creation.[58]

The death, burial, and resurrection attached to the biblical narrative of baptism spoke of the new creature's transition from old to new. Empowered by the new life of the Spirit, Christians reborn and transformed from their old, dead lives kept the Taufbund. Covenant breakers, on the other hand, disavowed their baptismal waters and followed the sinful passions of their natural birth.[59] Rebirth, therefore, found its place in Francke's baptismal theology as that spiritual event that enabled believers to abide by the obligations of the Taufbund. Rebirth became a part of the foundation for his belief that true Christians would remain faithful to their side of the baptismal covenant. Without rebirth, Francke would say, this faithfulness was impossible.

In the simplest construction, rebirth was a transformative act of God. Paraphrasing Jesus's response to Nicodemus in John 3:3, Francke states, "They must all be born *from above*, and therefore they must all come from God—they who intend to return to him and his blessedness."[60] Rebirth resulted from the grace of God, which led the individual heavenward, where salvation rested. Therefore it was important for Francke to consistently remind his listeners that they must be born from above; rebirth came from God. Francke's habit of creating a theoretical divide between heaven and earth and between godliness and fleshliness was reiterated in this emphasis on the location of rebirth. The new creature was bound to God's will in the heavenly realm and no longer bound to the power of Satan and the earthly realm.

Obligating himself to believers through his covenantal faithfulness, God provided two means of rebirth: Word and sacrament. Of these two, Scripture was foundational. God's revelation of the law showed individuals their sinful state, but the gospel brought about rebirth. Francke offered a warning with respect to the Word and rebirth. Scripture could not be seen as mere letters on a page. The power of God was revealed in the heart through the Word, and so Francke consistently spoke of new birth in light of how individuals handled Scripture.[61] As it derived its importance from God's Word, baptism was a sacrament of rebirth. The complicated nature of rebirth in Francke's theology is evidenced by his attempts to properly define baptismal rebirth in light of his Pietist leanings. While affirming the Lutheran doctrine of baptismal rebirth, he also recognized the problematic nature this doctrine held in the context of his congregation. Francke laments, "Someone asks one hundred, even one thousand Christians, 'What is rebirth? What things does it consist of, and have they experienced something from it in their hearts?' Few will know how to say anything more about it than that baptism is rebirth." Most Christians had misconstrued the doctrine of rebirth and equated it wholeheartedly with the act of baptism, and in their minds rebirth was baptism, and baptism was rebirth. But Francke desired to undo this misconception, putting rebirth in its proper place in relation to baptism: "Baptism is not rebirth, but rather a bath of rebirth and a means which God has ordered; that through it humanity is included in his covenant of grace, but rebirth, or the new creation, must occur beforehand in their hearts."[62] Francke's emphasis on rebirth in his theology was consistent with the prominence other Pietist figures gave the doctrine, but he described rebirth in ways particular to his own concern for conversion.[63] We especially notice this in his articulation of baptismal rebirth.

Francke believed that faith was the primary means to rebirth. Using 1 Peter 5:10, Francke constructed a fourfold order to the establishment and growth of faith in God. In a "living" and "true" faith there was to be a foundation, an empowerment, a fortification, and a preparation (for eternity). These four components, which at times overlapped in function and appearance, were fixed on the goal of taking hold of the heavenly garb of Christ's righteousness. Of foremost importance, Francke grounded faith on the cross. Using the story of Jesus's healing of a nobleman's son, Francke remarks, "If anyone would like to say, *How is, therefore, that [story] a foundation of faith?* Answer: *the cross, the cross* is the best foundation of faith. . . . Yes, if one looked in the Old and New Testament, all the examples would show that faith is received, born, maintained, and perfected *in the cross*, and without the cross the power of faith cannot be attested."[64] Through the cross, outward afflictions and trials reach the human heart and serve to impart to it a living trust in God. Carter Lindberg notices Francke's "radical consideration of the person in his totality," in which "there is no neutral sphere between good and evil." Thus Francke was concerned that living faith be rooted in self-examination, a struggle over sin, and a heart-conversion to Christ. For, according to Lindberg, "the life of a child of God is a life under the cross."[65] From this spiritual disposition the Christian held a living faith that produced true comfort.

Francke also made much of the empowerment and fortification of faith. By fleeing from sin to the cross of Christ, the individual's heart was enflamed by the light of faith. Believers were not only made aware of their forgiveness but were also granted a certainty of salvation. From this state of certainty, God comforted, readied, and empowered them to "go out" into the world.[66] God's grace enflamed their hearts, taught and led them, and prepared them to withstand the trials of life. Francke saw this empowerment and fortification as an experience of God in the innermost being. Just as quickly as true Christians entered the "gates of rebirth" through faith, they were accompanied on the "narrow way of heaven" by a true experience of God. Such an experience gave individuals a knowledge that they were born into the family of God and, furthermore, a recognition that they were not mere outward believers. The inner experience sealed their hearts with the certainty of God's grace toward them.[67] Thus the fortification and empowerment that proceeded from faith brought believers to a point where they could derive certainty not only from knowledge of their forgiveness but also from an inner experience of God.

At this point in Francke's doctrine of faith, his dichotomy between true faith and a false faith becomes evident. Faith could, according to Francke, follow in a godly manner and lead to a preparedness for eternal life, but faith could also have false attachments. Francke warned against a faith that sprang from a love of creatures; that is a willful ignoring of the inner implications of the cross for the sake of the comforts of outward, worldly things.[68] Francke typically rooted this type of faith in human reason and attached it to those learned Lutheran preachers and theologians who opposed his ideas. In addition, Francke often used the phrases "delusional faith" (*Wahnglaube*) and "historical faith" to describe those who trusted in outward symbols and acts instead of the inward work of the Spirit.[69] Instead of experiencing the application of preached truths to the inner being, those holding to a historical faith merely assented to a superficial narrative.[70] In his conversion account, Francke described his trust in God—especially during his theological training—as a delusional faith, and he willingly applied the same term to those around him who had not undergone what he believed to be true rebirth.[71] This historical and reason-based faith led his congregants to trust solely on the outward ritual of baptism and leave off the more important inner rebirth of the soul.

Francke claimed the significance and goal of rebirth rested on becoming a "new man."[72] Though justification in its initial work in salvation was tied to rebirth, Francke emphasized three benefits of rebirth in relation to the new man. First, the individual was born into a spiritual family. The child of the world became a child of God. There was a spiritual-genealogical exchange in the person. Thus it could be said that the baptized entered not only into membership in the church but also into familial communion with God. Francke used this shared aspect between rebirth and baptism to make socioeconomic claims upon the reborn. Were someone truly reborn, said Francke, there would be no place for divisions within the family of God according to wealth or social status. "If one came from a royal line or blood, or else from worldly greatness, then he has nothing more with all such supposed grandeur than merely a human nature. However, if man is born of God, then he receives a divine nature—a divine disposition, state of mind, and character."[73] Where the outside world saw a hierarchy between rich and poor, noble and common, the spiritual family of God saw it otherwise. It was not only that rebirth granted equality within the believing community, but also that the new birth brought with it a spiritual loftiness outstripping all worldly honors. The reborn stood above the earthly king, the wealthy merchant, and the educated official because they stood in direct relation to their heavenly King.

The last two great benefits of the new birth came by means of renewal in Christ's image. Francke commonly referred to this by speaking of the "new creature." "Furthermore through this [rebirth] the heart is truly changed," he remarks. "A completely new person and new creature, which is the central aspect wherein rebirth exists, is worked in us."[74] In rebirth the divine nature replaced the "old Adam," a reference to corrupted human nature. Those born into sin and death were now renewed in the image of Christ. Francke believed the personal change was dramatic. At one point, he employed the image of discarding old rags for a wedding dress. The new creature, born of God, was involved in an exchange of natures. This change in the person was not an improvement; it was a transformation. Individuals who attempted to correct bad habits and reform their sinful lives would always remain bound to worldly desires. Rebirth gave Christians a new will, new desires, and a new reference point.[75] There was no room for the new Christian to compromise this inner transformation, continue in sin, and use the excuse that he was a "beginner." Such a disposition "would reveal a false heart."[76] The desire to please and honor God, instead of the flesh, now defined the Christian life.

In this state, Christians became partakers in the glory of God. This last benefit evidenced the theological step Francke took away from his Lutheran opponents. Francke exemplifies what Lindberg calls Pietism's "anthropocentric reorientation of theology," where "the doctrine of rebirth [was shifted] from the *Christus pro nobis* to the realization of the *Christus in nobis*."[77] According to Francke, not only did rebirth introduce individuals into the priesthood of all believers but it also transformed them into the Temple of God.

So then take note: Jesus must step into the heart and drive out all ungodliness, so that the person will let go of the love of the world, as a lust of the eyes, a lust of the flesh, and a pride of life. It must *become a Temple of God*, in which *the Spirit of God lives*, according to 1 Cor. 3:16, 6:16 [*sic*; 6:19]. It must be made new, and be replaced by a completely different condition through Jesus Christ, so that it no longer seeks [after] itself, but rather [after] that which is of God and neighbor.[78]

Just as he elevated sanctification to the same level as justification, Francke set the divine indwelling alongside the priesthood of all believers. Christians were now both priests and temples; they were clothed and wed. Herein lay the meaning of being a partaker in the glory of God: Christians *gloried* in the righteousness of Christ and *glorified* God through the outworking of the Spirit. This pietistic emphasis allowed Francke to expect signs from the reborn, from the baptized. Believers, living as new creatures and holding to the Taufbund, bore the fruit of those indwelt by the Holy Spirit.[79] Without such signs of life—without a visible struggle against the work of Satan—Francke would not accept that the person was actually reborn.

The Bath of Rebirth and Rebirth

The belief that such a multitude of Christians had fallen away from their Taufbund and remained in their earthly attachments and worldly passions complicated Francke's teaching on rebirth. Assuming such a destitute state within the church, he continually emphasized conversion and applied the language of rebirth to the converted. This theological direction led him to deemphasize the role of rebirth in baptism. Though he affirmed the traditional formulations of baptismal rebirth, he evidenced a discontent with how the sacrament was understood in relation to new birth. He expressed this dissatisfaction both through his critique of "historical faith" and also in his distinction between the "bath of rebirth" and "rebirth."[80] The baptismal washing spoke of a means to rebirth, while actual rebirth described the converted soul. This distinction should be seen as Francke's qualification of baptismal grace. Though rebirth in baptism was no less a reality than the type of rebirth Francke commonly attached to conversion, baptismal rebirth was of a different quality. The quality Francke associated with postbaptismal rebirth experiences arose from, and was seen in relation to, the self-understanding or spiritual maturity of individuals. Consequently, Francke's doctrine of rebirth consistently appeared two-sided. On one side stood baptismal rebirth, which occurred in the life of the inexperienced and immature and thus lacked lasting efficacy. On the other side stood the rebirth of mature individuals, who recognized their desperate state and turned from their worldliness.

Francke's distinction between baptismal rebirth and a rebirth through conversion stood in contrast to Spener's more traditional, moderate Pietist view.[81] Though Spener did tend to attach importance to the rebirth that accompanied a sincere act of repentance and faith, he did not evidence a lessening of the importance of baptismal rebirth. He recognized that the former self was put to death in baptism, while the "old nature" was not completely done away with.[82] This explains to some degree why Spener would never expect conversion experiences in the lives of Christians.[83] His traditional view of baptismal regeneration bound his view of conversion. Furthermore, in the way he structured his section on baptism in his sermons on rebirth, Spener displayed a high view of the power of the sacrament. Unlike Francke, Spener carefully avoided separating rebirth and the bath of rebirth. While mentioning the powerless nature of mere water to affect inner change, he used the first portion of the sermon to affirm the reality and efficacy of baptismal rebirth through the divine ordination of, and the Holy Spirit's work in, the sacrament.[84] By doing so, he maintained a high regard for the transformation that occurred through the sacrament while allowing for his typical stress on personal faith.

Francke, on the other hand, appears to have followed in the footsteps of Theophil Großgebauer. The influence of Reformed and Puritan thought on Großgebauer's construction of baptismal rebirth is quite noticeable. In *Treuer Unterricht von der Wiedergeburt*, which was published in combination with *Wächterstimme*, Großgebauer remarks, "First it is to be noticed that Holy Baptism is not itself rebirth, but rather the sacrament of rebirth."[85] Großgebauer went so far as to claim that baptism did not bring about conversion. Expounding upon the misconception, he remarks, "Many rest in what they, unfortunately, have been taught and led to believe: that they were (so to speak) converted in baptism . . . that they are, from baptism on, converted Christians."[86] He was unwilling to attach the important idea of conversion to the sacrament and reinforced his division between the sacrament of rebirth and actual rebirth by equating baptismal rebirth to Abraham's circumcision, which was only a seal.[87] As a seal, baptism was not a means to rebirth; it was merely an outward sacrament. Großgebauer claimed individuals were in need of an inner circumcision of the heart, or with respect to the New Testament church, a baptism of the heart. In dismissing the sacramental grace of baptism, he rooted rebirth in a conversion experience of the individual and relegated the idea of baptismal rebirth to an outward teaching of the church.

Although tempered by traditional Lutheran teachings, Francke continued in Großgebauer's footsteps. Francke's distinction between the bath of rebirth and a later rebirth from conversion grew out his belief that individuals could not truly experience conversion in baptism.[88] They had no opportunity to rightly examine their lives in light of the worldliness in their hearts and all around them. As infants they had not taken a stand against Satan, the world, and their own fleshly desires. They had not experienced a change of heart. Thus Francke was willing to attribute true baptism not to the outward sacramental ritual but to the inward baptism of the heart.

> Thus we are right to say that he is not a Christian who is outwardly a Christian (one that outwardly attends the worship service with others). Also, a baptism is not one that occurs outwardly on the flesh, or is the removal of filth on the flesh, 1 Peter 3:21. Rather a Christian is one who is inwardly hidden; or who is the uncorrupted hidden man of the heart, or (as it is in the Greek) is *existing in immortality*, 1 Peter 3:4. And baptism is one which occurs in the Spirit and not in letters. In it the old man, with every sin and evil lust, is daily drowned and put to death, and in turn the new man is daily resurrected.[89]

Peschke rightly argues that Francke's teaching on rebirth must be seen in the broader context of his theology of conversion.[90] This is also true of Francke's teaching on baptism. Rebirth played an important role in Francke's thought as it corresponded to his overarching concern for the transformation of the human heart. This is typified by Francke's willingness to make conversion, rebirth, and a change of heart synonymous. Rebirth was a supernatural turning of the heart away from the world, and thus true baptism was rooted in the heart.[91] The sacrament of baptism, as an instrument of rebirth, found itself subsumed under conversion in Francke's theology. By setting both true baptism and rebirth in the heart of the individual, Francke could be considered a theologian of rebirth as much as he could be viewed a theologian of the heart.

Francke's stress on an inward conversion and "baptism of the heart" explains the position he held concerning baptismal exorcism. Although most early sixteenth-century Lutherans held the doctrine to be *adiaphora* (a thing indifferent), confessionalization and later infighting over crypto-Calvinist and Anabaptist tendencies helped elevate exorcism beyond what Luther or Melanchthon had intended. Divisions over the doctrine continued into the 1660s, in spite of several laws prohibiting polemics over exorcism from the pulpit. But through the influence of Pietism and rationalism, baptismal exorcism either disappeared or became insignificant by the late eighteenth century.[92] In Francke's case, his theology of conversion conflicted with baptismal exorcism. He identified the core elements of baptismal exorcism (Satan's spiritual captivity of individuals and his displacement from their hearts) in his language of Taufbund, but he associated them with a mature struggle of faith. Francke still attached an oath, in which one rejected the Devil, worldliness, and the flesh, to the sacrament, but the true casting out of Satan resulted from an outwardly discernible renouncement. Francke's occasional claim that believers should know the relative time of their conversion further demonstrated his denial of baptismal exorcism.[93] Power was no longer invested in the indiscernible faith at baptism but with a conscious act of repentance of sin and trust in Christ. Thus by February 1699, Francke and his assistant Johann Anastasius Freylinghausen had removed exorcism from their baptismal practices in Glaucha. The move apparently caused a stir, which pushed Spener to advise Francke five months later to show patience with such "side issues."[94] Like other reforming Lutherans, Spener did not want exorcism to be cast aside but rather properly explained to parishioners. Yet Francke defended his actions and the actions of his assistant in his response to Spener, claiming that they were following an earlier Brandenburg edict.[95] He likely found further support for halting baptismal exorcism through his colleague, Christian Thomasius, who in 1695 wrote against the practice.[96] What is certain is that Francke desired to do away with the "magical" aspects of baptism.[97] His rejection of exorcism in the sacrament was not a turn toward rationalism as much as a turn toward conversion. Baptismal exorcism stood in the way of Francke's emphasis on a true, inward faith and the believer's obligation to the baptismal covenant.

Even before Francke had developed his theology of baptismal rebirth, Lutheran theologians recognized the ability of believers to lose and receive anew the grace of rebirth found in their baptismal waters.[98] Rooted in this tradition but developing his own ideas concerning conversion and rebirth, Francke modified Theophil Großgebauer's division between baptismal rebirth and conversion. Though Francke did not deny the forgiveness granted in baptismal grace, he distinguished the bath of rebirth in baptism from a later, true rebirth that came from a "mature" conversion. He accepted and recapitulated the Lutheran standards, but he also developed a theology of the sacrament in line with his soteriological concerns. The consequence of his efforts was a tangible tension in his baptismal theology. On the one hand, he affirmed the salvific grace of the sacrament. On the other hand, he held such a negative view of the human condition that virtually everyone stood in need of true rebirth located beyond their baptismal waters. Baptismal grace, whether experienced or not, had become useless in Francke's articulation of the Christian life. Common Lutheran theological expressions like justification by faith were overshadowed by the Taufbund. As W. R. Ward correctly identifies in Francke's theology, "The church was based, not on baptism, but on the renewal of the baptismal covenant in conversion, on the personal appropriation of salvation and the priesthood of all believers."[99]

Moreover, those of the spiritual priesthood had also become temples of God. They were not only clothed with Christ's righteousness, but they were indwelt with the Spirit of glory, which brought with it an expectation of transformed lives. Still, Francke's beliefs on baptism did not draw broadly from the mystical writings he read during his university years in Leipzig or solely from Lutheran symbols.[100] Rather, he adopted and modified the innovations of Großgebauer, whose writings had an ongoing influence on his ministry. The baptismal covenant offered Francke a concept in which he could encapsulate his emphasis on inner conversion, the rejection of worldly desires, and the Christian obligation of faithfulness toward God. Thus he could dismiss baptismal exorcism and at the same time emphasize a mature renouncing of the Devil's influence. Along with Großgebauer's ideas, Francke incorporated the thought of Johann Arndt and Philipp Jakob Spener to root the meaning of baptism not in the experience of the infant dripping with consecrated water but in the reconverted life of the adult, who through a baptism of the heart maintained their vows to God. Francke's baptismal theology offered those around him, and those who came after him, an interpretation of the sacrament that focused on those already baptized. The supernatural characteristics attributed to the means of grace were pushed to background and the existential implications of the covenant between God and man took center stage.

As Francke's son, Gotthilf August, listened to the preaching of his father that summer day in 1714, his own experience would come to illustrate his father's teachings. Even though Francke's son had felt the waters of holy baptism, and even though he had maintained a life that had the appearance of godliness, "yet God still made himself known to [him]." Gotthilf August's baptism as an infant had not provided him the security of eternal life; rather it had served as a false comfort. He needed a conversion and rebirth that could only come with a mature encounter with God. This reflected a movement in his father's thought that had profound implications for his understanding of the Eucharist. Placing conversion and rebirth at the center of his theology meant that August Hermann had to construct ways in which he could not only communicate such a religious experience to his audience but also verify that congregants were "truly" reborn. How could one measure an inner experience of conversion and rebirth? Francke would turn to the confessional as a platform for building a pastoral confidence concerning the spiritual condition of his congregants.

6

CONFESSION

Any discussion of the Lord's Supper in early modern thought, whether Lutheran, Catholic, or Reformed, does not begin with the altar but with the confessional (*Beichtstuhl*).[1] This is no different for Francke. In a sermon published in 1699 Francke criticized the abuses surrounding the Eucharist, remarking, "It is understood [that] he who does not properly practice the Lord's Supper also does not properly practice confession, and he who does not properly practice confession also does not properly practice the Lord's Supper. For one depends on the other."[2] Francke emphasized this interdependence throughout his ministry, but it held special prominence during the first ten years of his Glaucha pastorate. In addition to his seemingly constant reference to confession in sermons on the Eucharist, Francke made the confessional one of the first places where he instituted his Pietist theology of the sacraments.[3] In a theology that emphasized self-reflection and a denial of worldly desires, confession was not merely the doorway into the celebration of the Eucharist. It was a time to confirm true faith, and the implications of being a worthy penitent followed the believer from the confessional to the altar.

This chapter will explore Francke's theology of confession. The development of Lutheran confessional practice, beginning with Luther's attempts to make confession a source of comfort and the conflict that occurred in Berlin during the first decade of Francke's Glaucha pastorate will serve as a historical contextualization for Francke's own attempts at reforming the practice. He held spiritual preparation before participating in the Supper in high regard and hoped that reforms would usher in an improvement in personal conduct and a renewal of the church. As a consequence of this hope, he attacked the false sense of security that confessional formulas provided the laity and the false "witness" of the clergy, who at times offered absolution in exchange for a confessional offering. Francke's various attempts to address what he assumed to be confessional abuses reveal his underlying concern that the Christian faith had been reduced to ritual performances. Whereas almost two centuries before, Luther had hoped confession would bring comfort to souls plagued by uncertainty, at the turn of the eighteenth century, Francke wished to interrogate individuals in confession as to whether their comfort was valid.

From Luther to Francke

Luther's break with the sacramental system of the Catholic Church brought with it a progressive redefining of confession during the first part of the sixteenth century.[4] His early understanding of confession invested sacramental value in the practice. But in *The Babylonian Captivity of the Church*, Luther conceded that confession lacked the word of promise, and he expressed concerns about the papal power intermingled with the practice.[5] Much of his early work on confession dealt directly with this abuse of power. Describing Luther's concern, Kurt Aland remarks, "[The confessor] must not attack people with power. Rather kindly and gently lead and instruct, and not provoke nor agonize their consciences, which is the Devil's work."[6] Luther reevaluated and revalued confession in light of his desire to see the penitent's faith strengthened. To the degree it was possible, Luther desired to strip the confessional of the layers of fear associated with it as a result of ecclesiastical abuses. In its most basic form, confession was to be (and to be understood as) the place where, according to Susan Karant-Nunn, the repentant person expressed "heartfelt regret and the resolve to improve one's life," and where the confessor offered the consolation of the gospel.[7]

As Luther further clarified and developed his position on confession, he threw off its sacramental status and turned his attention to the work of confirming personal faith and consoling the weak. He allowed his earlier suggestions, like the use of lay confessors, to fall by the wayside but strenuously defended others, like the doing away with auricular confession, during which it was expected that every sin would be recalled. What Luther retained and what he dismissed depended on whether the idea conformed to his belief that confession should be a place where Christians contemplate their sin, express their faith, and find consolation. Limiting how much personal sin the penitent confessed, for example, was primarily an attempt at removing fear from the practice. Not only was it impossible for the penitent to recall all her daily transgressions, but Luther believed the act of confessing gave clergy tantalizing details that could be held against the individual.⁸ Instead of attempting to account for every sin committed, Luther and his followers required an admission of sinfulness. And in the place of outward penitential acts determined by the priest, Lutheran confessional practice offered the words of absolution as an assurance of salvation by faith. These, among other changes, were an attempt to reorient confession away from cultivating fear in the hearts of believers and toward providing comfort and assurance to Christians who prepared themselves for the altar.

Yet in its preparatory role, confession quickly became more than just a place to console believers. It also became a place of instruction. Hans-Christoph Rublack notes this new "accent," remarking, "The hearing of every sin would be replaced with the *exploratio* of [the penitent's] knowledge of doctrine."⁹ Absolution could only comfort the troubled heart if the faith professed was in accordance with correct teaching. The Lutheran reform of confession naturally led to reestablishing the confessional as a place of doctrinal correction. Karant-Nunn claims, "rulers of the church were ... providing scripts that confessors must use in granting absolution."¹⁰ These scripts aided in correcting belief and codifying confessional practice, and alongside them, clergymen developed and published formulas for those confessing.¹¹ As parishioners gathered at church the day before the Eucharist celebration for a Saturday confession-service, they came prepared to repeat a formula of answers that outwardly rejected sin and the Devil and properly appropriated teachings on salvation and the church.¹² Though these formulas were not required nor standardized (they could vary from church to church and province to province), they aided in structuring the practice of confession. Moreover, they reinforced doctrine in the minds of the congregants, educating and confirming individual faith. The ability of the penitent to repeat the prepared formula granted the pastor a small degree of assurance that the congregant was not unworthily partaking in the Supper.

By the late sixteenth century, churches commonly practiced confession twice a year, usually before Easter and during the fall season. Luther suggested that there need only be one confession per year, but by the time Francke entered the doors of St. Georgenkirche in Glaucha, there was considerable freedom as to how many times believers were to confess, ranging from just once to four times a year.¹³ During this period of development, Rublack notes the confessional service also took on common features: "[The penitent] wore his Sunday clothes, distanced himself from the daily routine, [and] waited in the church, in the sacred place. He then removed himself from the other waiting congregants to the confessional, the specific place of the ritual which was either in the choir section or the room holding the sacramental elements [*Sakristei*], said the code of the confession of sins, and received in return absolution, [which included] for the most part a laying on of the hand. The penitent knelt there and further lowered himself thereafter."[14] Upon receiving absolution, the penitent sometimes gave the pastor a confessional offering (*Beichtgeld*), which was seen as a part of the pastor's income. The offering could be either required or given freely depending on the region or church, and the pastor was not to show preference to those who gave larger sums by holding different types or lengths of confession.[15] Many of these characteristics of seventeenth-century confessional practices, though likely arising from benign—even beneficial—grounds, became the foundation of complaints against confession by prominent reforming Lutherans.

By the beginning of the seventeenth century, works critiquing and seeking corrective measures of confession found their way to the printers. These books often decried the confessional offering and attacked the ignorance of those confessing.[16] A number of the penitent, it was claimed, still could not articulate basic Lutheran belief or mistook the efficacy of the ritual.[17] The very misunderstandings Luther hoped to remove from confession continued under the guidance of his disciples. These critiques became a major point of debate for prominent theologians seeking a broader church renewal.[18] One such reformer, especially important to Francke's sacramental theology, was Theophil Großgebauer.[19] His chapter devoted to confession in *Wächterstimme* was an attempt to support his own reform suggestions with what he understood to be the form of confession found in the early church. For Großgebauer, Lutheran confession was rooted in the "Latin Church" and held only faint glimpses of the early church practice. "Thus in each and every part, our private confession is different from early church confession."[20] Of main concern to Großgebauer was that private confession had lost the benefits of the common congregational confession in early Christianity. Instead of a believing community offering earnest, tearful prayers for fallen or newly converted Christians, and instead of pastors combining "true" prayer with the laying on of hands, Lutheran pastors offered little to nothing in the way of spiritual intercession for the penitent and laid their hands on people who expressed no understanding. Großgebauer mourned the absence of the foremost benefit of early church confession, discipline. The keys of binding and loosing (Matt. 16:19), a spiritual authority granted to the clergy, held no power in a practice that did not take sin, repentance, and faith seriously.[21] Großgebauer sarcastically remarks, "What occurs now? Those thoroughly poisoned and associated with unrighteousness are absolved and loosed at least two times every year. What kind of misleading practice is this? For either the pastor knows that his penitent is like this, or he does not know it: If he knows it, it is to his harm that he misleads the poor people. If he does not know it, what kind of overseer and keeper is he?"[22] All the abuses associated with confession and all the deficiencies in the church that resulted from these abuses pointed toward the clergy's neglect of church discipline. Parishioners continued in their sins and pastors embraced the entrapments of wealth and social prominence. The ritual continued but only vestigially, lacking the substance that discipline and godly living provided. The themes found in Großgebauer's complaints were representative of those made by reforming Lutherans during the middle of the seventeenth century and passed down to the first Pietists.

Philipp Jakob Spener's own suggestions concerning the confessional arose out of the influence of reforming writings like *Wächterstimme* on his ministry in Frankfurt, Dresden, and Berlin.[23] Though Spener apparently did not make his first official church confession until his mid-twenties, he never dismissed the practice, in part because of its role in aiding church discipline.[24] While in Frankfurt, Spener expressed a frustration, like Großgebauer, that it was impossible to properly examine the consciences of his congregants in just one day—even to the point of wondering whether it would be better to end private confession altogether, but his experience as head pastor of the Nikolaikirche in Berlin confirmed that the practice played an important role in preparation for the sacrament and in the improvement of personal piety.[25] Before arriving in Berlin, Spener had already written that he saw confession as *adiaphora*, a "church ceremony." He argued against the use of formulas and defended the need for true repentance in the penitent before they were absolved, but when Spener took on Francke's friend Johann Caspar Schade as a pastor at his large congregation, he could not have foreseen the controversy that would arise out his church's confessional practices.[26]

Orphaned as a child, Schade lived an impoverished childhood. In spite of this, he was able to study theology and philosophy at the university in Leipzig. It was there that Schade came under the influence of Francke, attending his collegium philobiblicum and being tutored by him in Hebrew.[27] As a participant in Francke's ministry, Schade watched as the Leipzig theological faculty censured his writings and investigated his conventicle activity.[28] Suspicions of Schade's Pietist tendencies followed him as he left Leipzig for Wittenberg in 1688, and rumors surrounding the Leipzig movement hindered him from acquiring a pastoral position in the surrounding region.[29] In 1691, a sympathetic Spener brought Schade onto his pastoral staff and shortly thereafter found himself entrenched in a battle over the confessional.

From the onset of his time in Berlin, Schade showed displeasure with Lutheran confessional practices. He could not reconcile his troubled conscience with the idea of offering absolution to someone whose faith he could not verify; moreover, Schade did not keep this inward conflict to himself, preaching vigorously in 1695 on the deficiencies in confessional practice. His complaints coalesced in the 1696 publication of *Von Conscientia errona*, in which the pastor offered his arguments against the current state of confession. Beyond repeating the complaints of earlier reformers, he included thirty questions that probed the inward disposition of the penitent and confessor. Schade attempted to write these questions in such a way that he believed only truly converted Christians could correctly answer them. As such, the questions acted as an indirect criticism of the church and consequently were not received well by church leadership.[30] As Schade's influence grew, more and more congregants questioned the validity of the practice, with some openly defying him.

In 1697, church leadership began an official investigation of Schade, at Spener's request. They were stirred by Schade's open attack on them, by a portion of his parishioners' abstention from confession while continuing to receive the Supper, by accusations of impropriety in his disciplining of two young girls.[31] The investigation was as much an effort to clear the air concerning proper confessional practice as it was an attempt to examine Schade's teachings. Spener was concerned that the quarreling over confession would push some of the Lutherans toward the Reformed faith of the court preachers in Berlin. He hoped to reach a compromise that would not diminish the confessional practice but would cut off the possibility of a partial exodus of his church members to the pews of the Reformed.[32] Thus he sought to mediate between those seeking freedom from the confessional and those seeking to continue according to Lutheran standards. After a contentious investigation and period of waiting, the civil authority (acting as the *Summus Episcopus*) issued its decree in 1698 concerning the conflict. It was decided (1) that the practice of confession would remain in its previous form; (2) that everyone who desired to take part in the Eucharist should attend a sermon on repentance (*Bußpredigt*) held on the preceding Saturday, which would afford them the opportunity for private confession; (3) that those who led Christian lives, but out of reasons of conscience did not desire to participate in private confession, should not be denied the Supper; (4) that those who did not participate in private confession were to meet with the pastor the week before they celebrated the sacrament; and (5) that the yearly allowance for the confessional offering was to be 200 Taler.[33] Though these softened the traditional standard that held confession as a prerequisite for participation in the

Supper—a weakening that concerned Spener—they addressed some of the misgivings surrounding the practice and brought an official end to the confessional conflict in Berlin.

Francke and the Confessional

The development and expression of Francke's ideas on confession were directly connected to the events in Berlin. Helmut Obst notes that though the relationship between Schade and Francke was frayed at moments, Spener looked to Francke as one who could to some degree "positively influence" Schade. After having the opportunity to visit and experience the controversy surrounding Schade and the confessional practices in Berlin, Francke formed his own opinion about the situation. In the end, claims Obst, "Schade's uncompromising and polemical way stood closer to [Francke's position] than Spener's diplomatic tactics."[34] Nevertheless, Francke sought to mediate between the two Pietists, believing that Schade's work could continue to have a positive impact.[35] Francke's role in the confessional conflict shows that he had already established his own particular position on the practice. In his first year as pastor in Glaucha, Francke began suspending parishioners from the Lord's Supper whom he deemed unrepentant at the confessional. This practice initially drew the tempered rebuke of Spener, but shortly thereafter, according to Terence McIntosh, Spener "retract[ed] his objections" to Francke's form of church discipline.[36] Four years later, in 1696, Francke began imposing what Veronika Albrecht-Birkner calls a "comprehensive and rigid" lifestyle expectation on his parishioners in Glaucha.[37] Francke believed that these social restrictions would bring honor to the Sabbath and turn away the wrath of God, and it resulted in the banning of fifty-three individuals from the Lord's Supper. In a 1698 report, the list of those who came under Francke's church discipline in relation to confession grew to sixty-four.[38] Thus, Francke's engagement with Spener and Schade in 1697 does not so much portray a change in Francke's point of view concerning confessional practices as it reflects a matured theology of confession that had been refined through controversy and conflict.

Coinciding with the conflict in Berlin, Francke published his first work on confession in 1697 under the title *Kurtzer und einfältiger Entwurf von den Mißbräuchen des Beichtstuhls*. In it he sounded his critique of the practice and offered suggestions for improvement, both to the penitent and the pastor. Though Francke had already been voicing complaints against confessional practices from the pulpit since his arrival in Glaucha, *Kurtzer und einfältiger*

Entwurf granted him the platform to specifically address his ongoing frustration with the use of formulas, the state of the clergy, and the confessional offering.

"People, when they first learn the confession formula, are not shown its meaning, but rather they merely memorize the words, which they do not even understand. . . . They cannot properly disclose the inner condition of their hearts with [the formula]."[39] In spite of whatever benefit confessional formulas offered the church, Francke believed they had become a source of confusion and corruption. The penitent rarely used the formulas as sources of self-reflection. Rather, they memorized them in their youth and repeated the formulas when necessary, at times without forethought. In a 1694 sermon, Francke seemingly mocks his congregants:

> [The penitent] should say the confession [formula], not babbling it with the mouth alone, but rather examining whether the words come from the heart. For it is hypocrisy before men, not to mention before the living God, when one says [the formula] with the mouth but he does not have any of it in his heart. What is more, they do not even think once about the words they say, nor understand just once the words they speak. And so they say that which they learned without any understanding, [as if] they had not said them once before. [To the phrase] "I ask that He hear my confession" they also say [the instructions], "Stand there, announce: I am a sinner," and namely they include "a female sinner" at the end. They say both [the masculine and feminine versions], "I am a male sinner, a female sinner." And they do the same thing when they are supposed to say, "at the Holy Eucharist." They say [the abbreviated], "at the H. Eucharist," just as they learned it . . . and there are thousands of similar instances.[40]

This dependence on mere rote words, claimed Francke, even led some to confess sins they never committed. Out of habit others would repeat the words of absolution back to the confessor, making a mockery of the office.[41] Using examples like these, Francke supported his assertion that confessional formulas facilitated a continuance of unbelief within the church and that, in reality, the problems surrounding confession lay deeper than just the surface-level memorization of the formulas.

At the very core of the abuse stood the unconverted individual's willingness to invest salvific qualities in the mere performance of confession. Francke believed that in the mind of the penitent, memorization and mere repetition of the formula became an instrument of salvation. "If one learned a confession [formula] in his youth, then he believes he can pass for a Christian for as long as he lives, and he does not concern himself with the state of his heart, with his words, with his works, and with how he worthily receives [the Supper]. It is enough if he can say the bare words of the formula in confession, and afterwards participate at the altar. He does not pay attention to how he might provide for life. O what a miserable condition!"[42] Penitents recited the confession formula with the hope that hands of absolution would be laid upon their head and that the act of absolution would grant them forgiveness. This direct connection between formula recitation and the expectation of salvation in absolution served as the backdrop to Francke's statements with regard to those who worried over forgetting the confessional formula. Parishioners came to confession under pressure, whether self-inflicted or not, to perfectly say a standardized expression of repentance, which had been set out for them in their youth. If they forgot a small phrase or said it incorrectly, claimed Francke, they feared for their souls. If they were interrupted by the pastor during their response (something Francke apparently did in order to both test his parishioners' faith and reveal the false assumptions they made in confession), they feared for their salvation. Even Francke's complaints about the unwillingness of the elderly to learn new confessional responses should not be merely interpreted as a pastor's complaints over spiritual laziness but as Francke's assumption that some in his congregation feared a misspoken word would result in the failure to receive absolution.[43]

The outworking of this relationship between the use of formulas and the expectations of salvation resulted in more than just interposing fear into an act that was supposed to communicate the comfort of true faith. In Francke's opinion, those who only outwardly recited such formulas replaced true repentance with the simple vocalization of words: "Namely, they think repentance exists in saying the confessional formula when one goes to confession [and] thereafter receiving absolution or the forgiveness of sins once one confesses. After that [he] participates in the Holy Eucharist."[44] Individuals equated repentance with saying the proper words and salvation with the simple response of absolution from the confessor. Thus, there was a theological concern at the core of Francke's critique of confessional formulas: they not only undercut a proper understanding of conversion but became a replacement for the religious act central to Francke's theology, true repentance. The inner, heartfelt turning away from the world and its entrapments was made outward, and it could be handled in outward ways. If simply saying the formula sufficed, then there was no need for preparation. Penitents could approach confession without sincere self-examination.[45] In addition, they did not need to seek an improvement of their lives, something Francke believed was at the core of confession, but believed they needed merely to repeat the confession they had learned as a child.

The visible effect of investing salvific value in the outward act of confession was the ability for parishioners to create a barrier between their own sinful lives and the confessor's knowledge of their spiritual condition. By making sin, repentance, and absolution outward observances, the penitent saw confession as an act in which the confessor did not serve as a representative but the administrator of God's grace. The embodied confession of one's formulaic response needs only the absolving touch of the pastor. Certain supernatural elements, such as God's wrath and anger against sin, were hidden behind and distorted by the earthly pastoral office. Rebuking the confessional practices of his Glaucha congregation, Francke remarks, "[The pastor] does not know your hate and jealousy, which you have in your heart. He does not know the resentment which you have. He could not know your proud heart. He could not know your blasphemy, which you pour out of your mouth. He could not know your lavishness, nor your eating or drinking, what you do at home, your coming and goings, and little of your nights and days. Behold how does it help you when no one knows? The all-seeing eyes of the Lord watch over everything."[46] Confessional formulas served as blindfolds, keeping penitents from truly acknowledging their sinfulness and God's impending judgment. Unwilling to look into their hearts, penitents went through their confessional habits with "natural eyes" blinded to Pietist themes of salvation.[47] Of utmost importance, this misappropriation of the role of the formula blocked the road to rebirth, and consequently interfered with Francke's conception of true Christianity. This frustrated Francke: "Therefore the confession formula often mixes up the work of conversion so that one cannot tell whether it was said by a regenerate or unregenerate [*Wiedergebohren oder Unwiedergebohren*]."[48] Although confession was to be a place where confessing reaffirmed the covenant between God and man, playing an important role in the process of personal renewal and maintenance of faith, it instead became a place where individuals could avoid the condition of their hearts and their need for rebirth and could thus "steal" absolution.[49]

Francke combated this by extending the boundaries of preparation for the Lord's Supper beyond confession on Saturday. Before penitents could sit in confession, they had to undergo a thorough investigation of their lives.[50] In step with confessional reforms instituted in his childhood home by Duke Ernst the Pious in 1654, Francke required his own parishioners to contact him for a visitation several days before going to the confessional.[51] He began practicing visitations in his first years in Glaucha and later advised his theological students to adopt a similar practice.[52] On the surface, visitations were attempts to ease the number of people being examined the day preceding the celebration of the Eucharist, something he complained about to Spener.[53] However, the practice allowed Francke to conduct his own vigorous investigation of congregants' lives without being limited by time. Francke elevated these visits to the level of the Saturday confessional practice, which in turn made the latter a confirmation of what had occurred during the former.[54] It was in these meetings that the confessor was to ask the hard questions, pushing beyond the expected formulaic responses to unearth the condition of the individual's heart. He was to pose questions that challenged the person's understanding of the Christian faith. Francke complained that pastors relied on the basic questions and responses provided in the catechism, which churchgoers could memorize and repeat without needing the ability to clarify their words: "It is not enough for children, who want to participate in the Supper, to say the catechism; rather, they must be able to rightly examine themselves."[55] The true test of the believer lay in this examination, and Francke used these preconfession visitations to test whether his parishioners, young and old, could discern their own spiritual state. It was during these interactions that believers needed not only to admit their condition but also to provide outward expressions of contrition.[56] In addition, confessors were to visit congregants in their respective houses, to examine the young and old in public and private, and even to inquire from housemates and neighbors about the lifestyles of individuals.[57] It even appears the controversies that surrounded Francke's practice of visitation in Glaucha led him to encourage young pastors to keep a log of their visits, in case parishioners challenged their pastor's evaluation of them.[58] In all of this one can see Francke's search for a level of certainty concerning the spiritual condition of his parishioners. He felt that confession had become just the mere repetition of formulas, diminishing its role as a time when sin was recognized and turned from. Thus he built a system that required a true confession of the heart.

If the congregant remained unwilling to undergo such an examination, Francke's final tactic was to use the confessional as a place of church discipline.[59] Those who did not regard his rebukes, who did not reject their worldly lifestyles, or who avoided his examinations were barred from the altar, something with both spiritual and social consequences. As noted above, the conflict between Francke and his own parishioners in 1692 arose from similar disciplining practices, and between the years 1696 and 1698, Francke banned anywhere from fifty-three to sixty-four from the Supper.[60] The visible result was that a number of those in the Glaucha congregation voiced their complaints to the Halle church leadership and had their confessions heard by sympathetic pastors within the city walls. In Francke's eyes, this drastically hindered the effectiveness of his control over spiritual matters in the church. In June 1695, Francke complained to Spener that his parishioners were able to avoid him and attend confession in Halle. A little over a year later he repeated his complaint, adding that now it was occurring in contradiction to a recent order of the consistory that pastors in Halle not take on any foreign penitents. In December 1696 he wrote to Spener about his own experience confronting those who were absent from his confessional, calling their activities a "conspiracy" and setting out a detailed list concerning his interaction with them and the misconduct occurring around confessional practice. The latter he did so that others could see from where the problems stemmed.[61] Francke remained unwavering, encouraging pastors as late as 1699 to leave their positions in the church if authorities permitted unworthy parishioners to attend the Supper. Francke insisted a proper handling of confession required the pastor not merely to examine the heart of the penitent and provide the comfort of the gospel, but also to bear the jarring discomfort of withholding certain "unbelieving" individuals from the Supper.[62]

This form of rigorous investigation required much from the pastor, and Francke laid great responsibility on the confessor's shoulders. Ultimately, he concerned himself with the clergy's spiritual state. For Francke, the ability to properly examine and direct believers depended on the confessor's heart. He chided wayward pastors: "Since they do not have a living understanding and experience of divine truth in their hearts, they do not know how to properly share the Word of truth."[63] Thus Francke warned of pulpits being filled with men whose heads were full of ideas and lives full of habits learned at the university but who had not studied at the "school of the Holy Spirit." They systematized the faith, learning the various intricacies of doctrine, but they did not have the very essence of the catechism in their hearts.[64] Francke believed this form of Christianity, grounded on the mere memorization of doctrine, was replicated in the confessional. Pastors required no more than the repeating of a formula because they themselves offered their parishioners no more than a standardized response. Francke claimed their unconverted lives led to a confessional of laziness, pride, and falsehood. Pastors either took on penitents without real concern for their actions or they accepted their formulaic answers without delving deeper into the spiritual condition of their parish.[65] Thus the clergy were as complicit as congregants in making salvation a completely outward act. They assumed their responsibility lay in the simple granting of God's forgiveness. The need for rigorous examination was brushed away by the hands of absolution. It was, then, of great importance to Francke that faithful pastors were installed in the church, and the pastoral training eventually offered by the Stiftungen should be understood in light of Francke's effort to change the composition of the Lutheran clergy.

The confessional offering also conflicted with Francke's attempts to reform the practices surrounding the Eucharist. If it was assumed by some that confession formulas were an outward means to obtaining forgiveness, then the confessional offering represented the penitent's outward response. In so far as memorized words were deemed true repentance, the gift of money was understood as the proper expression of gratitude. According to Francke, neither required individuals to amend their ways. Moreover, the confessional offering carried with it social implications. With a sizable offering, the rich could "buy" more time, longer talks, and more elaborate prayers. They were even able to acquire private confessions outside the normal Saturday gathering, which, unlike those conducted by Francke, allowed the penitent to cover over their misconduct.[66] The offerings also became a means of gaining a place of prominence in the congregation. Those who made paltry gifts risked being excoriated during confession or from the pulpit, and those with nothing to give would stay away. A lack of money brought with it fears over appearances and over meeting daily needs:

> 1) As a result of the failings of the confessional offering many keep from attending confession and the Holy Eucharist. For once it is the custom that one not appear before the priest empty-handed, then many a [penitent] becomes ashamed that he will not be able to bring anything, even though he is fine or rarely acts badly. He thinks, since he does not yet have the confessional offering, he will wait eight days. This does not only occur when they know that their pastor is greedy, but also when they know it might have nothing to do with him. 2) Most of the poor sigh as they give their confessional offering to the pastor, which they would have used for the great necessity of cherished bread.[67]

On the side of the penitent, the offering stood as both a social and spiritual barrier. It could be used to hide their hearts or expose their poverty. The former was a privilege of the wealthy and the latter a fear of the poor.

On the side of the pastors, Francke believed the confessional offering hindered their work in the congregation. It interfered with their responsibility to serve and build up their parishioners. The confessional offering became an "offering of sin" (*Sünden-Geld*), where the pastors accepted money out of avarice and not out of need. Francke warned this could result in God's punishment of hardship or even death.[68] In their greed, pastors turned the words of absolution into a commodity, and with their eyes turned toward earthly gains they shirked the responsibility to thoroughly examine their congregants. Moreover, these confessors intensified the social divisions within their church, showing favoritism toward those of higher social status. Francke believed their concern was in the growth of their own stature and not the growth of their congregations' faith. While advising pastors concerning ambition, he cautions "that one finds a greater danger in applause, than before when one was persecuted."[69]

From the outset of his Glaucha ministry, Francke assumed there to be dangers inherent in confessional offerings. Though he accepted such offerings early in his ministry, his interaction with Olearius during the first few months of his pastorate suggests that he did so with misgivings.[70] In a letter to Spener in the spring of 1696, Francke claimed he either did not accept his parishioners' offerings or he gave them to the poor, and three years later he explained to his congregation:

> At the beginning of my [pastoral] office I accepted confessional offerings and used them for my needs. As time went on, God strengthened my faith so that I trusted him, that he would provide for my needs in other ways. Thereafter, I accepted the confessional offering . . . but all that was given to me made its way to the needy members of Christ. But this also became a burden to me, which I could not shrug off because a lot of inconvenience arose from the confessional offering. Since I have a child-like trust that God, through a thousand different ways, will provide the poor that which appears to escape from under them, I will not stop myself from letting it go [i.e., letting the offering practice come to an end].[71]

Francke wished this same type of trust, which he claimed to display, in the lives of his fellow clergy. If their faith were strong enough, they would be able to trust that God would protect them from an impoverished life. Thus Francke used the confessional offering as a measuring stick of faith. To be dependent on it meant that the pastor held a weak trust in God, and in such a state, he could easily continue down a road in which the offering became a source of sacramental abuse.

For Francke the confessional offerings and the misuse of formulas came to signify shortcomings in the practice of confession during his time. The formula provided a false sense of security and a false understanding of true conversion. The inner rebirth and transformation, which Francke sought in the lives of his parishioners, was exchanged for the outward repetition of phrases learned from youth and devoid of personal meaning. With confessional formulas, penitent persons could avoid their sin or imagine that the mere speaking of the confession sufficed. The confessional offering, in turn, served as an assumed "fruit" of this outward, recited faith, and it became in the eyes of Francke a blessing to the rich and a curse to the poor. More important, the practice of confession had been reduced to outward acts. He complains, "People hear 100,000 sermons and confess themselves to death, and yet are not more godly. This will be punished [by God]."[72]

Francke, in contrast, demanded a vigorous search of the heart. He encouraged visitations, which would double as confessions, to occur several days before the Supper celebration, and he began banning unrepentant churchgoers from the altar. He also became outspoken concerning the clergy's spiritual state. Formulaic responses satisfied unconverted confessors. These pastors avoided challenging the ungodly in their churches and gladly offered absolution with the unspoken expectation of a sizable confessional offering. The comfort that Luther originally desired in his own confessional reforms had become lost in outward habits. Sin was not addressed and thus the soul went on undisturbed.

The shape of Francke's confessional critique is not merely the entrance into a discussion of his theology of the Lord's Supper. Rather, it is an inseparable piece of his overall theology of the sacrament of the altar. Though Großgebauer's work on the subject weighed heavily on Francke's own ideas, Francke never openly sought to establish a common, collective confession in the worship service. Instead, under his watchful eye confessional practice was actually elevated.[73] It served as the main tool in which he could evaluate the faith of his congregants, and it became the starting point from which his theology of the Eucharist could be understood.

7

THE EUCHARIST

To see the importance of the Lord's Supper in Francke's early ministry, one need not look any further than the pulpit. In 1693, the first full year of Francke's pastorate, he preached six times on the sacrament, and the following years did not bring a decline in his sense of urgency on this issue.[1] The altar became a place where communicants could publicly testify to their faithfulness to their baptismal covenant or where they could come under the judgment of God for participating with unconverted hearts. For the faithful, the Eucharist was a source of strengthening and empowerment. The discipline and obedience through which they remained in their Taufbund became a badge of honor that was displayed to all as they knelt before the sacrament. For the wayward, it represented a place of divine wrath. Certain that few had remained in their baptismal covenant, Francke carefully articulated a theology of the Eucharist that used ideas of worthiness and unworthiness to guard against impropriety at the altar.[2] Francke's handling of confession reflected this. The vigor with which he conveyed the need for self-examination—for a true confession arising from a true understanding of sin—resulted from his overarching concern for the communicant's worthiness.[3] It was Francke's hope that his parishioners would take the bread and wine as brides and lovers of Christ and not "murderers" of their Savior.[4]

This chapter will focus on the shape of Francke's theology of the Eucharist, paying special attention to the central role worthiness played in his articulation. To begin, we will consider how Francke interpreted communicant worthiness and incorporated visible signs of worthiness into his theology of the sacrament, something Peschke notes was contrary to Luther's theology.[5] Francke not only took up Scripture to justify his use of visible signs but also offered his audiences a complex spectrum describing sacramental worthiness made up of three unworthy types (the Epicurean, hypocrite, and ignorant) and three worthy types (the maid, virgin, and bride). Within this typology we find Francke wrestling to prove inner conversion with outer signs. His exhortations to be born again did not end with the heart but extended to the body, and participation in the Eucharist provided Francke a place to determine the spiritual condition of his congregants and to cultivate what Malte van Spankeren calls a "Pietist habitus."[6] Thus Francke's theology of the Eucharist stands as the culmination of his theology of the sacraments.

The Unworthy and the Worthy

Francke's interpretation of 1 Corinthians 11, the Pauline passage out of which the traditional words of institution originate, undergirds his emphasis on individual worthiness at the altar. In his exposition of the passage, Francke did not primarily attend to the implications of those verses that include claims of the real presence and the proclamation of Christ's death during the meal.[7] Instead he made much of the verses that followed, emphasizing participating in a worthy manner, self-examination, and the judgment of God. Francke's theology of the Eucharist reflects his understanding of verse 27: "The one who eats from this bread and drinks from the cup of the Lord in an unworthy manner is guilty of the body and blood of Christ."[8] He interpreted "unworthy manner" in a way that made the worthiness of his parishioners' eating and drinking contingent upon their spiritual state. This is one instance in which inner, subjective aspects of Francke's theology are pushed outward. According to his exposition of Scripture, only those whose lives were determined beforehand to be worthy were allowed to the altar.[9] Consequently, it was not just that the propriety of the outward act of participating in the Eucharist depended on the spiritual condition of the communicant, but that the prerequisite worthiness of communicants was determined to some extent by examining the spiritual fruit they brought to the altar. In order to justify this, Francke placed God's judgment (which Paul threatens in verse 29) on those "false" Christians who did not evidence the signs of a worthy life—a life bearing the fruit of godliness—and yet partook of the bread and wine. This is a notable theological step by Francke, in which he made the Lord's Supper a place for the repentant and not (for the most part) a place for the repenter. "It was instituted," remarks Francke, "in our [church] several years ago that each and every penitent was emphatically shown what belongs to a worthy participation in the Holy Eucharist, [and] that each person was warned that he should not come to the Supper or confession, where he does not deem himself in the state of repentance and faith."[10] Consider these words in comparison to Luther's Large Catechism: "People with such misgivings [about their sin] must learn that it is the highest art to realize that this sacrament does not depend upon our worthiness. For we are not baptized because we are worthy and holy, nor do we come to confession as if we were pure and without sin; on the contrary, we come as poor, miserable people, precisely because we are unworthy."[11] Francke's cautionary words appear to shift away from the catechism, and they express his attempts to reframe the Eucharist celebration. The visitations that Francke instituted after he took up the pastorate in Glaucha were to be meetings for discerning the penitential condition of individuals. If they were found unworthy, they were barred from the sacrament. Worthiness no longer solely depended on Christ's objective work or on how communicants ultimately approached or treated the sacrament, but on how they led their daily lives. Thus Francke could exhort his parishioners not to participate unless they did so as worthy Christians. As will be shown, he allowed for degrees of worthiness, but his interpretation of 1 Corinthians 11 enabled him to move away from a focus on a worthy partaking in the Eucharist to a worthy partaker.

The outworking of this emphasis on worthiness at the Supper led Francke to speak often on "signs" as evidence of faithfulness. The use of signs in evaluating individual souls played a broader role in Francke's pastoral theology. In his lectures on pastoral theology he writes, "It is nevertheless a major point [*Haupt-Stück*] of the office of pastor that one is able to paint [a picture] before his congregants that they are not yet converted; and on the other hand, that he can give certain signs of the state of grace [*signa status gratiae*]." Pastors were to hang this picture of both regenerate and unregenerate signs before their parishioners so that they might scrutinize their spiritual states. Francke cautioned pastors, however, to be careful over the amount of pressure they applied to those "converted" parishioners, who were easily made afraid, so that they would not be led into spiritual trials (*tentatio*). This warning may reflect a maturing in Francke's theology that occurred as a result of his emphasis on Anfechtungen in his radical, early ministry. Nevertheless, he confirmed the propriety of seeking out such signs of salvation, encouraging pastors to make use of the booklet *Kennzeichen eines wiedergebohrnen Menschen*, which appears to be a portion of Christian Hoburg's 1684 writing on rebirth, edited and published in 1711 by the Rostock medical doctor Georg Detharding.[12]

He supported this use of "signs" by applying it to the self-revelation of God in the Old Testament. God gave "signs" of his faithful character in creation and the Sabbath, Noah and the rainbow, Abraham and circumcision, and Israel's exodus and the Passover lamb. In describing these Old Testament acts of God, Francke used "memorial" (*Gedächtnis*) and "sign" (*Zeichen*) interchangeably.[13] This application of the term allowed him to claim that the Eucharist is itself a culmination of God's display of faithfulness in the Bible; it is the church's grand sign of God's love. By expositing Scripture in this way, Francke coupled what he openly called the goal of the sacrament to commemorate Christ's death with his own theological concern for individual worthiness.[14]

Scripture, therefore, also provided Francke the language of personal signs of worthiness: "For this reason Holy Scripture instructs us about the examination of ourselves, and gives us the proper and unmistakable identifying signs of true faith."[15] Like the two-sided baptismal covenant, on God's side the sign of faithfulness culminated in Christ's sacrifice, and on the human side the sign of faithfulness was epitomized in self-examination and the resulting marks of true belief. Thus to be worthy meant to be one who manifested the Christian fruit of their conversion. Conversely, to be unworthy meant that unregenerate individuals carried with them the marks of unbelief. These marks played such an important role in the meal, claimed Francke, that even the early church barred certain individuals from the altar if their professions of faith were not accompanied by the proper signs.[16]

The pastor was to act as a doctor and diagnose his patients. Using marks of faithfulness as identifying signs, he was to cautiously grant access to the altar or to do all in his power to show individuals their horrid condition.[17] For those who took their diagnosis to heart, they were not to be immediately granted absolution and access to the altar but were to wrestle with the state of their lives. For those unsure in their faith, Francke recommended that they first seek salvation from God before they be allowed to celebrate.[18] The judgment of God was an ever-present reality in Francke's thought, and the altar was one of the surest places to incur God's wrath. Thus Francke stressed that participants combine identifiable marks of worthiness with their repentance and faith. Just as in other areas of his theology, Francke described sacramental worthiness in degrees or stages. As individuals progressed or digressed in their relationship with God, they moved from one level of worthiness to the next. In his sermons on the Eucharist, Francke applied a typology consisting of two sets of descriptors to talk about unworthiness and worthiness. He defined unworthiness with the terms Epicureanism, hypocrisy, and ignorance; signs of worthiness fell under the descriptors of humility and tears, the Christian struggle (*Kampf*), and a burning love.

The Unworthy: Epicureans, Hypocrites, and the Ignorant

"But who, then, are the unworthy? Both the Epicureans and the hypocrites are."[19] In his 1697 Maundy Thursday sermon, Francke laid out a spectrum of those who fell into the category of unworthy communicant. It reflects his assumption that the unconverted, like the reborn, lived in degrees of unbelief. At the far left of this spectrum of unbelief, where those most distanced from God lived out extreme and blatant sin, stood the Epicurean. Even without Francke's warnings, most would have agreed that those who fell under the category "Epicurean," whoever they may have been in the community, should not have been allowed to the altar. Nevertheless, Francke felt it necessary to include the category in order to give both a balance and a foil to those who lacked the necessary marks of a worthy communicant but imagined themselves otherwise.

Francke most likely received the term from his own theological tradition, which derived the name from Paul's interactions with the inhabitants of Athens in Acts 17:28, but Francke provided his audience with a more contextualized description of the Epicurean as one who was in their midst. They were the thieves, the whores, and the debauchers. They were the wildest and most outstanding heathens. Like the atheist, their spiritual lineage traced back to those who mocked and disparaged Noah and were caught up in the floods of judgment. They shared the same spiritual genes as the neighbors of Lot, who were devoured in flames of wrath. Francke attached the Epicureans of his time to the gross evils of humanity.[20] In the context of the Supper, Epicureans not only threw off the responsibility to examine themselves but also threw off the very Christian faith to which the sacrament belonged.

Nevertheless, the root problem of Epicureanism lay not merely in sinful actions but in a state of being. According to Francke, Epicureans were distanced from the Supper because they were distanced from the very thing it signified, the blood of Christ. Without the regeneration of new birth, they remained children of the world, living out the desires of their hearts. With Epicureans in mind, Francke asked his congregation, "[Does our city] lack heavy drinkers? Does it lack Sabbath-breakers, whores, thieves, the greedy, or extortionists? Nevertheless they attend confession and the Supper every quarter-year. O what an abomination! What will God do when he looks upon it with his anger and ferocity?"[21] The type of people belonging to this category, these bold-faced sinners, stood squarely under the wrath of God. In light of their dire circumstances, Francke called them to avoid God's punishment and convert.

The Epicurean represented a category that did not apply to most of Francke's congregants. Instead, a large gathering quietly sat in the sanctuary, jealous of their prodigal brothers and sisters who went about sinning openly while still participating in the sacrament. Nevertheless, this silent majority found themselves in the same unworthy state as the Epicurean.[22] They were the hypocrites. With respect to the spectrum of unbelief they stood somewhere to the right of the Epicureans, but they received the same condemnation for their unconverted hearts. Along with their prodigal brothers, who chose the pig feed of worldliness over their heavenly Father's inheritance, hypocrites approached the altar in a state of unworthiness.

According to Francke, hypocrites did not take to open sin like Epicureans, looking instead to create the appearance of true belief at the altar while maintaining a life devoted to the flesh. Francke desired hypocrites in the church to be seen as the pretenders, as those who only offered a superficial version of Christianity. They followed the lead of the Devil, who pretended to be an angel of light. Nevertheless, their forerunners arose not from those outside the covenant of God, like the Sodomites, but from within. Francke linked hypocrisy with Pharisaism, which he viewed as the practice of offering nothing more than outward, empty expressions of faith in God. They were the offspring of the Old Testament Jews who with their ears heard the preaching of such prophets as Amos, but did not add a godly life to their hearing.[23] In defining hypocrisy Francke revealed the important role that outward expression of godliness played in his form of conversion theology. He claimed not merely that hypocrites needed a change of heart but that they needed to show consistency in their lives. Yet in a circular way, this consistency reflected the condition of their hearts. They could not merely promise improvement, say the necessary words, provide the appearance of holiness in church, and then return to their sinful habits the very next day. For Francke there was an interplay between the inner and outer life, in which the outer confirmed the inner: "At the same time, some pretend with [the words of] their mouths to be good, agree to becoming better, but then they continue in their sin. How is this not a terrible hypocrisy? Therefore do not imagine, when you present yourselves with outward piety, and yet still act badly, I say, do not imagine that the Lord God does not see into the nooks of your hearts, nor recognize how you actually are."[24] Notice that Francke preached against pretending to be truly converted with outward professions and acts, while simultaneously calling hypocrites to better their lives. Thus his theology of conversion wrinkles upon itself, the outward depending on the inward and vice versa. The nature of the unworthy condition of hypocrites, who professed to be followers of Christ but yet did not hold to or walk in a manner consistent with their profession, exposes this complicated, circular feature of Francke's thought.

Fundamentally, hypocrites had deceived themselves. Francke noted that, unlike the Epicureans, hypocrites actually imagined themselves to be good Christians. They said their morning and evening prayers, repeated their memorized statements of faith, and attended church services without fail, but their religion was merely outward ritual.[25] "Then man can see how he has used his Christian name, his baptism, his participation in church confession and the Supper only to paste over [his] inner wickedness and to build a fine reputation in front of other people."[26] Even unconverted teachers merely adorned themselves with their teachings and did not possess "in a pure conscience the mystery of faith and the love of Christ Jesus and his apostles."[27] Congregants and their church leaders had created a false righteousness, propped up by a language of piety, but they remained without visible signs of the power of salvation.

The most telling mark of their unregenerate condition was the unwillingness of hypocrites to follow Christ. For Francke these deceivers were not disciples. They lacked the desire to take seriously the commands of God and showed no sign that the preached word caused any change in their actions. The foremost mark of the nonchalant approach of hypocrites to their lives and the sacrament was their unwillingness to suffer according to their Savior's example. Hypocrites might say the right words and at moments act in accordance with the outward requirements of faith, but they were unwilling to take up the cross. Instead, the fear of man swayed their hearts, and the call of the world outweighed the call of God.[28] Within Francke's theological system they could expect a double judgment of God upon their lives for (1) recognizing the truth of God and (2) against their better judgment denying and hiding it in order to avoid suffering embarrassment from others around them.[29] Consequently along with Epicureans, Francke called hypocrites both to convert and to examine themselves in order to confirm that they were truly repentant.

Allied with the Epicureans and the hypocrites, but situated on the far right of the spectrum, were the ignorant. In Francke's opinion, many came to the altar without even a slight understanding of their own faith, and therefore they came unworthily.

> Since up until this point God the Lord has acted gracefully among us (albeit not many recognize [the responsibilities leading up to participating in the Eucharist] as grace, but rather they hold it to be a great austerity and irresponsible innovation. They greatly bemoan and complain that once they want to participate in the Eucharist, [the confessor]

always makes it sour to them), so it should be asked: What is still lacking and in what areas should one still wish for improvement? First we must lament how many don't give themselves nor turn to all the instruction given them. Rather, they dismiss all the warnings they hear and toss them to the wind, [while] others conceal themselves with hypocrisy.[30]

For Francke spiritual instruction did not solely deal with the acquisition of knowledge attached to the Supper, but with the ability of individuals to use their understanding of doctrine to examine themselves. If parishioners remained willingly ignorant of their faith, they participated—along with Epicureans and hypocrites—unworthily.

Francke's insistence that communicants form a base of knowledge concerning the Supper before participating led him to speak directly to the spiritual responsibilities held by each person. From early in their youth, children were to learn the doctrines applied to the sacrament and incorporate them into their lives. To provide for this education Francke required a training based on biblical texts. The catechizing for which he became both famous and despised was to support the personal reading of Scripture occurring in his parishioners' homes. He prodded his congregation concerning those who did not take spiritual education seriously: "But if they spurn his Word, how can they worthily participate in the Supper?"[31] Communicants who forsook biblical instruction did so at their own risk. They evidenced a "horrible ignorance" and brought God's judgment upon themselves at the altar. The responsibility to receive and apply instruction, and thus avoid God's wrath fell on the shoulders of those far beyond their youth. Neither age nor income exempted one from the need to understand what the Bible said concerning the sacrament. The responsibility also fell on the pastor to admonish, warn, and instruct those around him.[32] Spiritual instruction was not only to provide answers to questions of faith but was also to cultivate faithfulness. In particular, Francke emphasized training in order that his parishioners could examine their own hearts and, more important, prove themselves worthy when examined.

Attempting on Maundy Thursday 1694 to teach his congregants about the importance and honor that should be attributed to the sacrament, Francke used an analogy that also touched on his concern for taking spiritual instruction seriously. Preaching on the reasons that they called the sacrament the "Lord's Supper," Francke likened the sacrament to eating a meal at a king's table.[33] He emphasized how most would show excessive caution before such an honored encounter, making sure they said the right words and showed proper table manners. By drawing on the need to show caution in what a guest might say to a king, Francke subtly pointed to his underlying desire that the communicant approach the "Table of the Lord" with an even higher sense of caution.[34] For Francke, this caution was exemplified in the individual's carefulness, making sure that the matters of the head were informed by the disposition of the heart. To encourage this carefulness he offered three questions that one needed to answer in order to take part in the Supper worthily: (1) Why do you participate in the Supper? (2) How is it beneficial? and (3) What do you receive in it?[35] To have been able to answer these meant that communicants would have been able to speak to some degree on the real presence of Christ, on the sacrament as a commemoration and proclamation of Christ's death, and on the believer's disposition of gratitude. Nevertheless, Francke believed that these questions could be answered superficially, without the accompaniment of faith. Therefore he sought out signs that indicated believers had received spiritual empowerment from their inner doctrinal assent.[36]

Herein Francke revealed his understanding of the relationship between the head (doctrinal knowledge) and the heart (subjective experience). "It is supposed to be a help to him in heaven when he goes in and eats and drinks at the altar? For how can his heart be present, if he does not know that which he is supposed to believe and that upon which his heart should be grounded?"[37] The usefulness of spiritual training in preparation for the Eucharist only held value if the participant transitioned from objective doctrines learned, to subjective truths believed, to spiritual fruit that objectified inner belief. Communicants were to take instruction and moreover the spiritual condition of their lives seriously. Should they partake in the Supper without evidencing signs of a heartfelt understanding of their faith, they did so as unworthy participants.

This ignorance of spiritual matters applied to the young, who either neglected their training or were kept from it by their parents. It applied to the rich, who avoided Francke's examinations, and to the poor, who would not make time for catechization. Each in their own way evidenced signs of an unconverted heart and thus risked the judgment of God at the altar. With their brothers the Epicureans and hypocrites, the ignorant formed Francke's typology of unworthiness.

The Worthy: Maids, Virgins, and Brides

Late in the afternoon on 6 March 1718, Francke arrived in Nürnberg, and at the suggestion of a few of his friends, he entered into a conventicle meeting that was just letting out. As he passed into the room several of the attendees made their way out, but his arrival made them pause and turn around to see what might occur. Upon asking the pastor what had been discussed and finding out the topic was the Lord's Supper, he used the next hour to exhort his listeners concerning the three types of worthy participants in the sacrament: maids, virgins, and brides.[38] Shortly thereafter, the talk was published under the title *Anhang von drey unterschiedenen Stuffen oder Classen nach welchen diejenige so würdig zum Heil. Abendmahl gehen* and attached to his sermon delivered on Maundy Thursday 1712 concerning the worthy preparation for the sacrament. In it Francke offers a spectrum of worthiness, which begins at and extends from true conversion. Though Francke claimed that each of these types of participants understood their unworthy condition in light of their sin and the redemptive work of God, he nevertheless symbolically used these figures to describe his views on marks of worthiness at the altar. The signs of worthiness attributed to the maid, virgin, and bride were both literally and figuratively extended to their real-life counterparts. The maid, overcome and humbled by her sin, responded to God with tears of regret. The virgin took seriously the call to follow Christ and thus assumed the responsibility to struggle against the world. The bride, standing nearest to Christ, evidenced a passionate love for her groom. The following will describe the signs of worthiness Francke attached to each of these symbolic figures and how they extended into Francke's further articulation of the sacrament.

Either newly converted or weakened by her sin, the maid represented the lowest level of worthiness at the Supper. Just as she held no social status in the community, she participated in the Supper with a demeanor of complete unworthiness. In defining a maid-like disposition, Francke remarks, "Those, who are like maids, are like the sinner (to be read about in Luke 7:37–50), who expresses contrition and sorrow for her sins, with which she offended God and to which she was awakened in her conscience, or expresses contrition and sorrow in recognition of her deep corruption, which most have covered with an empty Pharisaism or hypocrisy."[39] Francke seldom missed the opportunity to remind his listeners of their corrupted state apart from God, and as expected, his first stage of worthiness spoke to this problem common to humanity. To come worthily to the altar required that individuals address beforehand that they were by nature "lost and damned child[ren] of Adam."[40] "Such [people like the maid] do not unworthily participate in the Holy Eucharist. For although up until that point they were great sinners, they now recognize and regret their sin in true repentance [and] are very undone and humbled."[41] Maids appeared at the altar so overcome with what self-examination revealed in their lives that they could not imagine themselves being anything other than unworthy for such a sacrament. With a "weak faith" like that of the disciples, who deserted Christ shortly after the Passover celebration, maids held to Christ's divinity and redemptive work but were demoralized by their own betrayal of God.[42] Their sins grew so large in their eyes that they failed to notice anyone else participating with them. Thus in Francke's construction, believers represented by the maid could claim a worthiness, but the weight of their sins determined their visible expression of worthiness.

In this state, communicants displayed one of the core qualities of worthiness. They were humble and humiliated. For Francke humility defined how all communicants were to come to the altar regardless of the symbolic category of worthiness to which they belonged, but he especially emphasized this human disposition when he spoke of maids. Maids were those who were "quite satisfied when they, like the lost but now repentant son, might simply be day laborers in their Father's house."[43] In light of the sinfulness they once embraced, Francke called these worthy communicants "poor worms" and "beggars," who were wounded as if half dead.[44] They exchanged the pride of the world for a spirit of humility. God stood as the pattern for humility and was pleased to see it reciprocated. Thus parishioners were to root the source of their humility in God the "beggar" and Christ the humiliated.[45] They were to approach the altar with a joy connected to "trembling" that took God's work on their behalf seriously, and brought with it an increasing "humiliation and humbleness of heart, which is pleasing before the Lord our God."[46] Thus humility at the sacrament was primarily understood as both a response to God's redemptive work and a reaction to the communicant's previous "unabashed" sin.[47] Moreover, there was a connection between this humility and a felt, emotional reaction in the hearts of believers. Their humility was not merely a repetition of words but could be tangibly observed.

In reference to the Supper, Francke often connected true humility to the shedding of tears.[48] Continuing with his initial definition of the maid, Francke writes, "for this reason [that is, the recognition of her sin] she does not consider herself valued enough to come before Christ's face, just as the aforementioned sinner sat behind his feet, cried, and began to wet his feet with tears, and to dry [them] with the hair of her head, and to kiss his feet and anoint them with oil."[49] The New Testament offered Francke several proof-texts that he used to link crying to heartfelt humility. One example is Mary, the sinful woman who washed Christ's feet with her tears in the aforementioned story in Luke's Gospel. This synoptic pericope was a recurring story that Francke incorporated into his sermons on the Eucharist. In one such sermon, Francke embellished the Lukan text and recalled that not only did Mary wet Christ's feet with her tears and dry them with her hair, but "she would not allow herself to be comforted until she heard the comforting words, 'your sins are forgiven.'" Francke continues, "Behold, there a proper faith was displayed." Francke also used the Apostle Peter's dramatic denial of Christ before his crucifixion as a proof-text: "When he denied Christ, he went out and cried bitterly. He cried bitterly, [and] that was proper repentance."[50] Above all, though, there were the tears of Christ, which he shed over unrepentant Jerusalem. In winter 1694 Francke preached a sermon entitled *Von den Thränenden Augen des Herrn Jesu*, in which he painted Christ's visible display of sorrow as the pattern for the tears shed over the sins of believers. "When a child of God cries—a servant of God cries, over our city and its degenerate state, you should believe with certainty that they are Christ's tears. What [tears] I or another shed, they are the tears which Christ sheds in you. Since they have seen the degeneracy that Jesus saw in Jerusalem, they shed their tears for humanity's great unrepentance, in which it continues."[51] Beginning with the divine sorrow of Christ, in which Francke joined Jesus's sufferings to his tears, crying in the face of sin became the mark of a humble heart. The tears of repentance (*Bußthränen*) shed by followers of Jesus took on the added significance of remorse for acting contrary to the will of God, and with respect to the Lord's Supper, tears indicated a worthy participation of those who remained in the early stages of faith.[52]

Francke's doctrine of tears did not remain in abstraction. In the same way that he did not require believers to know the exact date of their conversion, Francke did not make the shedding of tears a required act in his theology of conversion. Nevertheless, he attested to the validity of Christian crying in his own ministry. In one notable instance, Francke connected tears to the true conversion of Spener's dying son, Johann Jakob (1669–1692). The younger Spener, who with the encouragement of his father had spent time studying under Ehrenfried Walther von Tchirnhaus, matriculated at Leipzig in 1687 and took a position as professor of mathematics and physics at the university in Halle a few months before Francke accepted the Glaucha pastorate. In January 1692, Johann Jakob found himself on his deathbed and face-to-face with Francke. Francke wrote in his journal concerning the visitation, "Professor Spener allowed me to come visit him in the evening, and with many tears attested to the fear of his conscience and his longing for an earnest and true conversion."[53] The next day he wrote to the elder Spener,

> Yesterday he allowed me to visit and freely poured out his heart to me; how he completely recognizes that until then he had lived in a sinful condition, which could not please God, and that for this reason he was

afraid in his conscience. He wished nothing more than that God would help him and place him in a proper and perfectly pleasing position before him [i.e., the Lord]. I openly said to him how up until that moment not only I but his honorable father looked upon his condition, and how we would have wished that he might come to a living knowledge of God. I asked him not to let this momentum visitationis divinae pass him by without making good use of it, but rather to employ it to his proper, thoroughgoing conversion.[54]

In Francke's mind, the tears Johann Jakob cried over his spiritual condition pointed to an inner transformation found in conversion, one in which individuals turned from their sinfulness and humbled themselves before God. The same day that Francke wrote to the elder Spener about his experience, he again visited Johann Jakob, writing, "Mr. Spener once again granted me the pleasure of visiting, and he attested to a firm longing after God."[55] The second visit only confirmed what Francke already knew: the tearful marks of a maid evidenced by Spener attested to his living faith.

At this point in the spectrum of worthiness, Francke did not require an exemplary life as preparation for the sacrament. Those he classified as "maids" still remained immature in their faith, though Francke was certain they held a true faith. Shocked by their sin, maid-like communicants were humbled before the grace of God. They responded, as the disciples did after fleeing from the type of suffering Jesus underwent at the cross, with tears of remorse.[56] Nevertheless, they came to the Supper in a state of worthiness.

"Spiritual virgins" inhabit the next position in Francke's typology of worthiness. Francke derived his term primarily from the parable found at the beginning of Matthew 25, which depicts the plight of ten waiting virgins and their oil lamps. Five of the ten virgins wisely took extra oil for their lamps and were prepared when their bridegroom suddenly called in the middle of the night. With lamps alight, they followed their groom to the marriage feast. Francke contrasted their readiness with the spiritual immaturity of the maids. As Francke clarifies, "They [spiritual virgins] are not the ones which just now converted or are 'laying the foundation from repentance of dead works' (Heb. 6:1). Rather they have already converted to God from their godless wandering or, by divine grace, pressed through from a lukewarm state of being to a godly earnestness, and now they move forward in daily renewal into the image of God, applying themselves to being followers of Christ."[57] Within the broader elements of this brief definition, Francke reveals the major elements that formed his conception of the "virgin" communicant. He alludes to a stage of faith in which believers took seriously their responsibility to follow God and sought the Eucharist for the strengthening it offered. They were to "follow the Lamb"—connecting discipleship with suffering—and by faith kiss the hand of their groom, who kept them from wandering down the broad path. Francke exhorts spiritual virgins, "Watch carefully, that you do not fall from your fortress, [but] grow even more."[58] Implicit in this formulation is Francke's doctrine of struggle (*Kampf*). Much is made of his teachings on the repentance struggle (Bußkampf), but it is clear from his writings that the whole of the Christian life was to be seen as a struggle against the Devil, the world, and the flesh at a variety of spiritual levels. Spiritual virgins, as they participated at the altar, took seriously this call to follow Christ and struggle against the world.

Nevertheless, Bußkampf played a prominent role in Francke's theology of conversion. Standing at the beginning of the Christian life, the repentance struggle should remain a vivid experience in the worthy communicant's memory.[59] He described it as a process during which individuals underwent a dramatic experience that took them from spiritual death to life. It was an inner conflict between the "old man" and the "new life."[60] During the process, believers were awakened to their sin and their eternal predicament. On the one hand, the power of sin so entrapped them that they despaired of trying to be freed from it. On the other hand, God's impending judgment distressed their hearts to such a degree that they feared what was to come. This part of the process he termed the fear struggle (*Angst-Kampff*). In this awakened state individuals experienced "birth pains," waiting for the hidden God to reappear.[61] While waiting, doubts and inner sorrow over sin debilitated them. Only after divine grace broke through could they find relief: "[God's] creation of a new and pure heart in us is the hardest struggle and at the same time the central point in the whole repentance struggle [*Buß-Kampffe*]."[62] Though at one point Francke offered his congregation a complex description of Bußkampf that included six stages, it is important to note he did not presume that any of his discussions on the topic were to be understood as a standardized schema. Instead, Bußkampf represented his belief that adult conversion included a recognition of sin, human inability, and God's judgment, a despair caused by such devastating knowledge, and an urgent plea for rescue that found relief in the redemptive work of Christ.

Spiritual virgins, though, stood on the other side of Bußkampf. They, like the maids, had denied the world and its lusts and taken up the call of discipleship. Their worthiness was found not in merely repenting again of their sin but in battling against the temptations of Satan. Quoting 2 Timothy, Francke exhorted his congregants that they were to hold to the faith by fighting the "good fight."[63] With the Eucharist in view, spiritual virgins faced a twofold struggle in following Christ. First, the *Kampf* of worthy participants reflected the sufferings of Christ. Just as Christ struggled unto the shedding of blood, communicants at this stage in their faith were to live in light of the sufferings of Christ.[64] His pain offered them comfort and courage. Thus the Lord's Supper became a proclamation not only of the death of Christ but also a proclamation of the commitment of spiritual virgins to travel the same path as their groom. This was not a road of ease, and so these communicants were to expect struggles. Yet they were not alone in their circumstances. "The Lord Jesus will strengthen him there [at the altar] with his body and with his blood. Thus he must fight and struggle with more zealousness and manliness against the world, the Devil, and [his own] flesh and blood."[65] The Supper offered the empowerment needed to follow in the sufferings of Christ, and the body and blood of Jesus helped counteract the worldly disposed body and blood of the individual.

Second, communicants as spiritual virgins could not merely qualify their participation in the sacrament with the waters of their baptism but had to visibly proclaim Christ's death with fruits that resulted from their denial of worldliness.[66] Alongside Christ's sufferings, believers were to be daily conformed to his obedience: "I exhort [you], take yourselves seriously, and watch out that you use this grace with fear and trembling, in order that you do not again lose what has been offered to you. Always be bold, [but] do not fall into a false freedom.... Watch out that from day to day you ever increasingly pursue sanctification. For at the same time ... the power of the divine stirring will increasingly disclose itself in your hearts and you will come to share more richly in the gentle moving of the Holy Spirit."[67] Spiritual virgins were ever mindful of their obligation to the baptismal covenant, which required that they grow in a faith manifested in works of love. Thus the Christian struggle that Francke expected from worthy communicants consisted in the passive reception of Christ's sufferings and in the active process of sanctification, in which faithfulness evidenced itself in fruit.

"The third class of those who participate worthily in the Holy Eucharist is those who can be reasonably called *a chosen bride of Christ* their Savior due to their strong faith, to their fiery love which they bring him, and to their striving to live with him in the most heartfelt and inward unity." The bride type, which Francke proposed to his readers in *Anhang von drey unterschiedenen Stuffen oder Classen*, represented the pinnacle of the Christian faith and, thus, the highest order of worthy participants. The contours of Francke's bride category are seen in what he called the "bride-conditions," which participants in the class exhibited. First, for these brides, "Christ is all to them; their sole wisdom, their sole righteousness, their sole sanctification, their sole redemption, their sole honor, their sole passion, their sole joy, their sole fortune, treasure, and jewel."[68] In his catechism sermons published contemporaneous to this tract, he claimed that the commemoration in the Supper was properly celebrated when "[Christ] is great in our souls, when he is glorious in our hearts, when he is our all in all."[69] This first condition was the primary indicator of a bride. Brides no longer depended on the world or earthly things. They sought out a tangible change in their lives. Most important, they did away with their own way of thinking, which pursued things of "flesh and blood," so that Christ held sole possession of their hearts. Francke appears to differentiate brides from maids and virgins by their inner dispositions. Brides were in some degree closer to Christ.[70] Accordingly, the next few conditions focused on the love of Christ in their lives. Christ's love was to be with them when they lay down and when they arose, when they came and when they went. It was to make the "bitter cross lovely and pleasant to them."[71] Moreover, those with "bride-hearts" were compelled by a love for God to do what pleased their heavenly groom.[72] Thus in brides one found communicants who were not only disciples but who expressed a passion for God absent in other examples of worthiness.

In his sermons on the Eucharist, Francke described this level of commitment as a "fiery" or (more often) "passionate love" (*brünstige Liebe*). It was a mark of faithful brides who devoted themselves to their groom's will. Such a love began as merely a spark in the heart of believers, but their growing understanding of redemption stoked the small flame until it filled the whole heart. As loving brides, communicants responded to the strengthening and empowering granted in the Supper with passionate love, patience in suffering, and humility before God and man. Thus, brides did not leave behind the characteristics of the other two stages of worthiness but rather added the sign of passionate devotion to their marks. Francke exhorted his congregation, "If you desire to enjoy the proper fruit of the Supper, then your prayer must be even more zealous and passionate. In your Christianity more earnestly learn to sigh after God than has occurred up until this point."[73] Francke coupled this sighing passion for God with a true fear of the Lord and contrasted it to life without an understanding of the sacrament. Ultimately, brides distinguished themselves from other communicants by this overflowing love toward Christ in their hearts.[74]

In Francke's typology of the bride, we are confronted with tangible evidence of his mystical tendencies. Though it would be hard to defend the claim that Francke was a mystic, there is no question that he evidenced mystical tendencies in certain points of his thought.[75] His own conversion testimony reflects the early influence of both Arndt and the Spanish mystic

Miguel de Molinos.[76] The Bußkampf theology that he preached had clear traces of mystical ideas, especially in his teachings on the hiddenness of God. In addition, his emphasis on a passionate, burning love in the worthy communicant reveals that Francke, even as a mature theologian and pastor, gave room to mystical ideas. It also draws attention to the nature of those mystical tendencies in his theology. Although they may have played a role in Francke's early views on perfectionism, the characteristic notions of "emptying" and *Gelassenheit* that have prominence in mystical teachings are absent in Francke's works. Rather, Francke's mystical tendencies can be found in his emphasis on drawing nearer to God. The value of nearness was not rooted in divine locality but in creator-creature unity. Growth in holiness paralleled a decrease in the spiritual distance between believers and their redeemer. The Supper held a special mystical role because the commemoration Jesus commanded his disciples to celebrate at the altar was to occur most importantly in the hearts of believers.[77] The Supper was a place where believers drew closer to God or distanced themselves through unworthiness. While Epicureans could expect the judgment of God, brides were consumed with a nearness to God. Thus Francke could say, "Yes, [Jesus] provided [his disciples] a commemoration of his suffering and death, with which he desired that the hearts of his disciples be bound together in love; that just as a loaf of bread comes from many grains, and wine comes from many grapes, through them [the bread and wine] they may be one heart and mindset, and that they may be one in our highly deserved Savoir, Jesus Christ, sanctified through his blood."[78] Brides, therefore, not only offered a further sign of worthiness (their passionate love for Christ), but they also displayed Francke's mystic-like concern for nearness to God.

In Francke's spectrum of worthiness we see the outworking of his emphasis on approaching the altar with the necessary signs. Individuals could not properly celebrate Christ's death at the altar without an expressed form of personal worthiness. For Francke, the Eucharist continued to hold all the qualities Lutheran divines had attributed to it, resting peacefully in the sacristy of the church. But he erected a theology of the Lord's Supper that focused on those resting all-too-peacefully in the nave. Francke carved out a theology of worthiness, adding existential signs of worthiness to the divinely given qualities of the sacrament. Consequently, proper preparation for the Eucharist did not begin in corporate worship on Sunday, but in the confessional and pastoral visitations. Using the baptismal covenant as the criterion, he encouraged and rebuked his parishioners, sought the eyewitness testimony of neighbors, looked for signs of worthiness, and (when necessary) banned individuals from the sacrament. By ministering in this way, Francke exposed the impact of his Pietist soteriology on his theology of the Eucharist. Conversion and sanctification, in terms of rebirth, struggling in faith, and holy living, came to dominate how Francke articulated the Lord's Supper. For this reason, Peschke was right to call his theology of the Eucharist a "richly colored mosaic."[79]

EPILOGUE
The Church of the Heart

The previous chapters have sought to provide an introduction to Francke's sacramental theology, and in doing so, to offer a glimpse into how his emphasis on personal conversion, rebirth, and sanctification spilled over into every aspect of his religious thought. As has been shown, Francke could not speak of baptism or the Eucharist without bearing upon the minds of his audience the need for conversion and rebirth and the call to live according to the inward work of God. And just as Francke's emphasis on conversion pervaded every aspect of his sacramental theology, it also shaped what Francke intended the church to be.[1] This rich connection between the means of grace and the identity of the church played out in Sunday worship under Francke's leadership, where consistent rhythms of liturgy and the preached Word cultivated a clear sense of what it meant to become a Christian and how the community of believers should be recognized. In the sermons Francke delivered week in and week out, he bore upon the minds of his audience the contours of his Pietist theology of conversion, and he contextualized the identity of the church through the life of the believer. This is one of the reasons he often returned to the refrain of the unfortunate state of the "corrupted church" (*verderbte Kirche*) that worshipped "outwardly" through Word and sacrament. In 1699 Francke exclaims, "There are those that say, 'What am I doing wrong? I am fond of attending church. I participate in confession and the Eucharist, and so on.' If one looked upon their heart and mind, . . . they [would be seen as] being fond of worldly honor, wanting to be important people."[2] It was only by means of "true" faith that an individual could claim a proper conversion, and it was only as a new creature that such a person could "properly" participate in the corporate celebration of the sacraments. Should conversion go missing in this ordering, that which followed fell apart, including the identity of the church as seen in its worship.

This is why Francke's theology, especially his theology of the sacraments, provides an important glimpse into eighteenth-century notions of what constitutes the church.[3] Just as personal faith and conversion defined his views of the church's traditional boundary markers, so too they defined his understanding of the church. Without conversion and rebirth, there could be no proper worship of God in Word and sacrament, and this absence of proper worship spoke to an absence of believers in the congregation. Thus Francke juxtaposed a corrupt, dead church with a converted, "proper" church. At several points in Francke's pastoral ministry he attempted to articulate what it meant to be a "proper church according to the New Testament" and how this church "properly worshipped." In the movement of Francke's sacramental theology toward individual conversion and identifying true conversion, he inevitably moved toward redefining the church with reference to the condition of the individual heart.

The Proper Church According to the New Testament

In February 1699, Francke preached on what he presented as the proper way to attend Sunday worship. Working from the liturgical text Luke 2:22–23, where the evangelist describes the presentation of Jesus at the Temple by his parents, Francke applied his heart-centered biblical hermeneutic to the passage and pushed it in a direction that allowed him to address practices and habits in his congregation. His exhortations reflected his desire to cultivate a type of worship that he believed could only arise from a community whose hearts were converted to Christ.

To emphasize his point, Francke patterned worshipping individuals after Simeon, who is described in the Lukan story as "righteous and devout" (Luke 2:25).[4] Toward the end of his sermon, Francke exhorts his parishioners, "This [Simeon] waited upon the Comfort of Israel, and the Holy Spirit was in him. Take note that his heart was a proper church of the Holy Spirit. And you should learn from old Simeon that when you desire to properly attend church, you must get to know the proper church according to the New Testament."[5] Francke, like Spener in his *Pia Desideria*, placed great value on retrieving certain aspects of the early church.[6] Nevertheless, Francke's "proper" New Testament church appears inseparable from the individual hearts of his congregants, who he believed should follow the example of Simeon and be prepared for the inner work of the Holy Spirit. Interestingly, he warned that even attending "prayer hours" and catechesis, two activities Francke often encouraged for the renewal of the church, could become outward acts that covered the inward reality of an unregenerate heart. The only hope for individuals was that they "call upon the Holy Spirit from the bottom of their heart."[7]

Regarding this "church of the heart," Francke held forth to his listeners a synergist view of the relationship between the individual's and the Spirit's work. While Simeon was responsible to prepare himself for God's presence, it was the Spirit who erected a "chapel" (*Kirchlein*) in his heart. In these small confines the Word of God was made "powerful and living," for the Spirit taught Simeon. And it is in the church of the heart, exemplified by Simeon, that we find proper worship (*rechte Dienst*). This is likely one reason that Francke begins his sermon by claiming prayer is "the main piece [*Hauptstück*] of all of worship." Those who desired not to be "distant" from the "filling of the Word of our Savior Jesus Christ . . . should worship in Spirit and in Truth" (John 4:24).[8] A few months later in June, Francke pleaded with his audience, "Examine yourself further: What's the condition of your prayer? How impassioned [*brünstig*] is it? How zealously is it delivered to God? How do you praise God? . . . You've heard it said that you should keep Sunday holy, gladly hear and learn God's Word, treasure it also in a refined, good heart, and thereafter bear righteous fruit."[9] The prayers of the faithful played their part in the reception and outworking of God's Word communicated by the Spirit.

We need not look beyond Francke's example of Simeon and his concern for heartfelt prayer in Sunday worship to catch a glimpse of his understanding of the church. While Simeon provided a pattern for those who would worship properly, Francke points out that Christians are prone to fall into two types of people who distort church attendance. On one side are those with an "Old Testament mentality," who like the disobedient Israelites in the book of Exodus are only outward worshippers of God. In a sermon held in January 1699, he criticized those who dismissed his preaching on repentance as theologically dangerous. They, like the Israelites who persecuted the prophets, continued to practice "outward worship . . . ordered according to the old ways."[10] Francke's primary concern was the way in which individuals elevated the ritualized participation in the preached Word and sacraments of Sunday worship to the point that merely being in church made them worthy of salvation. He compared these types of people to "dumb animals" who remained in their "sin-sleep."[11] The "old ways" of outward worship neglected not only the need for personal repentance but also the law of God, which should press upon them their obligation to obedience.

The other type of Christians who failed to worship properly were separatists, who, according to Francke, believe "it is useless that people outwardly gather together; rather [they believe] . . . it is an Old Testament mindset, which doesn't please the Lord God and from which one also cannot obtain a true edification of his soul."[12] These individuals neglected the "community of gifts" (*Gemeinschafft der Gaben*), a gathering that edified and strengthened the believer. Not only had these separatists spurned the call of the book of Hebrews to avoid neglecting the fellowship of believers, but they furthermore ignored or misinterpreted the blessing of their Savior, who was present where "two or three were gathered" in his name (Matt. 18:20).

These words of Jesus from Matthew 18 are found two other times in Francke's sermon on church attendance. For the most part, the phrase where "two or three are gathered" provided him the space to present the church as a worshipping community not bound to a specific place. He instructs his parishioners that even though Mary and Joseph were obligated to go and present Jesus at the Temple in Jerusalem, this did not mean that worship was bound alone to the Temple. It was true that Jews were commanded not to build altars and conduct elsewhere the special worship that was ordered for the Temple. Nevertheless, Francke claims, "house or heart churches remained," where followers were to pray to God.[13] In a 1694 sermon, Francke called those "two or three gathered in his name" the "tabernacle of Christ" (*Hütte Christi*), which recognized itself as "the blessed community of the holy in light that is not known by the world."[14]

As he concluded his sermon on church attendance, Francke again returned to Matthew 18:20 in a discussion of the place of "house churches" in the life of the believing community. This reference to house churches should not be confused with the more modern, evangelical emanation. Francke was drawing upon Luther's doctrine of the three estates, in which the family household formed, as John Witte describes, "the foundation . . . of churches" that "was to teach all persons, particularly children, Christian values, morals, and mores."[15] Particular to Francke's understanding of the church, it is notable that he took this final moment in the sermon to chide those who spoke dismissively of their responsibilities to the family at home by giving "house churches" the disparaging name "conventicles" or "secret gatherings." In doing so they had made "an unfortunate division between public and private edification."[16] Whether done wittingly or not, Francke connected the spiritual function of the estate of the family to conventicle meetings. He did not in this moment qualify or distance one from the other, but instead he encouraged any activity that took to heart Paul's exhortation that Christians should "allow the Word to richly dwell among them and admonish each other in all wisdom" (Col. 3:16). In commending such activity, Francke displayed the Pietist tendency to believe the most beneficial Christian growth arose from smaller, close-knit communities.[17] He goes on to explain that Paul had not intended these words strictly for that which occurs in the church. The words of Christ in Matthew 18:20 are fulfilled, according to Francke, in those who prayed together and called upon Christ's grace, regardless of the walls that surrounded them. These are the same individuals who were derided and laughed at by "worldly people" [*Welt-Menschen*].[18] Though Francke was paying special attention to prayer throughout his sermon on church attendance, he consistently presented the church as inward (the "heart church") and outward. Nevertheless, both of these "churches" were united in the goal of fostering piety in the individual life.

Three years later, in January 1702, Francke turned to the language of the Apostles' Creed to further define the proper church as a "community of gifts," a phrase he used to rebuke separatists in his earlier sermon. In the context of the common Christian affirmation that believers form the "communion of the saints," Francke again focused on the individual heart in his attempt to provide a definition of the church. He began, nevertheless, by setting forth the centrality of Jesus in identifying the church, for Christ is "established as the foundation [*Grund*] of the community of the saints; that he is found in us and we in him, and [that we are] bound with him as members."[19] The "blessed community" of believers was maintained by a recognition of Christ's lordship and a union to his redeeming work.[20] Yet this binding to Christ through faith is something realized in the heart. "One must know that Christ is not only the foundation, but also that this foundation must be laid in our hearts.... Where this living Jesus lives and works in the hearts of men, and his agency [*Wirckung*] is given room, there, there is the true foundation of the community of the saints."[21] He then reminded his congregants that such a union, one in which believers call Christ their Lord, comes only through their possession of the Holy Spirit.

After addressing the role of the Spirit, Francke offers a list or an order of salvation particular to his discussion of the nature of the church. First, those belonging to the community of the saints, claimed Francke, truly recognize their unbelief, having been awakened by a "true contrition and sorrow over sin." Second, the Spirit's grace sets their hearts aflame, and as a result the Spirit consecrates them to God and orients them away from a worldly mindset. The final result is that they are dedicated and sanctified as a temple to God.[22] This particular order of salvation drew upon Francke's consistent expectation for the individual's deep concern for sin during the conversion experience, but it also reflected his attempt to convey a right understanding of the church. The converted individual not only experienced rebirth through the awakening of the heart but she became a temple to God, an image that in Francke's theology symbolizes the "church of the heart" reaching its fulfillment. Without denying the traditional Lutheran understanding of the church, grounded upon Christ's redeeming work, he presented the individual heart as the reference point by which the church was to be understood.

Francke turned to the phrase "community of gifts" in his sermon to provide an expression of embodiment for his language of the church. Though there were certain special gifts granted to all individuals, in the case of his 1702 sermon on Romans 12, Francke was concerned with delineating "common gifts" given by the Spirit to all those within the community of saints. Among these common gifts were a genuine, nonhypocritical love, an abhorrence of evil, a diligence in serving one's neighbor, a "hot passion" for the Word that spoke to the indwelling of the Spirit, a hope in tribulation, a hospitality and mercifulness to others, and a humility with regard to one's place in life. Underlying Francke's list of common gifts was the expectation that Christians not be preoccupied with "eating, drinking, sleeping, and the such," which was found among "lazy" people; rather they were to be diligent and busy with their vocations, as if they were "living for Christ." In what might have seemed like the same breath, Francke exhorted his congregants not to attempt to "climb off the cross." For, they were given the gift of participation in Christ's sufferings.[23] By expositing Romans 12:9–16 as a list, he connected his theology of the cross with vocational calling. This allowed him to move effortlessly in his sermon from diligence in one's vocation, to suffering with Christ, and finally to caring for the poor. The way in which Francke presented these three features of the gifted community lends itself to the claim that he was providing visible marks of neighborly love that could help structure the identity of believers in a worshipping community, which he complained had grown ritualistic in its participation in the Word and the sacraments.

Proper Worship According to the New Testament

As a community of gifts, the proper church according to the New Testament built and strengthened itself through gathering together in corporate worship.[24] Nevertheless, Francke's emphasis on the individual's spiritual condition in his characterization of the church carried over into how he articulated proper worship. In a sermon on Romans 12:1–2 delivered July 1709, Francke insisted Christians evidence a reasonable, proper worship of God in a "sincerity, integrity, and truthfulness of the heart." For the worshipper's "faith should be living in him; his love should be living in him; his hope should be living in him.... But now the Holy Scripture sets forth such clear words, we should 'present our bodies as an offering, which is living, holy and pleasing to God,' and worship is situated in this, [and] not in attending church, not in attending confession and the Eucharist, not in what one reads in a prayer book or sometimes reads in the Bible; rather [it is] in one's complete consecration and offering up of oneself to God for his glory."[25] Though Francke set forth the theological virtues in his language of worship, he nevertheless defined these virtues in relation to the individual heart and expressed them using the inward language of being an "offering." In doing so, he gave primacy to the inner life of the individual in corporate worship. Thus Francke's claim that public worship was to provide the context of the Christian community's edification was based upon his commitment to individual conversion being the end and not the means to what he calls "proper Sunday worship according to the New Testament." In his sermon on honoring the Sabbath, published in 1726, Francke specifically addressed this "proper Sunday worship," setting out six "days" in light of the Small Catechism's teaching on the third commandment. These days differ from the "steps" he offered in his 1694 catechism sermon on the same topic, but they provide a glimpse into how Francke defined public worship in relation to the individual heart.[26]

First and foremost, according to Francke, Sunday worship was to be a "repentance and conversion day." He grounds this claim on Jesus's call in the synoptic gospels to "repent and believe" in light of God's coming judgment (Mark 1:15). Though Jesus's words were directed toward the Jews of his time, they held the same weight and power for Francke's own congregation. Their lives were also to be defined by repentance and conversion in order to avoid God's wrath. Nevertheless, holiness and those passions associated with holy living, and not Christ's first sermon, formed the core and breadth of his argument concerning proper worship. The Small Catechism states that Christians "fear and love God, so that we do not despise preaching or God's Word, but instead keep that Word holy," but Francke remarks, "how can a true fear of God be actualized in us if we are without true repentance of the heart?" So too, Francke wondered how the unconverted could keep from despising God's Word and have a "desire and joy" to "gladly hear and learn it." The only proper remedy to the holy requirement of the commandment was conversion. "As long as the person is not changed, no day will ever be properly made holy; If we convert to God from the bottom of our hearts [*Herzens-Grunde*], then every day will be made holy.... But if Sunday should be properly spent, then it must be, before all things, ... employed to our true conversion."[27]

Francke's assumption that too many Christians did not hold Sunday to be a repentance and conversion day colored every aspect of his exhortation on the third commandment. He believed his parishioners held the same false, *ex opere operato* disposition in their minds for Sunday worship as they did for the sacraments. If they merely participated in it, they were identified and sanctified as God's children. He believed the sermons offered by his fellow clergymen also came to reflect this false notion of Sunday worship, neglecting the core of God's Word found in the call to repentance and conversion. In winter 1699, Francke complained to his parishioners, "So it is among us, and so it is in our so-called Lutheran churches. If one preaches repentance to the people, they hold it as a new [i.e., dangerous] doctrine."[28] For those contemplating his exhortation on the third commandment, should they have a "true and thorough change of heart and mind," Francke insists, "then all of Christianity has its proper and enduring foundation."[29]

If Sunday were properly celebrated as a "conversion day," then according to Francke it may be called a "faith day." As in his broader theology, so too in his theology of worship, repentance and faith play an inseparable role. One cannot have true faith, claimed Francke, without true repentance. This relationship between repentance and faith allowed Francke to draw on language associated with Bußkampf to note the way in which worshippers of God are betrothed to Christ through their conversion. He emphasized the individual's recognition of personal misery and spiritual corruption that resulted from sin. This should lead the person, claimed Francke, to "remorse and pain" and "contrition of his heart." At this point, Sunday could become a "betrothal day of his soul with the Lord Jesus."[30] Francke connected spiritual betrothal to Christ with the baptismal covenant individuals had broken. The false worship that occurred within the walls of his own church testified to his parishioners' broken vows and broken covenants. Those who wished to rightly worship on Sunday should seek with "hot tears" to reenter their covenant bond through the rejection of Satan and his works.

Third, Francke set forth Sunday as a "holy day," which was impossible to have without the Holy Spirit. He reminded his readers in his third point that the grace of repentance and a conversion of the heart necessary for Sunday worship arose from the work of God's Spirit. In order to emphasize this, Francke described the individual's heart as the seat of three salvific "offices." The Spirit's work of sanctification stood at the end of a particular historical ordering of redemptive offices that included John the Baptist and Jesus Christ. First, in repentance the individual experiences the office of John the Baptist. Then, through faith he experiences the "reconciling office" of Jesus Christ, and finally in all that pertains to the work of sanctification, the office of the Holy Spirit finds room in him. "For it is then a proper holy day, if the ordering of God is left in this way undivided." He concludes, "If it is not a repentance day, then it is also not a faith day; and if it is not a faith day, so it is not, at least to us, a holy day. On the other hand, if one truly repents, comes to faith in the Lord Jesus, and allows room for the Holy Spirit, then it is a holy day to him."[31]

The final three "days" of the sermon concern themselves with the outworking of a true conversion in light of Sunday worship. Francke insisted that where there is a repentance day, a betrothal day, and a day of the Holy Spirit, there is "day of discipleship" (*Tag der Nachfolge*). Though individuals were held back by the monotonous work of their vocations, and their frames of mind were scattered, nevertheless proper Sunday worship offered believers the opportunity to experience an eternal Sabbath rest by following the "Sun of Righteousness and the Light of Life."[32] In proper corporate worship believers were refreshed and strengthened for the week ahead of them. In his 1694 catechism sermon on the same commandment, Francke identified the future Sabbath rest with an end to poverty, toil, and tribulation, which may explain why he called his fifth day of proper worship a "Day of the Cross."[33] For Francke there was an interplay between the rest experienced through discipleship and the tribulations of the cross. Discipleship is cultivated by participating in the storm of "hail and lightning" found in the cross of Christ, and Francke adds, "We cannot come to a proper and consistent rest if [participation in the cross] does not occur through discipline." The person who took part inwardly and outwardly in the cross of Christ experienced the "power of godly peace" and through proper Sunday worship, empowered by the preached Word, was able to overcome "all the storms, which befall him from Satan and mankind."[34] Finally Francke calls proper Sunday worship a "day full of good fruit." The Christian life as expressed in holiness was to be a natural consequence of the previous "days." Had individuals properly celebrated the "days" presented by Francke, from conversion day to the day of the cross, personal holiness would be a natural outworking. As he remarked in his 1694 sermon on the third commandment, "just as a person naturally grows in his age, so too he grows in his Christianity."[35] Spiritual fruitfulness, along with discipleship and cross-bearing, served as marks or signs for Francke that pointed back to their source, personal conversion. As the primary focal point in Francke's ordering of God's salvific work, conversion served as his goal for what he called "proper Sunday worship."

Francke believed this elevation of conversion as an identifier of the church, especially its corporate worship, was biblically based. Christ's words to the woman at the well in John 4:23 that Christians were to worship "in Spirit and in Truth" created a theological barrier to "holy worship" that Francke believed only rebirth could overcome.[36] While simultaneously acknowledging in his sermons on the church that those involved in outward worship fell into categories of "good and bad among each other" (*corpus permixtum*), his constant turn toward "proper" inward worship shifted the attention away from the visible community and toward the invisible condition of the individual soul.[37] The language of the church, for Francke, began with the heart, led to the true community united to Christ, and only then was to be identified with the outward practices of the church.

Francke's role in establishing German Lutheran Pietism through his pastoral activity, writings, and the ministries of his foundations in Halle provides ample reason to examine his ecclesiology. Nevertheless as they have come to represent German Pietism, his ideas arose at a time when seventeenth-century confessional ties were weakening within certain religious communities on the Continent and when a wave of attempts to reform and strengthen the church ran through German Lutheranism. Pietism, as it represents one such attempt at reform, inherently and intentionally drew attention to the condition of the church and offered theological assertions as to how it might be renewed.[38] Francke's theology cannot be understood outside of this Pietist commitment to rebirth in all areas of the church, and attempts to construct his religious thought without the framework of church reform inevitably fractures the cohesiveness of his theology. Francke's Pietist theology was a theology of conversion that sought individual rebirth for the sake of an awakening of the church and a reforming of the world. For this reason, his theological constructions concerning the sacramental practices of the church not only offer a window into the contours of Francke's theology, but they also provide a case study of ecclesiological innovations that foreshadowed abstract conceptions of the church found in parts of the Awakening movements and subsequent Protestant denominations.

As Francke approached the topic of baptism, his concern for a personal conversion experience, in which the individual comes to a recognition of her spiritual wretchedness and finds great relief and certainty in experiencing the love of Christ and the empowering of the Spirit, led him to speak often of individuals in relation to their baptismal covenant. This covenant, which on one side was enacted by the person at the baptismal font, provided Francke the theological language in which he could press his audience as to whether or not they recognized how their sinful lives had ruptured their relationship with Christ. In hope of cultivating this awareness, Francke drew further attention to their need for a baptism of the heart. This emphasis on a mature acknowledgment of sin inevitably pushed baptismal regeneration of infants to the background, and as Francke flirted with the Reformed-leaning ideas of Lutheran pastor Theophil Großgebauer, he walked a path in which he paid his respects to traditional Lutheran teachings on baptismal rebirth but subverted those same teachings with his emphasis on a definable conversion experience. Lurking in the background of Francke's teaching on baptism was his conviction that individuals gained their identity in the church not through their baptismal waters but by means of their conversion.

The boundaries of the believing community would inevitably take on the character of the abstract, inward nature of rebirth language. Francke had no apparatus in his theological arsenal that could confirm the inward transformation of the individual heart without mediation. Therefore, confession became a mediator of sorts by which he could identify those who evidenced a converted life. The individual conscience continued to speak to the "good" or "bad" spiritual condition of the person, and through interviews and in the act of confessing, Francke was able to bring the conscience into the public sphere. At the same time, he attacked those practices in which repentance was subverted by outward acts that he deemed empty of spiritual significance. The confessional offering embodied this subversion of true faith and stood in conflict with the heartfelt testimony of a follower of Christ. Nevertheless, what for Luther was to be a means of comfort became for Francke a means of identifying the converted, sanctified life.

Thus the celebration of the altar turned into an introspective evaluation of personal worthiness before the Lord. Francke was careful to never claim this was a human-merited worthiness. "Though," Gary Sattler rightly estimates, "one is not totally convinced by his language."[39] Those, according to Francke, who had truly experienced the self-giving love of Christ cultivated a life that evidenced the transformative power of God's unmerited favor. These were the faithful few who participated in the Eucharist worthily. Nevertheless, there were visible proofs, or signs, that Francke felt pastors could turn to, which granted them a greater certainty regarding the spiritual condition of specific individuals. Francke would even go so far as to offer a typology of maids, virgins, and brides to help characterize the nature of worthy participation in the sacrament.

This application of Francke's Eucharistic theology nevertheless pointed to a complex dynamic in Francke's overall religious thought. He had made the transformation that arises from conversion and rebirth the theological feature that essentially connected individuals to the Christian community. By presenting conversion as a personal encounter with God, this inward act of transformation and not the outward, visible signs of the sacraments became the way in which the church was identified. In their essential character, the means of grace offered by the church became ways in which the transformative religious experience was to be provoked or confirmed. The sacraments were specifically calls to a new life in Christ, and in this context orthopraxy would come to reassure the claims of an inward spiritual "newness." But Oswald Bayer notes, "in and of itself . . . orthopraxy does not provide clear *nota ecclesiae*, since [as Luther says] 'even some heathens are so practiced in such works and clearly at times seem to be holier than Christians.'"[40]

Francke's "church of the heart" language is the embodiment of his conversion-driven sacramental theology. The goal of rebirth had so permeated his theology that any attempt at identifying the character and nature of the church must begin for Francke with the individual conversion experience. Thus he complained against those who believed their participation in corporate worship established their inclusion in the community of the saints. These misguided individuals, according to Francke, had mistaken the order by which the body of Christ could be identified. Only by beginning with individual rebirth could one rightly speak of those other elements of belief and practice that defined the community.

This draws attention to Francke's place among the various developing early modern understandings of the church. His theology stands as a case study of how ecclesiologies were being stretched in the late seventeenth and early eighteenth centuries. The traditional marks of the church were being pushed by religious figures like Francke in directions that would cause them to eventually take a backseat to what Molly Worthen calls "the traditional evangelical 'sacrament': the personal decision for Christ."[41] One need not look further than the Pietist playground, Pennsylvania, to see the transatlantic ripples of Francke's theological influence. Gettysburg theologian Samuel Simon Schmucker (1799–1873), whom Mark Granquist calls "the most important figure within American Lutheranism in the first half of the nineteenth century," believed he was following in the spiritual footsteps of Francke as he sought to redefine American Lutheran understandings of the sacraments.[42] He hoped this would better situate American Lutheranism in a widening evangelical "scene" that had its roots in Second Great Awakening revivalism.[43] In order to do so, Schmucker sought to remove what he considered the unbiblical doctrines of the real presence of Christ in the Eucharist and baptismal regeneration. Reasons for Schmucker's ecclesiological accommodations may also run in the direction of rationalism, but his recourse to German Lutheran Pietism reflects the often overlooked influence that Francke's theology had on transatlantic Protestant understandings of the church. The ongoing influence of Francke's Pietism on later American Lutheran ecclesiology likely led nineteenth-century Reformed theologian John Williamson Nevin (1803–1886) to mourn the ways in which views like Schmucker's had "forsaken" traditional understandings of the Supper.[44]

The importance of August Hermann Francke in understanding Protestant theological innovations occurring in the eighteenth and nineteenth centuries should not be underestimated. As George Whitefield's ministry was to the Great Awakening, so too was Francke's to German Pietism. His published sermons and tracts, his attempts to renew the church through the training and sending of pastors, and his own personal travels to provoke church renewal in German regions all point to his influence during a period when in some religious communities confessional lines were fading and being replaced by denominationalism or weak forms of religious toleration. For this reason, this study provided a walk down one of the main corridors of the house of Francke's theology. As we have considered the architectural contours of his thought, we are nevertheless reminded of important steps that need to continue in research addressing Francke. The most obvious of these is the need for substantial biographical work to supplement historical-theological studies like this one. Gary Sattler's dated biography remains the only recent attempt in the English language at a thorough account of Francke's life. Furthermore the works of scholars like Veronika Albrecht-Birkner and Jonathan Strom remind us of the need for research into specific periods of theological developments in Francke's life. This compels us not only to take seriously the early, more radical expressions in Francke's theology, but also to take into account later periods of theological development as they can be ascertained from his sermon manuscripts and correspondence. How did he approach liturgical passages of Scripture at different stages in his ministry? How did advances in his ministry affect the content of his preaching? Francke is a glaring reminder that early modern sermon manuscripts provide an important corrective to historical-theological research that has primarily based its narrative on official or published books and tracts. The unpublished sermon offers an uncensored look into how religious leaders applied their theological predilections to the life of the church. Finally, an examination of Francke's theology reminds us that Lutheran Pietism has traditionally dominated the nature of research on Continental Pietism. Francke's Reformed tendencies, evidenced at moments in his sacramental theology, call our attention to the history of German Reformed Pietist thought. Should we draw more exhaustively upon developments in German Reformed Pietism, we may be able to piece together a fuller picture not only of the overlap and exchange of theological ideas, but the broader reaches of Pietist networks in German-speaking regions. The life and theology of August Hermann Francke presents an invaluable glimpse into one of the more provocative—if not at times drifting—expressions of early modern experiential Protestantism that for Francke was embodied in Pietism.

NOTES

Unless otherwise indicated, all translations are mine. All references to German words reflect the spelling of the original.

INTRODUCTION

1. Ernst Neumann, *Der Missionar am Volta*, 111. The story of Eddi and his gift is itself an anecdote derived from the front cover inscription of the author's copy of the book.
2. Ibid., 100.
3. D. Brown, *Understanding Pietism*, 26; H. Brown, *Heresies*, 389. Sträter notes that after his conversion Francke consistently held an "apostolische Selbstbewußtsein," even addressing himself to Spener in a letter as "Paulus von Glaucha." Sträter, "Spener und August Hermann Francke," 91.
4. Mori, *Begeisterung und Ernüchterung*, 15.
5. Shantz claims that Pietism "represents the most significant Protestant renewal movement since the sixteenth century." Shantz, *Introduction to German Pietism*, 1. Strom says Francke brought a "wider currency" to Pietism in "Problems and Promises of Pietism Research," 537. See Hirsch, *Geschichte der neuern Evangelischen Theologie*, 2:91.
6. See Jenson, "Church and the Sacraments," 207. Bradley and Muller claim that "the best model for the history of doctrine is certainly the integral or organic model that attempts a synchronous understanding of the development of the central ideas of Christianity." Bradley and Muller, *Church History*, 30.
7. Orsi, *History and Presence*, 66.
8. *Book of Concord*, 42–43.
9. Peschke, *Studien*, vols. 1–2; Peschke, *Bekehrung und Reform*. See also Matthias, "Gewissheit und Bekehrung," 11–31; Albrecht-Birkner, *Francke in Glaucha*; Albrecht-Birkner and Sträter, "Die radikale Phase," 57–84.
10. Beyreuther, "Der Ursprung des Pietismus," 137.
11. H. Schneider, "Understanding the Church," 15.
12. R. Lehmann, *Die Transformation des Kirchenbegriffs*, 185–338. Erhard Peschke offers the most recent study of Francke's sacrament theology: Peschke, "Die Abendmahlsanschauung," 128–39.
13. Swain, "Lutheran and Reformed Sacramental Theology," 363.
14. Campbell, *Religion of the Heart*, 7–8. For an example of this in colonial America, see Winiarski, *Darkness Falls on the Land of Light*, 42–53. Concerning the sacraments and Pietist self-identity, Roeber notes, "For subscribers to the Augsburg Confession, . . . the sacramental dimension of the Christian church—especially the importance of baptism and the Lord's Supper—remained indispensable reference points." Roeber, "Waters of Rebirth," 53.
15. Gordon, "Theologies of the Sacraments," 261.
16. See Jung, "Impact of Pietism," 226.
17. For information of the history of the Stiftungen (also called the *Glauchasche Anstalten*), see Obst, *August Hermann Francke und die Franckeschen Stiftungen in Halle*. For Francke's own account, see *Segens-volle Fußstampfen*.

18. For a short history of the *Pietas Hallensis*, see Yoder, "Rendered 'Odious' as Pietists," 17–26. See also Brunner, *Halle Pietists in England*; Brecht, "August Hermann Francke," 514–31; Hindmarsh, *Spirit of Early Evangelicalism*, 24–25.

19. Yoder, "Rendered 'Odious' as Pietists," 18.

20. Whitmer, *Halle Orphanage*, 35.

21. Untermöhlen, "Rußlandthematik im Briefwechsel," 125–26.

22. Wallmann proposes three primary characteristics of Pietism: conventicles, personal reading of the Bible, and chiliasm. See Wallmann, *Der Pietismus*, 85; Wallmann, "Was ist Pietismus?," 20–27. This "strict constructionist" view of Pietism has become the prevailing model and is reflected in the more recent works of Strom and Shantz. Shantz adds renewal, rebirth, and social activism to Wallmann's three aspects. See Lindberg, "Introduction," 2; Strom, "Pietism," 600–603; Shantz, *Introduction to German Pietism*, 7. The following discussion adopts Wallmann's definition and adds to it rebirth.

23. Wallmann, *Der Pietismus*, 79–80, 82–84. Tappert in the introduction to his translation of the *Pia Desideria* summarizes Spener's suggestions as, "reform of theological education, criticism of scholastic theology and theological polemics, advocacy of interconfessional toleration and understanding, emphasis on a religion of the heart as well as the head, demand for a faith that expresses itself in life and activity, cultivation of personal holiness with a tendency toward perfectionism, upgrading of the laity, recommendation of private meetings for the fostering of piety, development of the spiritual priesthood of believers, endorsement of mysticism, etc." (p. 19).

24. Spener's *Pia* stood in contrast to the reform plan of Theophil Großgebauer, who suggested that a renewal of faith must begin with the clergy. See Sträter, *Meditation und Kirchenreform*, 150–52.

25. A. Deppermann, *Johann Jakob Schütz*, 352. See also Wallmann, "Kirchlicher und radikaler Pietismus," 36.

26. Wallmann, "Eine alternative Geschichte des Pietismus," 56; Mori, "Conventicle Piety of the Radicals," 203.

27. The prominence of conventicles in the early stages of the work of Spener and Francke casts doubt on whether it is proper to associate the origin of German Pietism with the earlier work of Johann Arndt or William Perkins. For broad conceptions of German Pietism that include Arndt and Perkins, see Martin Brecht, "Pietismus," 607–8 and Stoeffler, *Rise of Evangelical Pietism*, 49–58. Were conventicle practices removed as one of the key features of Pietism, the broader views proposed by scholars like Brecht and Stoeffler would have greater traction. Nevertheless, the regional, historical, theological, and practical distinctives that corresponded to the rise of Pietism under Spener and its extension under Francke, not to mention the various communication networks associated with their activity, strengthen arguments for a narrow view of the term, like that found in the works of Wallmann.

28. Herzog, *European Pietism Reviewed*, 4.

29. Schicktanz notes Spener's sermon from 1669 in which he expresses a longing for Christians to meet together for spiritual edification. Schicketanz, *Der Pietismus von 1675 bis 1800*, 56. Interestingly, Shantz notes, "The greatest influence on Spener was Jean de Labadie's 1668 work on reform through the pastorate." Shantz, *Introduction to German Pietism*, 91. For information on Labadie, see Goeters, *Die Vorbereitung des Pietismus*, 139–284.

30. Wallmann, "Labadismus und Pietismus," 195.

31. Strom and Lehmann, "Early Modern Pietism," 403. Such a suspicion was not limited to the conservative theologians. A few centuries later, Weber would call them the "religious aristocracy of the elect." Weber, *Protestant Ethic*, 131.

32. Wallmann, *Der Pietismus*, 78–79.

33. Ibid., 68. The term "confessional Pietism" appears to have its origin in studies of North American Christianity. In an early example of this, Frantz claims that "Reformed and Lutheran confessionalists" were "committed to their particular traditions [i.e., the Heidelberg Catechism

and Augsburg Confession]." Frantz, "Awakening of Religion," 281–82. More recently, Holifield applies "confessional Pietism" to his discussion of American Pietists. Holifield, *Theology in America*, 400. "Confessional Pietism" better describes the dispositions and efforts of Pietists like Spener and Francke. It was not that these men were simply devoted to the edification of their parishioners, but they were devoted to the confessions that gave shape to their form of worship. Much as in Luther's early attitude toward the Church in Rome, these German Pietists were committed to traditional Lutheran categories and practices in reforming their churches. The term "confessional Pietist" best explains Francke's efforts to undermine the Berlin court's *Unionspolitik* and to maintain a military chaplaincy committed to Lutheran teachings. See Marschke, "Halle Pietism," 224; Marschke, "'Wir Hallenser,'" 3–85.

34. Strom and Lehmann, "Early Modern Pietism," 404. See also Dingel, *Geschichte der Reformation*, 57–58. Wallmann remarks, "Die Notwendigkeit des Bibellesens hat Spener verknüpft mit dem zweiten Vorschlag seiner 'Pia Desideria,' der Aufrichtung und Praktizierung des allgemeinen Priestertums der Gläubigen (in Speners Terminologie des 'geistlichen Priestertums')." Wallmann, "Was ist Pietismus?," 23.

35. Strom, "Common Priesthood," 48.

36. Strom, "Early Conventicles in Lübeck," 19. See also H. Lehmann, "Europäisches Christentum," 9–16.

37. Francke complains, "Also ist es noch mehr am Tage, daß, nach der Zeit, wie andern Ländern die alldortigen Kriegs Revolutien [!], so in Teutschland insonderheit der dreyßigjährige Krieg, in alle Stände, bevorab aber in dem Lehr-Stand, viele und große Unordnungen und ärgerliche Mißbräuche eingeführet, woran man den Schaden noch biß diese Stunde zu fühlen und zu beklagen hat." Francke, *Der Große Aufsatz*, 79.

38. H. Schneider, "Der evangelischen Kirchen," 59.

39. Strom and Lehmann, "Early Modern Pietism," 403. Kolb sets 1580–1750 as the period of Lutheran Orthodoxy. Kolb, "Lutheran Theology," 451.

40. Schicketanz, *Der Pietismus*, 15.

41. Wallmann, "Die Nadere Reformatie," 420.

42. Strom and Lehmann, "Early Modern Pietism," 403.

43. Schmidt, *Wiedergeburt und Neuer Mensch*, 171–75.

44. Campbell, *Religion of the Heart*, 7–8.

45. Sträter, *Meditation und Kirchenreform*, 149–57.

46. Strom and Lehmann, "Early Modern Pietism," 403.

47. To the degree that rebirth is linked to reform, it has been the case among scholars like Lehmann to connect Pietism to a broad "series" or "chain" of "revival" movements during the period. See H. Lehmann, "Pietism in the World,"17; H. Lehmann, "Four Competing Concepts," 318. There is merit to Lehmann's effort to situate Pietism in a broader discussion of transatlantic religious movements of the period, but placing it in the rubric of "revivals" is problematic. We need to take into account the implications of applying "revival" to groups of confessionally committed early modern Lutherans, who would not have understood Lehmann's modern implications of "revival" nor likely accepted such a label. The contrast of mentality between Lutheran Pietists and figures in the First Great Awakening, like Jonathan Edwards, can be seen in the latter's description of revival as periods of "sudden conversions . . . whenever there is an extraordinary pouring out of the Spirit of God." Murray, *Revival and Revivalism*, 20. Neither Spener nor Francke was acquainted first-hand with such revivals. Rather they sought reform and renewal within their congregations. The revival that Edwards experienced while pastoring was considerably different from Francke's pastoral experience. See Marsden, *Jonathan Edwards*, 194. Edwards's own claim that Francke's work in Halle was a "remarkable revival of power and practice of religion" may have been met with curious looks from Francke, who himself evidences a different understanding of "revival" when he called Luther a "revived" (*erwecket*) witness of God. Francke, "Von der äusseren Kirche," in *Buß-Predigten*, 1:215.

48. Hinrichs, *Preußentum und Pietismus*, 12–13.

49. Wallmann, *Philipp Jakob Spener*, 206. See also Schmidt, *Wiedergeburt und neuer Mensch*, 141n112; Strom, "Pietism and Revival," 173–218. The sermon, particularly in Lutheranism, should not be dismissed as one of a myriad of church activities. Rather it held the *locus primus* in early modern Protestant worship and in the Christian life, and what was spoken from the pulpit eventually resulted in a vast seventeenth-century print culture. Kolb notes, "The sermon was the most important medium for communicating the Reformation message in the sixteenth century, and it continued to be the chief way in which pastors conveyed the message of the church to the people and tried to shape their lives." Kolb, "Lutheran Theology," 442. Not surprisingly then, printed sermons have become invaluable texts for scholars of literature and sources for theologians and historians of religion. This is especially true for Pietism research. See Wallmann, "Prolegomena zur Erforschung der Predigt," 284–304.

50. Karant-Nunn, *Reformation of Feeling*, 6.

51. All texts unpreceded by an author's name are to be attributed to Francke. Italicized words and phrases in this work reflect the original texts from which they were taken.

52. Francke, "Kurtzer und einfältiger Entwurf," 92–93.

53. For a brief description of how Francke's sermons were handled, see Wallmann, "Prolegomena zur Erforschung der Predigt," 295.

54. Ward, "Evangelical Identity," 13.

55. Pelikan, *Spirit Versus Structure*, 114.

56. Kolb, "Martin Luther," 148.

57. This can be seen in Willimon's discussion of Pietism and the sacraments: "Pietism also stressed a personal, conscious, experiential conversion experience as the only normal method of entrance into the kingdom of God—a belief which sometimes led them into anti-intellectualism or condemnation of those who failed to duplicate Pietistic conversion patterns." Willimon, *Word, Water, Wine and Bread*, 96. Harold O. J. Brown remarks, "By making religion increasingly individualistic and by being relatively unconcerned about doctrine, the Pietists helped to make the old distinction between orthodoxy and heresy seem artificial and irrelevant to those who came after them." H. Brown, *Heresies*, 389.

CHAPTER I

1. Matthias, *Lebensläufe August Hermann Franckes*, 25–29, 101. Hermann von der Hardt is assumed to be Francke's *Tischwirth*; See Matthias, *Lebensläufe*, 137. For a discussion of the role of personal testimonies like Francke's *Lebenslauf*, see Strom, *German Pietism*, 15–27; Strom, "Pietist Experiences," 293–318; Vogt, "In Search of the Invisible Church," 293–311.

2. Hiestand and Wilson, *Pastor Theologian*, 39–41. They apply the label "Protestant clerical theologian" to pastor theologians and write, "What is more, they [pastor theologians] were catalysts for revival and yet critiqued revival; they preached learned sermons and yet counseled the downtrodden; they wrote philosophical essays and yet weighed in on civil matters; they offered theological rationale for global missions and yet founded colleges and tutored budding theologians" (12).

3. Vanhoozer and Strachan, *Pastor as Public Theologian*, 82. For the use of "pastor theologian" in an early modern context, see Ryken, "Thomas Boston as Pastor Theologian," 93–107.

4. Eire offers helpful insight into the ideological and theological conflicts encountered in early modern Christianity. Eire, *Reformations*, 158–84.

5. Brecht, "Luther's Reformation," 134–35.

6. Luther, "Babylonian Captivity of the Church," in *Luther's Works*, 36:11–126; Luther, "To the Christian Nobility," in ibid., 44:123–217; Luther, "Freedom of a Christian," in ibid., 31:333–77.

7. Kramer, *Beiträge*, 60; Kramer, *August Hermann Francke*, 1:18.

8. Beyreuther, *August Hermann Francke: Zeuge des lebendigen Gottes* 39; Kramer, *Beiträge*, 59; Kramer, *August Hermann Francke*, 1:15.

9. Although the academic title "magister" is often translated "master," there is a significant difference in training and education between the two, and therefore "magister" will be used throughout this text.

10. Beyreuther, *August Hermann Francke: Zeuge des lebendigen Gottes*, 42–44; Kramer, *Beiträge*, 60–61. For a recent study of Francke's conventicle work, see Kevorkian, *Baroque Piety*, 147–94.

11. Hopf, "Anton, Paul," 319–20.

12. Brecht, "August Hermann Francke," 442. Cf. See also Kramer, *August Hermann Francke*, 1:20.

13. Kramer, *August Hermann Francke*, 1:23–25; Francke, "August Hermann Franckes Lebenslauf," 20–23; Brecht, "August Hermann Francke," 442–43; Stahl, *August Hermann Francke*. See also Baird, "Miguel de Molinos," 1–20.

14. H. Brown, *Heresies*, 366.

15. Matthias, *Lebensläufe*, 19–21; McGinn, "Miguel de Molinos," 21–39.

16. Peschke, *Bekehrung und Reform*, 38–39. The three areas of Molinos's influence are derived from Peschke's analysis.

17. See Matthias, "Gewissheit und Bekehrung," 13. Matthias points out the tendency of earlier scholarship to put too much emphasis on Molinos's influence on Francke.

18. Wallmann, "Labadismus und Pietismus," 191.

19. For an interpretation of the educational themes in Francke's conversion narrative, see Yoder, "'Temples in the Hearts of Heathens,'" 181–86.

20. Matthias's work regarding the influence of Johannes Musaeus on Francke's theology sheds light on the tension in Francke's conversion account. Even though his experience reflects Musaeus's lectures on conversion, Francke still depended on what Matthias calls the, "supernatural intervention of God." Matthias, "Gewissheit und Bekehrung," 24.

21. Strom's recent research sheds much-needed light on previous assumptions about the influence of Francke's conversion story on later Pietist conversion narratives. See Strom, *German Pietism*, 15–27.

22. Beyreuther, *August Hermann Francke: Zeuge des lebendigen Gottes*, 65–66; Kramer, *August Hermann Francke*, 1:39.

23. Martin, "More Than Piety," 12.

24. Beyreuther, *August Hermann Francke: Zeuge des lebendigen Gottes*, 67. Kramer also identifies this important period of Francke's intellectual development and acknowledges the complexity of labeling this Hamburg period as the beginning of Francke's interest in the training and cultivation of children: Kramer, *August Hermann Francke*, 1:40–41.

25. Kramer, *August Hermann Francke*, 1:40.

26. Beyreuther, *August Hermann Francke: Zeuge des lebendigen Gottes*, 68.

27. Ibid.; Kramer, *August Hermann Francke*, 1:40. It is noteworthy that theologian Johann Müller in Hamburg had previously been contacted by Superintendent Menno Hanneken about the controversial conventicle activity in Lübeck. See Strom, "Early Conventicles in Lübeck," 27.

28. Albrecht-Birkner and Sträter, "Die radikale Phase," 59–65. Their argument that Francke held an extreme view of perfectionism rests heavily on a letter from Spener to Francke in which the Berlin pastor—in light of later testimonies of intense spiritual trials by early followers of Francke—asked Francke to earnestly think back to whether he had taught something contrary to traditional understandings of justification. For another treatment of the relationship between radical Pietism and Francke, see Mori, *Begeisterung und Ernüchterung*.

29. Cf. Wood, "Origin, Development, and Consistency," 33–55.

30. Albrecht-Birkner, "Franckes Krisen," 93.

31. Albrecht-Birkner and Sträter, "Die radikale Phase," 61–62.

32. Albrecht-Birkner and Sträter note this lack of evidence. Ibid., 59. Beyreuther, on the other hand, casts a very sympathetic light on Francke's early theology when he writes, "Er vermag sie [Lange and Zeller] auf gesunde und nüchterne biblische Bahnen zurückzulenken und aus aller religiösen Überstiegenheit zu lösen." Beyreuther, *August Hermann Francke: Zeuge des lebendigen Gottes*, 68. It might be helpful to recognize that at some level Francke's association to radicals sprang from a mutual interest in rebirth, biblicism, and the instruction of laity, and not primarily in the doctrine of perfectionism, while also recognizing that Francke probably held perfectionistic ideas, especially during the year directly after his conversion experience.

33. Francke, "Von der äusseren Kirche," in *Buß-Predigten*, 1:224, 226. This portion of Francke's sermons represents one of his largest defenses of his teaching on obedience to God's law.

34. H. Brown, *Heresies*, 368. Brown goes on to claim, "Protestantism began as a zeal for truth, and for decades seemed to leave good works, or at least the doctrine of good works, entirely to the papacy. It was Pietism that gave works back to Protestantism" (389).

35. *Gerichtliches Leipzig protocoll*, TGP II.1:68; Kramer, *Beiträge*, 114–15n2.

36. Kramer, *August Hermann Francke*, 1:42–45. It is clear Spener had a stake in weeding out radical enthusiasts from those associating themselves to Francke; and furthermore, the friendship between Spener and Francke resulted in a concerted effort to counter various attacks against Pietism. See Albrecht-Birkner and Sträter, "Die radikale Phase," 61–65.

37. Kramer, *August Hermann Francke*, 1:44.

38. Ibid., 1:47; Francke, "Schriftmäßige Lebensregeln," in *Werke*, 350–55.

39. Kramer, *August Hermann Francke*, 1:45.

40. *Gerichtliches Leipzig protocoll*, TGP II.1:95.

41. Ibid., 87, 110.

42. Francke's continued desire to see a reform of the clergy can be seen in his lectures on the vocation of pastoring, published posthumously by his son. See Francke, *Collegium Pastorale*.

43. Kramer, *August Hermann Francke*, 1:48; Wagenmann, "Carpzov, Johann Benedict II," 21; Beyreuther, *August Hermann Francke: Zeuge des lebendigen Gottes*, 77; Carpzov, "Vorrede," 14. Carpzov offers a description of his sermon in the "Vorrede." For a recent assessment of the conflict between Carpzov and Francke, see Schuster, "Johann Benedict Carpzov und August Hermann Francke," 183–202.

44. Brecht, "Philipp Jakob Spener," 336.

45. Ibid., 333. Interestingly, Carpzov encouraged similar gatherings in 1685. See Koch, "Johann Benedict Carpzov und Philipp Jakob Spener," 161–82.

46. Carpzov, "Vorrede," 15.

47. Ibid., 16.

48. Beyreuther, *August Hermann Francke: Zeuge des lebendigen Gottes*, 78; Kramer, *August Hermann Francke*, 1:48–52.; TGP II.1:5–7.

49. Kramer, *August Hermann Francke*, 1:46.

50. *Gerichtliches Leipzig protocoll*, TGP II.1:11.

51. Ibid., 12–13.

52. The complete set of questions asked can be found in *Gerichtliches Leipzig protocoll*, TGP II.1:14–18.

53. Later Francke indirectly addressed this accusation, stating, "daß die Kraft des Wortes und der Sacramente doch nicht von dem Ministerio dependire, und also (schliesset man gantz ungereimt daraus) sey es gleich viel, was für einen man zum Pfarrer bestelle, und läge nicht viel daran, der Candidat möge bekehret seyn oder nicht, es könne es einer so wol taufen als der andere, einer so wol das Abendmahl halten als der andere, und so fort," *Der unverantwortliche Mißbrauch des heiligen Abendmahls*, TGP II.9:535.

54. A. Deppermann, *Johann Jakob Schütz*, 81–125.

55. *Gerichtliches Leipzig protocoll*, TGP II.1:14, 18.

56. Carpzov, "Vorrede," 51–54, quote on 51.

57. Ibid., 57–58.

58. Ward, *Early Evangelicalism*, 41.
59. After being barred from holding seminars for the theology students, Francke began seminars in other fields of study (for example, philosophy). Carpzov believed all of these took on the character of those he taught for the theological faculty and that Francke acted deceptively by merely calling his conventicles by other names to avoid the ban. Carpzov, "Vorrede," 52.
60. Boehm, "Short Account," 19. For a study of Böhme's life, see Sames, *Anton Wilhelm Böhme*.
61. For an interesting depiction of the culture in late seventeenth-century Leipzig, which Francke critiqued, see Wiggin, "Geography of Fashionability," 315–29.
62. Francke uses this analogy in his "Apologia," *Gerichtliches Leipzig protocoll*, TGP II.1:107.
63. Yoder, "Pietas et Apologia," 121–43.
64. Francke, "Apologia," *Gerichtliches Leipzig protocoll*, TGP II.1:82–83, 92, 106–7.
65. Francke, "Apologia," ibid., 84, 90, 95.
66. Francke, "Apologia," ibid., 93. Francke echoes this in his later instruction to theology students, "Es lehret die Erfahrung daß wohl hundert andere Collegia ehe gehalten werden als ein einiges erbauliches Collegium über die Heil. Schrifft." Francke, "Timotheus zum Fürbilde," in *Werke*, 158.
67. Döring, "Seckendorf, Veit Ludwig von," 117–18.
68. Kramer, *August Hermann Francke*, 1:52–53; Beyreuther, *August Hermann Francke: Zeuge des lebendigen Gottes*, 86–87; Brecht, "August Hermann Francke," 448.
69. Kramer, *August Hermann Francke*, 1:52; Beyreuther, *August Hermann Francke: Zeuge des lebendigen Gottes*, 91.
70. Beyreuther, *August Hermann Francke: Zeuge des lebendigen Gottes*, 88; Biereye, "Francke und Erfurt" (1925): 42–43. For a summary of Pietism in Erfurt during this period, see Wallmann, "Erfurt und der Pietismus," 325–50.
71. Beyreuther, *August Hermann Francke: Zeuge des lebendigen Gottes*, 34.
72. Aland, "Breithaupt," 576.
73. Wallmann, "Erfurt und der Pietismus," 337, 341.
74. Biereye notes that people from several of the churches gathered to show their support for Francke shortly after his sermon on April 21. Biereye, "Francke und Erfurt" (1925): 48.
75. See Francke, "August Hermann Franckes Lebenslauf," 6.
76. Kramer, *August Hermann Francke*, 1:69. Concerning the dream, see Beyreuther, *August Hermann Francke: Zeuge des lebendigen Gottes*, 94–95.
77. Wallmann, "Erfurt und der Pietismus," 339.
78. Ibid.
79. Biereye, "Francke und Erfurt" (1925): 54–55.
80. Francke did preach while in Leipzig, but his ordination in Erfurt allowed him to do so in an official and consistent manner.
81. Biereye, "Francke und Erfurt" (1925): 55.
82. Wallmann, "Erfurt und der Pietismus," 340; Albrecht-Birkner, *Francke in Glaucha*, 30–35.
83. Freylinghausen's claim is found his Lebenslauf and quoted in Kramer, *August Hermann Francke*, 1:73.
84. Kramer, *August Hermann Francke*, 1:74.
85. Biereye, "Francke und Erfurt" (1925): 54–55.
86. Kramer, *Beiträge*, 118.
87. Biereye, "Francke und Erfurt" (1925): 55. Breithaupt served as an "Ephorus" for the gymnasium. For a clarification of the word, see Zedler, *Grosses vollständiges Universal Lexicon*, 1366.
88. Biereye, "Francke und Erfurt" (1925): 50.
89. Kramer, *August Hermann Francke*, 1:65. Wallmann notes that during Francke's tenure in Erfurt there were no Pietist sympathizers within the city leadership. Wallmann, "Erfurt und der Pietismus," 340–41.

90. Kramer, *Beiträge*, 111.

91. Ibid. For information on Casper Schwenckfeld and his relationship to Pietism, see Shantz, *Crautwald and Erasmus*.

92. Kramer, *Beiträge*, 112. For information on Georg Lehmann, see Albrecht-Birkner, *Pfarrerbuch der Kirchenprovinz Sachsen*, 5:309. It may also be of interest to note that Lehmann preached the burial sermon for Joachim Feller, the professor made famous for his poem on Pieitism; see G. Lehmann, *Der Gefallene aber nicht weggeworffene Berechte*.

93. Brecht, "Philipp Jakob Spener," 344–52.

94. Kramer, *Beiträge*, 114.

95. Ibid., 114–15.

96. Biereye, "Francke und Erfurt" (1926): 33–34. Though the commission's claims are in reference to a document written before January 1690, the allegations and characterizations continued after the commission was officially established.

97. Kramer, *August Hermann Francke*, 1:90–91.

98. Breithaupt also offered letters of defense.

99. Sagittarius, *Theologische Lehr-Sätze*; Sagittarius, *Untheologische*; Sagittarius, *Gründlicher Beweiß*.

100. Sagittarius, *Gründlicher Beweiß*, C3v. Cf. 1 John 2:20, 27. Mori notes, "The 1691 indictment of the Erfurt preachers charged that Pietists addressed each other within their group as 'brother' and 'sister,' regardless of age, class, and gender, and 'conducted conversations with each other in an unusual way,'" in "The Conventicle Piety of the Radicals," 208.

101. Ibid., D1r.

102. Ibid., F1v. Sagittarius was referencing Matthew 6:19–20.

103. Kramer, *Beiträge*, 134–38.

104. This "remotion-decree" can be found in ibid., 147.

105. Kramer, *August Hermann Francke*, 1:100–101.

106. Ibid., 1:102; Kramer, *Beiträge*, 163; Brecht, "August Hermann Francke," 453; Albrecht-Birkner, *Francke in Glaucha*, 18; Klaus Deppermann, *Der hallesche Pietismus*, 62–68.

107. Kramer writes, "Von größerer Wichtigkeit war, daß er [Francke] den in der Regierung maaßgebenden Persönlichkeiten genau bekannt geworden war, und deshalb in den Kämpfen, die er auch in der neuen Stellung erwarten mußte, um so sicherer auf Schutz rechnen konnte." Kramer, *August Hermann Francke*, 1:103.

108. Ibid., 1:102–3; Kramer, *Beiträge*, 158–59; Brecht, "August Hermann Francke," 453.

109. See Neuß, "Das Glauchaische Elend," 19–27.

110. See Howard, *Protestant Theology*, 87–104.

111. Marianne Taatz-Jacobi, "Ein prekäres Beschäftigungsverhältnis," 9.

112. Kramer, *Beiträge*, 159–60; Albrecht-Birkner and Sträter, "Die radikale Phase," 57–58.

113. Kramer, *Beiträge*, 166, 168.

114. For information on Olearius, see Albrecht-Birkner, *Francke in Glaucha*, 20n103.

115. Kramer, *August Hermann Francke*, 1:104–5.

116. Brecht, "Philipp Jakob Spener," 362; Brecht, "August Hermann Francke," 456. The content and quotes of *Imago Pietismi* were reconstructed using Veit Ludwig von Seckendorf's rebuttal, *Bericht und Erinnerung*.

117. For work on the problematic nature of labeling the university at Halle a "Pietist" university, see Sträter, "Aufklärung und Pietismus," 49–61.

118. Seckendorf, *Bericht und Erinnerung*, 32. At one point in Francke's courting of Anna Magdalena von Wurms, they reflected their Pietist commitments by addressing each other as "brother" and "sister." See Lißmann, "'der Herr wird seine Herrlichkeit an uns offenbahren,'" 147.

119. Seckendorf, *Bericht und Erinnerung*, 39.

120. Ibid., 37–38, 44.

121. Francke, recalling an early conversation with Olearius about the *Imago*, remarks, "Ich sagte, es wäre ein Pasquill, der Autor hätte seinen Namen, und dann auch den Beweiß dazu

setzen sollen. Denn man könte ja viel Beschuldigungen bringen, wenns nicht auff den Beweiß ankäme," Kramer, *Beiträge*, 167.

122. Ibid., 167.
123. Ibid., 167, 175.
124. Albrecht-Birkner, *Francke in Glaucha*, 21.
125. Neuß, "Das Glauchaische Elend," 23. Neuß numbers the death toll in Halle and the surrounding communities at 5,566.
126. Albrecht-Birkner, *Francke in Glaucha*, 12.
127. Kramer, *August Hermann Francke*, 1:106; Neuß, "Das Glauchaische Elend," 22.
128. Albrecht-Birkner, *Francke in Glaucha*, 17.
129. K. Deppermann, *Der hallesche Pietismus*, 72; Neuß, "Das Glauchaische Elend," 23; Brecht, "August Hermann Francke," 456.
130. Albrecht-Birkner, *Francke in Glaucha*, 21, 118.
131. Kramer, *Beiträge*, 191.
132. Albrecht-Birkner, *Francke in Glaucha*, 117.
133. Ibid., 118.
134. *Gerichtliches Leipziger Protocoll*, TGP II.1:98.
135. Kramer, *Beiträge*, 179.
136. Ibid., 191.
137. Albrecht-Birkner, *Francke in Glaucha*, 28. McIntosh notes that Spener eventually retracted his objections to Francke's confessional practices. McIntosh, "Pietists, Jurists, and the Early Enlightenment Critique," 640.
138. McIntosh, "Pietists, Jurists, and the Early Enlightenment Critique," 631–41.
139. For Francke's association to radical prophetesses called the "begeisterten Mägde," see Mori, *Begeisterung und Ernüchterung*, 185–250; Wustmann, *Die "begeisterten Mägde,"* 76–84, 111–72. See also Kramer, *August Hermann Francke*, 1:112ff; Brecht, "August Hermann Francke," 458.
140. Francke offered a response in 1692 to the publication of the letters: *Entdeckung der Bosheit*, TGP II.1:145–59.
141. Kramer, *August Hermann Francke*, 1:116.
142. Ibid., 1:117, 118.
143. Ibid., 1:105, 106.
144. Wallmann, *Der Pietismus*, 117.
145. Kramer, *Beiträge*, 187.

CHAPTER 2

1. Lindberg, *Third Reformation?*, 139. George writes, "The Luther corpus contains many diverse genres of writing. . . . In none of this, however, is there anything remotely resembling a systematic theology." George, *Theology of the Reformers*, 56.
2. "Studium Theologicum est cultura animi." Peschke, *Studien*, 2:130. Peschke clarifies the translation of "animis": "Man würde ihn mißverstehen, wenn man animus mit Geist, Bewußtsein oder Gedächtnis übersetzte. Im Herzen, nicht im Verstand, in der Erfahrung, nicht im Denken kommt es zur Begegnung zwischen Gott und dem Menschen" (130).
3. Peschke and Brecht offer multiple areas of Francke's theology, but the three presented in this work represent a reduction of his theology to areas that will be expanded upon throughout the rest of the chapters. See Peschke, "Die Theologie August Hermann Franckes," 42–61; Brecht, "August Hermann Francke," 462–73; Matthias, "August Hermann Francke," 100–114.
4. As a small child Francke undertook private tutoring in Gotha, and when he turned thirteen, he entered the *classem selectam* in Gotha's gymnasium. For the brief year he spent in the classroom, Francke was taught by Johann Heinrich Rumpel, who after receiving his magister in

1672 held lectures on ancient/biblical languages ("orientalische Sprachen") at the University of Leipzig. Rumpel served as a *subkonrektor* during Francke's time at the school, and later in life became the superintendent of Salzung. Though Francke's sister read to him from the Bible, Johann Arndt's *Wahren Christentum*, and other books when he was a child, it is reasonable to see his gymnasium experience as the beginning of his love for languages. For biographical information on Rumpel, see M. Schneider, "Die Lehrer des Gymnasium," 16; Brückner, *Neue Beiträge zur Geschichte deutschen Alterthums*, 579–81; Reichart, *Davidischer Hertzen*, 1–44 (Rumpel's "Lebenslauf" appears pp. 17–24).

5. Matthias, *Lebensläufe*, 31. Quoted from Yoder, "'Temples in the Hearts of Heathens,'" 183.

6. Howard, *Protestant Theology*, 94n187.

7. Wallmann, "Was ist Pietismus?," 25–27.

8. Matthias, "Die Grundlegung der pietistischen Hermeneutik," 190. He further explains, "Das Problem der Gewissheit stellte sich ihm hermeneutisch als Problem einer speziellen Form des Verstehens" (191).

9. For an examination of Lutheran conceptions of the nature of Scripture, see Preus, *Theology of Post-Reformation Lutheranism*, 1:254–376.

10. Francke, *Collegium Pastorale*, 338. This contrasts Dayton's inclusion of Francke with Pietists who "were more open to ideas of 'progressive' revelation that implied historical development and to the idea of 'degrees of inspiration.'" Dayton, "Pietist Theological Critique," 82.

11. Francke, *Catechismus-Predigten*, 53.

12. Francke, "Timotheus zum Fürbilde," in *Werke*, 166.

13. Ibid., 158.

14. Francke, "Einfältiger Unterricht," in *Werke*, 216–17.

15. Describing Francke's hermeneutic, Peschke writes, "Die Inspiration des Heiligen Geistes verfolgt nicht das Ziel, Glaubenslehren zu vermitteln, sondern lebendige Frömmigkeit zu schaffen." Peschke, "August Hermann Francke und die Bibel," 82.

16. Francke, "Einfältiger Unterricht," in *Werke*, 217.

17. Brecht, "August Hermann Francke," 467.

18. Ibid., 469; Peschke, *Studien*, 1:57–61. Reflecting on Francke's connection between understanding and godliness, Matthias writes, "Biblische Hermeneutik hat es also mit Veränderung des Willens zu tun." Matthias, "Die Grundlegung der pietistischen Hermeneutik," 191.

19. Wallmann, "Was ist Pietismus?," 22–24.

20. Francke, "Einfältiger Unterricht," in *Werke*, 216–17; Francke, "Timotheus zum Fürbilde," in *Werke*, 158, 164; Peschke, *Studien*, 1:101.

21. Francke, "Christus der Kern Heiliger Schrift," in *Werke*, 236, 243, 245–46.

22. See Francke's discussion "De Tentatione" in *Collegium Pastorale*, 208–10. See also Bayer, "Lutherischer Pietismus," 11–12.

23. Francke, "Einfältiger Unterricht," in *Werke*, 219. See also Peschke, "August Hermann Francke und die Bibel," 84.

24. Francke, "Christus der Kern Heiliger Schrift," in *Werke*, 246.

25. Peschke, "Francke und die Bibel," 60–69; Peschke, *Studien*, 2:15–31.

26. Matthias, "August Hermann Francke," 105.

27. Peschke, "Francke und die Bibel," 65, 66–67; Matthias, "August Hermann Francke," 105.

28. Francke, "Einleitung zur Lesung der H. Schrift," in *Werke*, 224.

29. Francke, "Christus der Kern Heiliger Schrift," in *Werke*, 243.

30. Ibid., 239–41.

31. Peschke, "Francke und die Bibel," 83, 86.

32. Francke, "Christus der Kern Heiliger Schrift," in *Werke*, 244.

33. Witt, *Bekehrung, Bildung, und Biographie*, 75.

34. Francke, "Von der äusseren Kirche," in Buß-Predigten, 1:226.
35. Lindberg, Third Reformation, 149.
36. Beyreuther, August Hermann Francke: Zeuge des lebendigen Gottes, 67.
37. Francke, "August Hermann Franckes Lebenslauf," 6.
38. Schrenk, Gottesreich und Bund, 308–9.
39. Weiske, Francke als Philologe, 7.
40. Yoder, "Hildebrand, Carl (Baron von Canstein)," 326; see also Schicketanz, Carl Hildebrand Freiherr von Canstein; Schicketanz, Der Briefwechsel Carl Hildebrand.
41. Francke, Wie der Gemeinde und Schulen zu helfen, 2198.
42. Peschke, "Die Theologie August Hermann Franckes," 42. For a thorough methodological discussion of "conversion," see Becker, Conversio im Wandel, 59–102.
43. Strom, German Pietism, 145. Strom contradicts those, like Witt, who claim that in Halle, Francke's conversion formed a standardized basis and expectation for individual conversion. See Witt, Bekehrung, Bildung, und Biographie, 77.
44. Matthias, "Bekehrung und Wiedergeburt," 58.
45. Francke had a multitude of reasons for the programs he established, but in his official writings and sermons he continued to return to his goal of glorifying God and converting the wayward Christian.
46. On 15 March 1692, Francke tells Spener, "Die copia von meinem lebenslauff ist nicht gar fertig worden." Spener, Briefwechsel mit August Hermann Francke, 96. Pollmann notes, "An essential function of the conversion narrative is to explain and justify change, and therefore to legitimize the conversion." Pollmann, "Different Road to God," 52.
47. Matthias, "Gewissheit und Bekehrung," 11–32. See also Matthias, "Pietism and Protestant Orthodoxy," 27–32; Matthias, "Franckes Erweckungserlebnis und sein Erzählung," 69–79.
48. Mader, "Conversion Concepts in Early Modern Germany," 34. In the context of missionary evangelization, Mahlmann-Bauer describes the difference of transitive and intransitive conversion as: "'Konversion' ist, neutral und formalllogisch betrachtet, eine mehrstellige Relation. . . . 'Sich bekehren' wird intransitiv gebraucht, analog zu 'sich (zu einer Glaubensgemeinschaft oder einem Glaubenssystem) bekennen.' Der aktive Gebrauch impliziert einen Willensakt und Selbstreflexion. Wird das Verb im Partizip Perfekt Passiv verwendet, signalisiert das grammatische Subjekt seine Passivität, wobei ein charismatischer Religionsstifter, ein Missionar oder ein spirituelles Erlebnis Auslöser und Ursache der Bekehrung sein können. Das transitive Verb 'bekehren' unterscheidet hingegen verschiedene Akteure." Mahlmann-Bauer, "Zeugnisse frühneuzeitlichen Konvertierten," 108.
49. Quoted from Mahlmann-Bauer, "Zeugnisse frühneuzeitlichen Konvertierten," 108n47.
50. Matthias, "Gewissheit und Bekehrung," 16.
51. Wagner, "Bekehrung II," 459–63.
52. Brecht, "August Hermann Francke," 463.
53. Francke, Catechismus-Predigten, 88; Die Gnade Gottes in Christo Jesu, 42.
54. Matthias, "Gewissheit und Bekehrung," 24.
55. See Strom, German Pietism, 42–45, 63–70.
56. Wagner, "Bekehrung II," 460. See also Wallmann, "Das Melanchthonbild im kirchlichen," 168–81.
57. Matthias, "Gewissheit und Bekehrung," 24–25.
58. Matthias, "Bekehrung und Wiedergeburt," 62–64. For a discussion on putting a date to Francke's conversion, see Matthias, Lebensläufe, 135–38.
59. Peschke, "Die theologischen Voraussetzungen," 106.
60. Whitmer, Halle Orphanage, 15. Kurt Aland would have his readers remember that Francke followed in the footsteps of Spener's "sozialen Leistung"; see Aland, "Der Pietismus und die soziale Frage," 105.
61. Breul, "Theological Tenets and Motives of Mission," 50; Francke, Der Große Aufsatz, 154.

62. Peschke, "Die theologischen Voraussetzungen," 103; Peschke, *Studien*, 2:206.
63. Francke, *Der Große Aufsatz*, 70, 72.
64. Peschke, "Die Reformideen des Comenius," 379.
65. *Gerichtliches Leipzig protocoll*, TGP II.1:92.
66. Peschke, "Die theologischen Voraussetzungen," 103.
67. Francke, *Der Große Aufsatz*, 58.
68. Lindberg, *Love*, 138.
69. Peschke, "Die theologischen Voraussetzungen," 98.
70. Francke, *Der Große Aufsatz*, 102.
71. Whitmer, *Halle Orphanage*, 21–28, 54–56. Writing to Prussian crown prince Friedrich II, Francke comments, "The frequent observation of [a model of the city Jerusalem] and the comparison of it with the Holy Scriptures . . . can yield all kinds of benefits, so that the [W]ord of God is approached with more and more desire" (75).
72. Ward, *Protestant Evangelical Awakening*, 61.
73. Lindberg, *Third Reformation?*, 142.
74. Pohl, "Hallesche Wahrheitszeugen," 44; Breul, "'Hoffnung besserer Zeiten,'" 270–74.
75. Yoder, "Pietas et Apologia," 135.

CHAPTER 3

1. *Von Sacramenten insgemein*, TGP II.10:602–13.
2. Beyreuther, *August Hermann Francke: Zeuge des lebendigen Gottes*, 79–86, 93–122; Brecht, "August Hermann Francke," 448–53.
3. A. Stein, *August Hermann Francke*, 141–53.
4. Francke followed an established tradition in the seventeenth century of preaching through the Small Catechism. Jetter, "Katechismuspredigt," 760–65.
5. *Von Sacramenten insgemein*, TGP II.10:603–4.
6. Epistemology (*Erkenntnistheorie*), as it relates to Francke's theology, is being applied here to the Christian study of the relationship between the knowledge of God (i.e., "truly" knowing God), faith, and the ability of individuals to rightly understand reality. Karl Barth exemplifies this use of the term "epistemology" when he writes, "Christian faith is concerned with an illumination of the reason," and, "as Christians we may live in the truth of Jesus Christ and therefore in the light of the knowledge of God and therefore with an illumined reason, we shall also become sure of the meaning of our own existence and of the ground and goal of all that happens." K. Barth, *Dogmatics in Outline*, 23, 26.
7. Spener, *Pia Desideria*, trans. Tappert, 109.
8. *Gerichtliches Leipziger Protocoll*, TGP II.1:31–33.
9. Francke would even turn attention away from questions on the dating of one's own conversion. As Beyreuther notes, "Eineinhalb Jahre vor seinem Tod hat Francke auf die Frage einiger Studenten, ob einer, der zu Gott bekehrt sein wolle, eine gewisse Zeit wissen müsse, eine öffentliche Antwort gegeben. Francke lenkt die Frage sofort auf ein anderes Gleis. Wir haben nicht zu fragen: Bist du bekehrt? Wann wurdest du bekehrt? Sondern: Was bedeutet dir Christus? Was hast du persönlich mit Gott erlebt? Ist dir in deinem täglich Leben Christus notwendig?" Beyreuther, *August Hermann Francke: Zeuge des lebendigen Gottes*, 57.
10. *Von Sacramenten insgemein*, TGP II.10:603–4.
11. Francke's concern for a daily experience of God is most clearly seen in his admonishment for believers to take up their cross daily and seek daily spiritual growth. He ended his sermon *Von den falschen Propheten* with a list of the attributes of a true teacher of the gospel, a list that should not be confined to the office of preacher. He writes: "7. Keines weges soll er Creutz-flüchtig seyn, sondern vielmehr eine rechte Liebe zum Creutz haben, es täglich auf sich nehmen,

... und es dem HErrn Jesu willig nachtragen.... 21. In der Tugend und allem guten soll er täglich wachsen und zunehmen, so, daß seine letzten Wercke die ersten übertreffen." TGP II.9:482.

12. The influence of Arndt also played a major role in Francke's understanding of humanity's spiritual condition. Arndt's articulation of fallen humanity focused on the division between fleshly and heavenly existence. See Peschke, *Bekehrung und Reform*, 17–30, 38–40.

13. Brecht, "August Hermann Francke," 442; Kramer, *August Hermann Francke*, 1:18–20.

14. The Latin version of the Augsburg Confession states concerning original sin, "They teach that since the fall of Adam all human beings who are propagated according to nature are born with sin, that is, without fear of God, without trust in God, and with concupiscence." *Book of Concord*, 37, 39. Francke exemplifies a similar stance in his critique of Lutheran Orthodox preachers: "Da zeiget unser Heyland an, so sey es immerdar ergangen, nemlich, daß diejenigen, so die Wahrheit denen Leuten vor die Stirn gesaget, die sich vor Menschen nicht gefürchtet, sondern ihnen ihr Verderben und Sünde vor Augen gestellet haben, keine Liebe bey der Welt gefunden." *Von den falschen Propheten*, TGP II.9:466.

15. Luther writes, "But original sin really means that human nature has completely fallen; that the intellect has become darkened, so that we no longer know God and his will and no longer perceive the works of God; furthermore, that the will is extraordinarily depraved, so that we do not trust the mercy of God and do not fear God but are unconcerned, disregard the Word and will of God, and follow the desire and the impulses of the flesh; likewise, that our conscience is no longer quiet but, when it thinks of God's judgment, despairs and adopts illicit defenses and remedies," in Luther, "Lectures on Genesis, Chapters 1–5," in *Luther's Works*, 1:114. For insight into Luther's conception, see Pelikan, *Christian Tradition*, 4:141–42.

16. *Die siebente Predigt über das siebente Gebot* (1726), TGP II.10:406. Francke applies the terms "thief" and "murderer" to fallen humanity in his rebuke of the false prophets in the church. He expressed his reason for using these descriptors for sinners: "Denn wenn einer zeitlich Gut stiehlet, so achtet man es nicht zu hart, daß man einen solchen einen Dieb nennet; so jemand den Leib tödtet, so achtet man es nicht so hart, daß man einen solchen einen Mörder nennet: Solten den die nicht Diebe und Mörder genennet werden, welche nicht zeitlich Gut, sondern die Seelen der Menschen stehlen, welche nicht den Leib tödten, sondern die Seele ermorden?" *Von den falschen Propheten*, TGP II.9:451. Francke was primarily concerned with the "inner" aspect of descriptors. Individuals were thieves and murderers in their hearts, regardless of whether they outwardly committed the acts.

17. *Die siebente Predigt über das siebente Gebot*, TGP II.10:406.

18. In this sermon on the seventh commandment Francke did not fail to remind his congregants of the connection between their unbelief and the sacraments: "Der gantze mensch taugt da nichts, auch in seinen besten Wercken. Wenn er am heiligsten thut, wenn er betet, wenn er GOTTes Wort betrachtet, wenn [407] er in die Kirche und zum heil. Abendmahl gehet, und in allem, was er etwa sonst vornimmt, ist er nur eir Greuel vor GOTT, so lange eder Unglaube in ihm die Oberhand hat, und so lange diese böse Wurtzel aller Sünden in ihm nicht angegriffen, und in wahrer Busse ertödtet wird," *Die siebente Predigt über das siebente Gebot*, TGP II.10:406–7.

19. Though not broadly used, Francke's application of "atheism" to the fall of man was not original. Hans-Martin Barth traces its use to the Reformed theologian Theodor Undereyck. See H-M. Barth, *Atheismus und Orthodoxie*, 133–34.

20. Walch, *Philosophisches Lexicon*, 211–13. Walch goes on to make several subdivisions of this category (for example, "einmal als Fehler" and "philosophische Atheisten"), providing a brief analysis of the major atheistic theories: Aristotle, the Stoics, Epicureans, and Spinoza. Concerning practical and theoretical (or "philosophical") atheism, see H-M. Barth, *Atheismus und Orthodoxie*, 77–86.

21. Walch, *Philosophisches Lexicon*, 215. Zedler, in his 1732 lexical work, provided a similar description of the two variations of atheism: "Ein Atheus Theoreticus soll derjenige seyn,

welcher den Satz zu behaupten suchet, daß kein Gott sey. Vor einen Practicum giebt man hingegen denselben aus, welcher durch sein ruchloses Leben dezeuget, daß er von keinem gottlichen Wesen wisse." Zedler, *Grosses Vollständiges Universal-Lexicon, Band 2,* 2017.

22. Francke evidences three degrees of idolatry: the building of physical, tangible gods; the turning of possessions, activities, or personal honor into gods; and most important, the misdirection of the heart that turns its love toward earthly things. See Yoder, "The Economics of the Unconverted: Idolatry, Greed, and Theft in August Hermann Francke's Theology of Wealth," in *Pietismus und Ökonomie (1650–1750),* ed. Alexander Schunka, Wolfgang Breul, and Benjamin Marschke (Göttingen: Vandenhoeck & Ruprecht, forthcoming).

23. Walch, *Philosophisches Lexicon,* 215.

24. See *Auffrichtige und gründliche Beantwortung* (1706), TGP II.1:260. Francke also makes reference to an "atheist" student he counseled in *Collegium Pastorale,* 184–85. More often than not, Francke connected atheism to "pharisaism," which gave it the form of practical atheism: *Das Geheimniß der Boßheit,* TGP II.9:503, 506.

25. Brecht, "August Hermann Francke," 443.

26. Francke, "August Hermann Franckes Lebenslauf," 26, 27.

27. Albrecht-Birkner notes Francke's atheism reflects his theological desire for certainty. See Albrecht-Birkner, "Franckes Krisen," 82.

28. Francke wrote to Spener on 15 March 1692, "Wegen des jüngst uns zugesandten brieffes eines mit dem Atheismo luctirenden Menschen sende hiebey den anfang und fortgang meiner bekehrung, . . . Es kommet doch alles darauff an, daß die vernunfft sich dem Glauben unterwerffe, und der Mensch nicht den ruhm behalte, daß er es selbst erlauffen habe, sondern daß sich Gott über alles erbarme." Spener, *Briefwechsel mit August Hermann Francke,* 91.

29. Ibid., 100. These letters can also be found in Kramer, *Beiträge,* 220–21. See also Weigelt, *Pietismus-Studien,* 1:62.

30. Obst, "Elemente atheistischer Anfechtung," 34.

31. It should also be noted that Spener's major work on atheism, *Geminum de Athei conversione Judicum, quod diverso tempore rogatus dedit* [. . .] (Halle, 1703), did not appear in print until more than ten years after Francke's *Lebenslauf* was written. See H-M. Barth, *Atheismus und Orthodoxie,* 46–50.

32. Albrecht-Birkner and Sträter, "Die radikale Phase," 60–61.

33. Obst, "Elemente atheistischer Anfechtung," 38.

34. Francke, "August Hermann Franckes Lebenslauf," 26. Obst argues the same in "Elemente atheistischer Anfechtung," 36.

35. Francke, "August Hermann Franckes Lebenslauf," 25–26.

36. Obst, "Elemente atheistischer Anfechtung," 37.

37. Francke, "Glauchisches Gedenck-Büchlein," in *Werke,* 75, 79–84.

38. Brecht notes, "Kortholt gehörte zu den von Arndt mitgeprägten frommen orthodoxen Theologen und stand Spener nahe." Brecht, "August Hermann Francke," 441; Beyreuther, *August Hermann Francke: Zeuge des lebendigen Gottes,* 34. See also Weigelt, *Pietismus-Studien,* 1:53; Halfmann, *Christian Kortholt,* 1–5, 9. Interestingly in 1680, a year before Francke's departure from the university, Kortholt published *De tribus impostoribus magnis liber,* which was a critique of the atheistic philosophies of Edward Herbert, Thomas Hobbes, and Baruch Spinoza; see Schmidt, "Atheismus," 355.

39. Beyreuther, *August Hermann Francke: Zeuge des lebendigen Gottes,* 34. See also Strom, *Orthodoxy and Reform,* 195–221; Schmidt, "Großgebauer, Theophil," 153.

40. In his *Lebensnachrichten,* Francke indirectly praises Großgebauer's *Wächterstimme* as a work that correctly instructs pastors how to lead their congregations; Kramer, *Beiträge,* 62. Francke's emphasis on the importance of Großgebauer's work is evidenced in the writing of his spokesperson in London, Anton Wilhelm Böhme. Böhme sent his work to Francke for his approval before having it published. In his *Short History of Pietism,* Böhme writes, "This Book [Großgebauer's *Wächterstimme*] was attended with a great Blessing, and like a rouzing Trumpet

awakened many Divines from their Sloth and Deadness into a greater Fervency and more real Sense of spiritual Matters. One of the most learned Men whose Eyes were first opened by the Means of this Book, was Philip James Spener." August Hermann Francke, *Pietas Hallensis*, 9. See Yoder, "Rendered 'Odious' as Pietists," 17–26. For the influence of the *Pietas Hallensis*, see Brunner, *Halle Pietists in England*, 85.

41. Quoted in H-M. Barth, *Atheismus und Orthodoxie*, 44.
42. *Die siebente Predigt über das siebente Gebot*, TGP II.10:410.
43. Matthias, "Ordo salutis," 318–19.
44. See K. Barth's discussion of the conscience in *Word of God*, 9–27. Barth, his critique of what he described as "Pietism" notwithstanding, evidences this existentialist view of the consciences while describing it as a great mediator between man and the righteousness of God.
45. See Sattler, *Nobler Than the Angels*, 58–63.
46. *Von den falschen Propheten*, TGP II.9:447.
47. Peschke, *Studien*, 1:40–41.
48. *Von den falschen Propheten*, TGP II.9:453–54. For an example of Luther's early construction of the conscience, see Baylor, *Action and Person*.
49. *Von Kampff eines bußfertigen Sünders*, TGP II.10:25.
50. *Von den falschen Propheten*, TGP II.9:458.
51. Ibid., 460. See Preus, *Theology of Post-Reformation Lutheranism*, 2:23.
52. *Die Freyheit vom Tode*, TGP II.10:113–14.
53. *Von Kampff eines bußfertigen Sünders*, TGP II.10:21, 29.
54. Francke saw the role of the preacher, especially as a *Bußprediger*, to aid in stirring the hearer's conscience. See *Von den falschen Propheten*, TGP II.9:458.
55. *Von Kampff eines bußfertigen Sünders*, TGP II.10:25–26.
56. *Von den falschen Propheten*, TGP II.9:471. In this particular passage Francke overlaps his call to test the teaching of spiritual leaders in the church with the call to self-examination. The Spirit not only grants the individual understanding to discern her faith but also to discern between true and false teaching. In fact, the ability to discern false teaching is contingent on the Spirit's revelation and the individual's self-examination. See *Von den falschen Propheten*, TGP II.9:472.
57. Peschke notes that in Spener's theological system the conscience could be "asleep," "sick," or "suppressed." Peschke, *Bekehrung und Reform*, 88. Concerning injuring the conscience, Francke remarks, "So lange der Mensch nicht den Zweck hat, daß er gern sein gantzes Wesen und Thun nach GOttes Wort einrichten will, sondern sich selber ein Christenthum nach seiner eigenen Phantasey schnützet, und sich nach den meisten und grössesten Haufen richtet, daß er es so, und nicht anders, als andere Menschen mache, damit er nicht für einen Sonderling gehalten werden möge, ob er gleich darunter sein Gewissen auf mancherley Weise verletzet." *Von den falschen Propheten*, TGP II.9:471.
58. Schmidt, *Der Pietismus*, 265.
59. "Aber ich frage euch auf euer Gewissen: Habt ihr das wol jemals erwogen in euren Hertzen?" *Vom Kampff eines bußfertigen Sünders*, TGP II.10:31.
60. Schmidt, *Der Pietismus*, 265.
61. Sträter, *Sonthom, Bayly, Dyke und Hall*, 4–18. Schicketanz goes a step too far in claiming that devotional literature, broadly speaking, was the most important means of communication in the period leading up to the rise of Pietism; see Schicketanz, *Der Pietismus*, 22. There has been a longstanding debate over the identity of "Emanuel Sonthom." Recent scholarship has followed Höltgen's conclusion that Emanuel Sonthom was Emanuel Thompson, son of Thomas Thompson of the town of Stade. See Höltgen, "Wer war Emanuel Sonthom?," 154–56.
62. Brecht, "August Hermann Francke," 443.
63. Schmidt, "Biblizismus und natürliche Theologie," 75. There are two copies of *Good Conscience* (1652 [sig. 54 C 9] and 1670 [42 E 3]) in the holdings of the AFStH.

64. Dyke, *Good Conscience*, 35–46. Dyke gives a short definition that expresses these two aforementioned functions of the conscience: "Conscience *is a power and faculty of the Soule taking knowledge, and bearing witness of all a mans thoughts, words and actions, and accordingly excusing or accusing, absolving or condemning, comforting or tormenting the same*" (9).

65. Schmidt, *Der Pietismus*, 265.

66. Marschke, "'Wir Halenser,'" 81–93; Marschke, "Halle Pietism," 217–28; Peschke, *Studien*, 1:68.

67. Krüger, "Gewissen III," 12:222–24.

68. Weyer, "Gewissen IV," 12:227.

69. See Calvin, *Institutes of the Christian Religion*, II.7.12–17.

70. Dyke, *Good Conscience*, 22.

71. Schmidt writes, "The idea of conscience leads to an emphasis on actual sin and so prepares German Pietism. Perkins insists on the connection between conscience and gospel as well as on that of conscience and law. But his disciples diminish the relation of conscience to the gospel, so that finally, there remains a simple moral conception of conscience, even with Bunyan." Schmidt, "Biblizismus und natürliche Theologie," 87. But J. I. Packer more appropriately describes the common Puritan conception of the conscience, saying, "The Puritans' teaching on the conscience reflected their view of *personal religion*. Godliness, to the Puritans, was essentially a matter of conscience, inasmuch as it consisted in a hearty, disciplined, 'considerate' (thoughtful) response to known evangelical truth, and centred upon the getting and keeping of a good conscience." Packer, *Quest for Godliness*, 114. See Bozeman, *Precisianist Strain*, 121–44; Beeke and Jones, *Puritan Theology*, 909–26.

72. Francke, "Schriftmäßige Lebensregeln," in *Werke*, 351.

73. H. Brown, *Heresies*, 362–63.

74. Peschke briefly addresses Francke's use of "Eid" in relation to the sacraments, but he does not examine the theological implications of Francke's use of oath, in Erhard Peschke, "Die Abendmahlsanschauung,"129–30. See Prodi, "Der Eid," 5–35. Scaer discusses Johann Gerhard's recognition of sacraments as oaths, or "promises" of commitment to God. Scaer, "Johann Gerhard's Doctrine of the Sacraments," 293, 299.

75. Jetter, "Katechismuspredigt," 760–65.

76. Spener, *Was die sacramenten seyen und was sie nutzen?*, 448–49.

77. Ibid., 449–53, 452.

78. Francke's practice of preaching from the Scripture text and not the catechism reflected his attempts to incorporate one of Spener's major reform ideas. Spener believed a thorough reform of the church could only come if believers came to know their identity as "spiritual priests" and learned directly from the Bible. See Spener, *Pia Desideria*, trans. Tappert, 94.

79. Francke believed the current state of preaching lacked the direction of God's Word: *Von den falschen Propheten*, TGP II.9:455. Francke exemplified his concern for personal use and application of the Bible in "Glauchisches Gedenck-Büchlein," in *Werke*, 77–78.

80. These presuppositions are found early in Francke's ministry. During the investigation in Leipzig, Francke was accused of open air preaching and holding academic meetings in German instead of Latin; see *Gerichtliches Leipziger Protocoll*, TGP II.1:36–48.

81. *Von Sacramenten insgemein*, TGP II.10:604–5.

82. Ibid., 605. For a consideration of Francke's use of "oath" in the context of military images, see Yoder, "'Königtum' und militärische Bilder," 160–66.

83. Scaer, "Johann Gerhard's Doctrine of the Sacraments," 299. Scaer notes, "Tertullian was the first to refer to the *sacramentum* of baptism and the Lord's Supper as promises or oaths made by believers."

84. Luther, "Sermons on St. John, Chapters 1–4," in *Luther's Works*, 22:286.

85. *Von Sacramenten insgemein*, TGP II.10:604–5.

86. Ibid., 605.

87. Stephens, *Zwingli*, 80; George, *Theology of the Reformers*, 148.

88. The exact date of Bayly's birth is not known, but Trueman notes that he received his BD from Oxford in 1611. Trueman, "Lewis Bayly," 52. For an early dating of his birth, see Wallmann, *Philipp Jakob Spener*, 17.

89. Trueman, "Lewis Bayly," 53.

90. Sträter, *Sonthom, Bayly, Dyke und Hall*, 8–9; Wallmann, *Philipp Jakob Spener*, 17. See also Wallmann, "Die Nadere Reformatie," 421; Wallmann, "Labadismus und Pietismus," 180; Kamp, "Die Einführung der christlichen Disziplinierung," 11–19.

91. Wallmann, *Philipp Jakob Spener*, 112, 160. Wallmann challenges Kantzenbach's earlier assumption that Spener's association to English edification literature arose from his time learning under Johann Conrad Dannhauer in Straßburg. See Kantzenbach, *Orthodoxie und Pietismus*, 135.

92. Peschke, *Bekehrung und Reform*, 65.

93. Bayly, *Practice of Piety*, 212, 220. In Bayly's *Praxis Pietatis* "oath" is translated as "Eid."

94. For an example of such associations, see Mori, *Begeisterung und Ernüchterung*, 219–21.

95. Whitmer, *Halle Orphanage*, 79.

96. Wallmann, *Philipp Jakob Spener*, 120n122; Brunner, *Halle Pietists in England*, 29; Yoder, "Rendered 'Odious' as Pietists," 23. Ward notes Spener also countered Quakers, who were "intruding upon Germany." Ward, *Early Evangelicalism*, 23.

97. *Gerichtliches Leipziger Protocoll*, TGP II.1:99. See Yoder, "Pietas et Apologia," 121–43.

98. Fox, *Small Treatise Concerning Swearing*, 6, 24. Fox writes, "And now you may see in the New Time, Christ saith, *But I say unto you, Swear not at all*: and what *you*, were these? was it not to the multitude of the Jews, and his Disciples that were Jews that he taught upon the Mountain: now by the Law of God and the Prophets, in their old time, they *were not to forswear themselves, but perform their oath to the Lord*: now in Christs *new time*, he saith, *Swear not at all*" (33).

99. Ingle, *First Among Friends*, 35–39.

100. *Von Sacramenten insgemein*, TGP II.10:605.

101. Ibid., 610.

CHAPTER 4

1. There is a long tradition in Christianity to see Christ's baptism as the "model" for the church's practice. See Wilken, *First Thousand Years*, 32.

2. *Book of Concord*, 359.

3. *Von der H. Taufe*, TGP II.9:587.

4. Peschke, *Bekehrung und Reform*, 13. Francke did not have a problem with the essential teachings of the church on baptism, but rather with what role they played, or in what way the Christian interacted with the sacrament. See *Aufrichtige und gründliche Beantwortung*, TGP II.1:249.

5. *Von der H. Taufe*, TGP II.9:589.

6. *Die Lehre unsers HErrn JEsu CHristi von der Wiedergeburt*, TGP II.9:174–75.

7. *Der Glaube an den HERRN JESUM*, TGP II.10:279.

8. The Large Catechism states, "Christians always have enough to do to believe firmly what baptism promises and brings—victory over death and the Devil, forgiveness of sin, God's grace, the entire Christ, and the Holy Spirit with his gifts. In short, the blessings of baptism are so boundless that if our timid nature considers them, it may well doubt whether they could all be true," *Book of Concord*, 461. Althaus remarks, "Baptism does not give a particular grace, not only a part of salvation, but simply the entire grace of God." Althaus, *Theology of Martin Luther*, 353.

9. *Von der H. Taufe*, TGP II.9:594.

10. *Book of Concord*, 42, 183–84, 359–62, 456–67.

11. *Von der H. Taufe*, TGP II.9:592.

12. For an example of Francke's biblical theology, see CHRISTUS *Der Kern*, TGP II.4:209–339.

13. *Von der H. Taufe*, TGP II.9:588. Francke's use of "all righteousness" in this context is to be understood as Jesus's active obedience to God in fulfilling the law.

14. Ibid. This follows the teaching of Luther. See "Predigt am Sonntag Lätare, nachmittags (10. März 1532)," in Luther, *Martin Luthers Werke*, 36:127.

15. CHRISTUS *Der Kern*, TGP II.4:284.

16. Francke, *Der Liebe Sohn des himmlischen* VATERS, 12, 21.

17. Ibid., 29–30.

18. Ibid., 14.

19. Ibid., 29–30.

20. Peschke, *Studien*, 1:59. Peschke actually structures much of his primary work on Francke's theology after the Pietist's propensity to see salvation as steps or phases. It is against this soteriological construction, structured by Francke and furthered by the Halle theologians working beside him, that Zinzendorf reacted in his own formulation of personal conversion. See Atwood, *Community of the Cross*, 48–49; Ward, *Early Evangelicalism*, 103–4.

21. *Book of Concord*, 360.

22. Spener, *Von der Bedeutung der Tauff*, 535.

23. The Luther translation of 1 Corinthians 15:45, "Wie es geschrieben steht: der erste Mensch, Adam, 'ward zu einer lebendigen Seele,' und der letzte Adam zum Geist, der da lebendig macht."

24. *Von der H. Taufe*, TGP II.9:592. Elsewhere, Francke writes, "Denn siehe da dein Erlöser ein solcher war wie Er dir jetzt beschrieben ist der Glantz der Herrlichkeit Gottes und das Ebenbild seines Wesens so wurde Er in einem Vieh-Stahl gebohren und in eine Vieh-Krippe geleget ob du bey solchem äusserlichen Zeichen seine weit tieffere Erniedrigung bedencken möchtest daß Er sich nicht geschämet in unsere so elende Hütte zu kommen und seine grosse Majestät damit zu bekleiden. O welch eine tieffe Erniedrigung!" CHRISTUS *Der Kern*, TGP II.4:299. "Doch, will Johannes sagen, habe er in solcher Niedrigkeit hier und dort einen Strahl seiner Herrlichkeit blicken lassen, daß er nemlich in solcher seiner Menschheit sey ein reiner Tempel GOttes, *in welchem die gantze Fülle der Gottheit wohnet leibhaftig*, Colossians II. V. 9, [Col. 2:9] *Offenbahrung der Herrlichkeit Christi*, TGP II.9:91.

25. *Von der H. Taufe*, TGP II.9:592–93. Luther writes, "It would be proper, according to the meaning of the word *Taufe*, that the infant, or whoever is to be baptized, should be put in and sunk completely into the water and then drawn out again," Luther, "Holy and Blessed Sacrament of Baptism," in *Luther's Works*, 35:29.

26. *Von der H. Taufe*, TGP II.9:593. Luther writes, "Therefore this whole life is nothing else than a spiritual baptism which does not cease till death, and he who is baptized is condemned to die. It is as if the priest, when he baptizes, were to say, 'Lo, you are sinful flesh. Therefore I drown you in God's name and in his name condemn you to death, so that with you all your sins may die and be destroyed.' ... Therefore the life of a Christian, from baptism to the grave, is nothing else than the beginning of a blessed death. For at the Last Day God will make him altogether new." Luther, "Holy and Blessed Sacrament of Baptism," in *Luther's Works*, 35:30–31. Summarizing the eschatological theme in Luther's theology of baptism, Althaus writes, "We might say that the death of our physical bodies fulfills the meaning included in baptism. The sooner we die, the sooner the meaning of baptism becomes an actuality. The more we must suffer, the more properly we conform to our baptism. Baptism and death, baptism and suffering, baptism and martyrdom, belong together." Althaus, *Theology of Martin Luther*, 355.

27. *Einleitung Zur Lesung Der Heiligen Schrifft Insonderheit Des Neuen Testaments*, TGP II.4:140. See also *Von der H. Taufe*, TGP II.9:592. The predominant tendency in Luther's work was to see the event in which the Spirit descends as a dove as a commissioning of Christ's preaching and teaching ministry. See Kingston-Siggins, *Martin Luther's Doctrine of Christ*, 52, 76.

28. *Von der H. Taufe*, TGP II.9:593.

29. Ibid., 592. This inclusion of the Ascension, which is found in Francke's theology of baptism, does not appear in Luther's exposition on the same passage nor in Spener's *Kurtze Catechismuspredigten*. See "Eyn sermon von der tauff Christi, aus dem dritten capittel Matthei, an dem tag der heyligen drey koning tag," in Luther, *Martin Luthers Werke*, 20:227–31.

30. Speaking on John 16:7, where Jesus discusses his earthly departure, Francke remarks, "Das ist der rechte Dienst, davon auch der Herr Christus bey dem Johanne XVI,7. redet, wenn er daselbst darauff seine Jünger weiset: er wolle ihnen den Tröster den Heiligen Geist senden, der solle sie in alle Warheit leiten." Francke, *Ein Unterricht vom Kirchengehen*, TGP II.9:625.

31. *Über das VII. Gebot*, TGP II.10:559.

32. *Einleitung Colosser*, TGP II.4:205.

33. *Besondere Einleitung Colosser*, TGP II.4:205.

34. See Francke, *Der Liebe Sohn des himmlischen* VATERS; *Von der H. Taufe*, TGP II.9:592. See also Breul, "Theological Tenets and Motives of Mission," 41–60. Beyreuther makes a strong argument to see Francke's interest in missions in light of his upbringing in Gotha under the rule of Ernst the Pious, but Francke's biblicism and universal reform plan must take precedence when determining the origins of his impulse for missions: Erich Beyreuther, *August Hermann Francke und die Anfänge der ökumenischen Bewegung*, 27–32. For a brief introduction to Duke Ernst I of Gotha, see Venables, "Pietist Fruits from Orthodox Seeds," 91–109. From Leipzig to Erfurt to Halle, Francke always rooted his work in biblical interpretation and education, and these themes came to dominate his work in other regions. Bible translations, exemplified in the East Indies mission, and religious instruction were part and parcel of the transregional work of the Stiftungen. Furthermore, this concern for missions in Francke's thought was mirrored in his baptismal theology. Just as Jesus's baptism stood as the basis for the practice of the church, so too, the declaration of God at Christ's baptism grounded the far-reaching work of Francke's Stiftungen.

35. For an example of Francke's transregional work, see Schunka, "Protestanten in Schlesien," 271–97.

36. Brecht, "August Hermann Francke," 515–17. See also Wilson, "Heinrich Wilhelm Ludolf," 83–108; Schunka, "Zwischen Kontingenz und Providenz," 82–114.

37. Brecht, "August Hermann Francke," 515, 519.

38. Müller-Bahlke, "The Mission in India and the Worldwide Communication Network of the Halle Orphan-House," 1:57–78.

39. For another example of Francke's habit of spiritualizing Scripture, see Yoder, "'Königthum' und militärische Bilder," 153–66.

40. Peschke, *Studien*, 2:17.

CHAPTER 5

1. Stürmer, Brief von Christian Stürmer an August Hermann Francke, 4.

2. Müller-Bahlke, "Mission in India," 60.

3. Wallmann, *Der Pietismus*, 116–17.

4. Francke, *Alles und in allen Christus*, 1177–78.

5. Knapp, "Des sel. Herrn Consistorialraths; D. Gotthilf August Franckens, Lebenslauf," 25.

6. Ibid., 8, 24–25. See also Sträter, "Gotthilf August Francke," 211–32.

7. For Francke's own recapitulation of these ideas, see *Von Sacramenten insgemein*, TGP II.10:612–13.

8. Luther writes, "Furwar wer Gottis gnaden nit alßo achtet, das sie yhn als eynen sunder dulden und selig machen werd, unnd alleyn seynem gericht entgegen geht, der wirt gottis nymmer frolich, mag yhn auch widder lieben noch loben. Aber ßo wyr hoeren, das er yn der tauff bund unß sunder auff nympt, schonet nnd macht unß reyn von tag zu tag, und das festicklich

glewben, muß das hertz frolich werden, gott lieben und loben," Luther, *Martin Luthers Werke*, 2:737.

9. Spinks, "Luther's Timely Theology of Unilateral Baptism," 32, 37.
10. Chemnitz, *Eine Tauffpredigt*, C2v.
11. Ibid., D1r–D1v.
12. Gerhard, *Außführliche Schrifftmässige Erkläring*, 83–84. Scaer writes, "The idea of reciprocity reappears in Gerhard's discussion of Old Testament sacrifices as sacraments. Before Abraham, sacrifices were the means through which God gave grace to his people. What the people sacrificed to God became the sacraments through which he gave good gifts to them. So 'in a certain way sacraments and sacrifices fit together.' Man's sacrifices to God became God's sacraments to man." Scaer, "Johann Gerhard's Doctrine of the Sacraments," 299–300.
13. Spener, *Kurtze Catechismuspredigten*, 495. In his catechism sermons, Spener mentions both the human and divine elements of the covenant in the context of the "gnaden-bund" (484). See Pless, "Liturgy and Pietism, Then and Now," 20.
14. See Kurten, *Umkehr zum lebendigen Gott*, 116.
15. Francke, *Die Gnade GOttes In Christo JESu*, 44.
16. Kurten, *Umkehr zum lebendigen Gott*, 104. Francke does mention remaining faithful to the *Gnaden-Bunde*, but he predominantly uses the term Taufbund with regard to the covenant. See Francke, *Die Gnade GOttes In Christo JESu*, 64.
17. *Von der H. Taufe*, TGP II.9:596.
18. Kurten, *Umkehr zum lebendigen Gott*, 106. Francke elsewhere states, "Es ist ja höchstnöthig, daß solches mit Fleiß erinnert werde, weil es heut zu Tage leider! so gar schlecht mit den meisten stehet, die sich Christen nennen, in der Kindheit getaufet sind und auf ihre Taufe sich verlassen, da sie doch längst den Bund entweder durch grobe äusserliche Schande und Laster, oder doch den fleischlichen Sinn, den sie in ihrem Leben haben über sich herrschen lassen, übertretten haben," *Von der H. Taufe*, TGP II.9:597. See also Francke, *Die nöthige Prüfung*, 12–13; Bartz, *Die Wirtschaftsethik August Hermann Franckes*, 16.
19. Francke, "August Hermann Franckes Lebenslauf," 6, 14–15.
20. *Von der H. Taufe*, TGP II.9:597.
21. *Von Sacramenten insgemein*, TGP II.10:606, 612.
22. Francke, *Die Gnade GOttes In Christo JESu*, 65.
23. Ibid., 74.
24. *Der Glaube an den HERRN JESUM*, TGP II.10:279. Concerning the relationship between the conscience and the Taufbund, Francke remarks, "Euch rede ich denn ietzo an, die ihr in eurem Tauf-Bund blieben sind, oder, so ihr denselben verlassen habt, welches euch euer eigen Gewissen sagen wird, dennoch wieder gefurcht habt, in göttlicher Ordnung in denselben aufs neue einzutreten; euch sage ich: Ihr seid selig." Francke, "Lehre von der heiligen Taufe," in *Catechismus-Predigten*, 535.
25. *Von der H. Taufe*, TGP II.9:597.
26. Francke, "Lehre von der heiligen Taufe," in *Catechismus-Predigten*, 545.
27. See Stolt, *Martin Luthers Rhetorik des Herzens*, 49–57.
28. Francke, "Lehre von der heiligen Taufe," in *Catechismus-Predigten*, 543.
29. Peschke, *Studien*, 1:135.
30. *Von Sacramenten insgemein*, TGP II.10:612.
31. Francke, *Very Necessary Examination of a man's self*, 1, 5. This sermon was translated into English and sent as part of his correspondence by Francke to England. The grammar reflects the original translation.
32. *Der Glaube an den HERRN JESUM*, TGP II.10:280.
33. Francke, "Die dritte Predigt," 90. See also Kurten, *Umkehr zum lebendigen Gott*, 120–21.
34. Francke, *Die Gnade GOttes In Christo JESu*, 71.
35. *Der Glaube an den HERRN JESUM*, TGP II.10:280.

36. *Lehre vor der Wiedergeburt*, TGP II.9:184.
37. Francke, *Die Gnade GOttes In Christo JESu*, 91–92.
38. Schmidt, *Wiedergeburt und neuer Mensch*, 197–98.
39. *Von der H. Taufe*, TGP II.9:596.
40. Ibid., 599–600.
41. Ibid., 597. Elsewhere Francke attached comfort to the Word of God, *Der Glaube an den* HERRN JESUM, TGP II.10:287. These two statements are not in contradiction. Baptism, as a sacrament founded on the gospel, was a visible sign of the comfort of salvation.
42. *Die Güter des Heyls So da ist in CHristo JESu*, TGP II.10:160.
43. *Der Glaube an den* HERRN JESUM, TGP II.10:293.
44. *Von der H. Taufe*, TGP II.9:599.
45. Arndt, *Wahren Christenthum*, 2.2.6.
46. Ibid., 1–14.
47. Ibid., 51–54.
48. See Peschke, "Die Bedeutung der Mystik," 304–6.
49. *Von der H. Taufe*, TGP II.9:594.
50. Der Glaube an den HERRN JESUM, TGP II.10:280, 299.
51. Francke, "Lehre von der heiligen Taufe," in *Catechismus-Predigten*, 529.
52. Ibid., 537.
53. *Lehre von der Wiedergeburt*, TGP II.9:184.
54. Schmidt, *Wiedergeburt und neuer Mensch*, 198; Schmidt, *Der Pietismus*, 14–33. See also Rüttgardt, "Zur Entstehung und Bedeutung," 1–96; Friedrich, "Philipp Jakob Spener," 40–42. For another perspective consider Shantz, "Origin of Pietist Notions," 29–41.
55. Wallmann, "Wiedergeburt und Erneuerung Spener," 7–31.
56. *Lehre von der Wiedergeburt*, TGP II.9:168.
57. Matthias, "August Hermann Francke," 107. Matthias is translating a German quote he makes in "Bekehrung und Wiedergeburt," 58. Though his English version states "other than Spener" his German states "anders als Spener," which in this instance is better translated "unlike Spener."
58. Lindberg concisely summarizes Lutheran views of rebirth: "Lutheran theology up to Pietism used the concept of rebirth in various senses. The Formula of Concord, without sanctioning a particular interpretation, has a threefold usage of the term rebirth: (1) the totality of justification (forgiveness of sins) and the consequent sanctification; (2) only justification (Melanchthon in the Augsburg Confession); and (3) only the sanctification and renewal which follows justification (Luther's major perspective)." Lindberg, *Third Reformation?*, 164.
59. *Lehre von der Wiedergeburt*, TGP II.9:183–84.
60. Ibid., 173.
61. Ibid., 178.
62. Ibid., 169–70.
63. See Matthias, "Bekehrung und Wiedergeburt," 49–82.
64. *Vom rechtschaffenen Wachsthums des Glaubens*, TGP II.9:9–10, 11, 12–13. Francke probably calls faith "living" due to its connection to rebirth; *Vom rechtschaffenen Wachsthums des Glaubens*, TGP II.9:17.
65. Lindberg, *Third Reformation?*, 173.
66. *Vom rechtschaffenen Wachsthums des Glaubens*, TGP II.9:16–17.
67. Ibid., 19–20. Stated in the positive, Francke remarks, "In dem *Innerlichen* erfähret er von GOtt, von Christo und sich selbst, was er durch die äusserliche Predigt gelehret ist. Hat er gelernet, wie GOTT allmächtig, allgegenwärtig, allwissend sey, so wird dieses alles durch eine Erfahrung in ihm versiegelt, daß er an GOttes *Allmacht, Allwissenheit, Gütigkeit, Treue* und *Wahrheit* gar keinen Zweifel haben kan" (20).
68. *Vom rechtschaffenen Wachsthums des Glaubens*, TGP II.9:12.

69. Francke, "Lehre von der heiligen Taufe," in *Catechismus-Predigten*, 540; *Lehre von der Wiedergeburt*, TGP II.9:187. For discussions of the doctrine of faith in the Reformation, see Althaus, *Theology of Martin Luther*, 43–71; Pitkin, *What Pure Eyes Could See*, 9–69.

70. *Vom rechtschaffenen Wachsthums des Glaubens*, TGP II.9:20.

71. Matthias, *Lebensläufe*, 28–32. Cf. Francke, "August Hermann Franckes Lebenslauf," 28–29. For a discussion of Francke's views of his "academic" faith, see Yoder, "'Temples in the Hearts of Heathens,'" 181–86.

72. *Lehre von der Wiedergeburt*, TGP II.9:201–2.

73. Ibid., 175.

74. Ibid., 192.

75. Francke, *Die Wenigkeit der rechten Kinder GOttes*, 339–40, 345–46, TGP II.9; Peschke, "Speners Wiedergeburtslehre," 214. The claim that change in the person was not merely an improvement of life is also apparent in Arndt's work.

76. Francke, *Collegium Pastorale*, 181. Just preceding this in the same Observation (32), Francke provides a thorough argument concerning the break with sinfulness that rebirth brings.

77. Lindberg, *Third Reformation?*, 149.

78. *Die höchnöthige Kirchen-Hauß- und Hertzens-Reformation*, TGP II.9:284.

79. Francke, "Lehre von der heiligen Taufe," in *Catechismus-Predigten*, 546.

80. *Lehre von der Wiedergeburt*, TGP II.9:179. See also Schäufele, "Taufe und Wiedergeburt," 219–28.

81. Matthias, "Bekehrung und Wiedergeburt," 58.

82. Wallmann, "Wiedergeburt und Erneuerung Spener," 28.

83. Strom, *German Pietism*, 14.

84. Spener, *Der hochwichtige Articul*, 110.

85. Großgebauer, *Treuer Unterricht Von der Widergeburt*, 57 [§ 10]. Großgebauer's instructions on rebirth can be found as the second part of his *Wächterstimme*. Regarding Großgebauer's use of Reformed thought, see Lieburg, "Dutch Factor in German Pietism," 57.

86. Großgebauer, *Wächterstimme*, 72 (ch. 5). Strom notes, "[Theophil] Großgebauer consciously broke with the Lutheran understanding of baptismal regeneration, which he argued led individuals to believe they were converted in baptism. He linked conversion to the idea of regeneration and the metaphors of rebirth." Strom, "Pietist Experiences," 296.

87. Großgebauer, *Treuer Unterricht von der Widergeburt*, 57 [5.10]. See also Matthias, "Bekehrung und Wiedergeburt," 52.

88. Peschke, *Studien*, 1:31.

89. *Lehre von der Wiedergeburt*, TGP II.9:199–200.

90. Peschke, "Speners Wiedergeburtslehre," 224.

91. *Lehre von der Wiedergeburt*, TGP II.9:193; *Von Sacramenten insgemein*, TGP II.10:612.

92. Nischan, "Exorcism Controversy and Baptism," 33–40, 46. As scholars continue to wrestle with identifying the father of Pietism, it is interesting that Arndt was quite opposed to the depreciation or removal of baptismal exorcism, and therefore stood at odds with later Pietists like Francke, whose concern for inner rebirth lessened the value of exorcism. See also Nagel, "Exorzismus III," 753–56; Kelter, "Der Taufexorzismus," 137–48.

93. Peschke, *Bekehrung und Reform*, 39; Matthias, "Bekehrung und Wiedergeburt," 62–64.

94. Spener, *Briefwechsel mit August Hermann Francke*, 614–15.

95. Ibid., 617. The edict, *Die Drey Confessiones*, is found 617n11.

96. Nagel, "Exorzismus III," 755.

97. Jacobi, "Das Bild vom Kind," 33. This would appear to add nuance to the claim that churchly Pietism, like radical Pietism, viewed alchemy and "natural magic" positively. See Shantz, *Introduction to German Pietism*, 19.

98. Beyreuther, *Geschichte der Pietismus*, 46–47.

99. Ward, *Early Evangelicalism*, 44.

100. Ward attributes Francke's belief to the influence of Miguel de Molinos in *Early Evangelicalism*, 41–44.

CHAPTER 6

1. While the Reformed churches did institute a common confession of sin in the service to replace the practice of private confession, they did not do away with the examination process that preceded participation in the Lord's Supper. The clearest evidence of this was the tokens (*méreau*) given to congregants before the celebration of the Supper: Gresch, *Die Hugenotten*, 204–5. See also Bezzel, "Beichte III," 424–25; Mentzer, *Sin and the Calvinists*. I will be using "the confessional" in a broader sense, signifying the place (whether in the choir section of the sanctuary or in an actual confessional) where confession occurred.

2. *Der unverantwortliche Mißbrauch des heiligen Abendmahls*, TGP II.9:526–27.

3. Gawthrop is mistaken when he writes, "Francke personally disliked the institution of the confessional." Gawthrop, *Pietism*, 129. Gawthrop is likely reading Francke's distaste for the confessional offering into his broader views of confession.

4. See Aland, "Die Privatbeichte im Luthertum," 452–519; Rittgers, "Embracing the 'True Relic' of Christ," 377–93; Althaus, *Theology of Martin Luther*, 315–18.

5. Luther, "Babylonian Captivity of the Church," in *Luther's Works*, 36:81–82:

For this sacrament, like the other two, consists in the word of divine promise and our faith, and they have undermined both of them. For they have adapted to their own tyranny the word of promise which Christ speaks in Matthew 16[:19] and 18[:18].... By these words the faith of penitents is aroused for obtaining the forgiveness of sins. But in all their writing, teaching, and preaching, their sole concern has been, not to teach what is promised to Christians in these words, or what they ought to believe, and what great consolation they might find in them, but only through force and violence to extend their own tyranny far, wide, and deep.

6. Aland, "Die Privatbeichte im Luthertum," 457. Aland describes Luther's position up to 1521 as "conservative."

7. Karant-Nunn, *Reformation of Ritual*, 95. Aland remarks, "Diese Beichte besteht aus zwei Stücken: der Klage unserer Sünden und dem Begehren nach Trost sowie der Absolution, die zwar vermittels eines Menschen, aber durch Gott geschieht." Aland, "Die Privatbeichte im Luthertum," 470.

8. Karant-Nunn, *Reformation of Ritual*, 95–96. It was Luther's opinion that early Christians rarely, if at all, practiced ritual confession: Aland, "Die Privatbeichte im Luthertum," 460.

9. Rublack, "Lutherische Beichte und Sozialdisziplinierung," 131.

10. Karant-Nunn, *Reformation of Ritual*, 99.

11. Aland offers the example of Windener's 1558 *Eine gemeine Form zu Beichten*, in "Die Privatbeichte im Luthertum," 481.

12. Rublack, "Lutherische Beichte," 131–32, 139–40.

13. Aland, "Die Privatbeichte im Luthertum," 466. For evidence that Francke held confession four times a year in Glaucha, see *Die Lehre von Erleuchterung*, TGP II.9:394; Francke, *Vom rechten Verhalten*, 457; *Der unverantwortliche Mißbrauch des heiligen Abendmahls*, TGP II.9:525; *Von der äusseren Kirchen*, TGP II.10:96; Francke, *Am grünen Donnerstage*, 556–57.

14. Rublack, "Lutherische Beichte," 134.

15. Aland, "Die Privatbeichte im Luthertum," 480.

16. Ibid., 491–93; Berthold, "Kritik," 11–48; Brecht, "Die deutschen Spiritualisten," 223.

17. It should be noted that some of these issues with confessional practice could be understood either as remnants of Catholic sacramentalism or as a deficiency in Lutheran practice and educating. See Aland, "Die Privatbeichte im Luthertum," 493.

18. Obst, *Der Berliner Beichtstuhlstreit*, 5.

19. Francke mentioned Großgebauer in his discussions on confession, including both of his major works on the topic. See Francke, "Kurtzer und einfältiger Entwurf," 99; *Der unverantwortliche Mißbrauch des heiligen Abendmahls*, TGP II.10:519–20. Compare this to Großgebauer, *Wächterstimme*, 75–78. See also *Die Erlassung und Behaltung der Sünde*, TGP II.9:150.

20. Großgebauer, *Wächterstimme*, 180, 183.

21. Francke addressed the keys in his sermon *Die Erlassung und Behaltung der Sünde*, TGP II.9.

22. Großgebauer, *Wächterstimme*, 196.

23. Wallmann, *Philipp Jakob Spener*, 220. For Spener's interaction with Großgebauer's *Wächterstimme*, see Sträter, *Meditation und Kirchenreform*, 150–51; Yoder, "Rendered 'Odious' as Pietists," 21–22.

24. Wallmann, *Philipp Jakob Spener*, 132, 220–21. See McIntosh, "Pietists, Jurists, and the Early Enlightenment Critique," 631–37.

25. Großgebauer writes, "Wie könten wir deß Sonnabends innerhalb drey oder vier Stunden bey achtzig und mehr Personen verhören?" Großgebauer, *Wächterstimme*, 187. See also Spener, *Pia Desideria*, 67.

26. Drese, "Der Berliner Beichtstuhlstreit," 64, 68, 70.

27. Obst, *Der Berliner Beichtstuhlstreit*, 11–12.

28. Carpzov writes, "Zum achten thun sie sich bereits mit Schrifften herfür darinnen sie ihr Wesen ausbreiten und defendiren wie alle zu thun pflegen welche Neuerungen und Spaltungen anrichten. Wir haben zwar M. Schadens beyde tractat, so er heraus gegeben einen unter dem Titel was fehlet mir noch? den andern: Was muß ich thun? nach dem ich der Decanus, sie censiret und alles Verdächtige geändert zu drucken vergönnet anzuzeugen daß wir dergleichen libellos asceticos, die ihren guten Nutzen haben allerdings billigen wenns nicht mit derer Edirung zur Behauptung des Pietismi angesehen." Carpzov, *Doppelte Verthäidigung*, 57. The report on Schade is found in *Gerichtliches Leipziger Protocoll*, TGP II.1.

29. Obst, *Der Berliner Beichtstuhlstreit*, 13.

30. Ibid., 22, 29–32; Drese, "Der Berliner Beichtstuhlstreit," 94.

31. Schade used corporal punishment to discipline two girls who avoided his catechism training and who were in the habit of lying; see Obst, *Der Berliner Beichtstuhlstreit*, 47–48. See also the letter from Spener to Francke, 16 February 1697, in Spener, *Briefwechsel mit August Hermann Francke*, 489–90. For a description of the liberties being taken by Schade's followers, see Spener's letter to Francke on 31 December 1697 in *Briefwechsel mit August Hermann Francke*, 523. On Spener's request, see Obst, *Der Berliner Beichtstuhlstreit*, 64–65.

32. Drese, "Der Berliner Beichtstuhlstreit," 97.

33. Obst, *Der Berliner Beichtstuhlstreit*, 115–16.

34. Ibid., 62. Schade served as godparent to Gotthilf August Francke; see Spener, *Briefwechsel mit August Hermann Francke*, 447.

35. Francke wrote to Spener on 30 March 1697, "Des bin ich gewiß, daß sein [Schades] Werck nicht den Krebsgang gehen wird." Spener, *Briefwechsel mit August Hermann Francke*, 507.

36. McIntosh, "Pietists, Jurists, and the Early Enlightenment Critique," 640.

37. Albrecht-Birkner, *Francke in Glaucha*, 39.

38. Ibid., 38–39.

39. Francke, "Kurtzer und einfältiger Entwurf," 93.

40. Francke, *Vom rechten Verhalten*, 425–26.

41. Francke, "Kurtzer und einfältiger Entwurf," 93, 97.

42. Francke, *Vom rechten Verhalten*, 403.

43. Francke, "Kurtzer und einfältiger Entwurf," 93–94; Francke, *Vom rechten Verhalten*, 425.

44. *Von Kampff eines bußfertigen Sünders*, TGP II.10:22.

45. Francke, *Vom rechten Verhalten*, 422.

46. Francke, *Von den Thränenden Augen*, 444–45.
47. Ibid., 394–95.
48. Francke, "Kurtzer und einfältiger Entwurf," 94.
49. Francke, *Am grünen Donnerstage*, 560.
50. Francke emphasized the importance of self-examination and pastoral examination before participation in the Eucharist when he states with regard to 1 Corinthians 11:28–29, "Welches uns denn zeiget, wie der Apostel diese Prüfung als eine höchstnöthige Sache angesehen habe." Francke, "Die sechzehente Predigt," 583.
51. Terence McIntosh argues Duke Ernst's reforms directly influenced Francke's later confessional practices in "Das 'Werck der Christlichen Disciplin,'" 68.
52. "Es ist auch dafür der Gnade GOttes demüthig zu dancken, daß von geraumen Jahren her die Christlöbliche Verordnung gemacht ist, daß die Confitenten, ehe sie zur Beicht und Abendmahl gehen wollen, sich erst alle angeben müssen, wie dann GOtt Lob! nunmehro diese gute Ordnung in dem gantzen Hertzogthum Magdeburg, vermöge des ergangenen Churfl. Gnädigsten Edicti, wird eingeführet werden. Davon wir denn diesen Vortheil haben, daß man diejenige, welche man ihres Zustandes halben besonders zu erinnern nöthig findet, zu sich bescheidet, und mit ihnen nach erheischender Nothdurft redet und handelt." *Der unverantwortliche Mißbrauch des heiligen Abendmahls*, TGP II.9:542. See McIntosh, "August Hermann Franckes Behandlung," 132–33.
53. Francke complained to Spener on 5 November 1692 that his time was consumed by, and that he was exhausted from, hearing such a large number of confessions. See Spener, *Briefwechsel mit August Hermann Francke*, 217.
54. *Die Erlassung und Behaltung der Sünde*, TGP II.9:151. The "elevation" which I am claiming here should be seen in the fact that Francke in this statement was assuming that the meeting he conducted would bear the markings of an actual confession where the congregant recognized and dealt with their sin (see Francke, "Kurtzer und einfältiger Entwurf," 95), leaving the Saturday confession to become merely the declaring of something already agreed upon: the penitent's sin and God's forgiveness.
55. Francke, "Kurtzer und einfältiger Entwurf," 96.
56. Francke, *Das geschäffte des Hertzen*, 673.
57. Francke, "Kurtzer und einfältiger Entwurf," 105.
58. McIntosh, "August Hermann Franckes Behandlung," 132–33.
59. *Der unverantwortliche Mißbrauch des heiligen Abendmahls*, TGP II.9:541. See Peschke, "Die Abendmahlsanschauung," 135.
60. Albrecht-Birkner, *Francke in Glaucha*, 28–29, 39–40. Spener did not fully approve of Francke's practice of banning from the altar. He worried Francke had been going too far in determining the spiritual state of his congregants.
61. Spener, *Briefwechsel mit August Hermann Francke*, 397, 462, 478–83. See Albrecht-Birkner, *Francke in Glaucha*, 38–39. Several years later, Francke complained to his congregants: "Ja es haben sich bishero noch immer hier und da Lehrer gefunden, die diejenigen zur Beichte angenommen, welche wir abgewiesen haben, dadurch sich denn die Leute in der Boßheit gestärcket, und gemeynet, sie hättens doch nun auf diese Weise erwischet, sind daher in den Läster-Geist hinein gerathen, und in des Satans Stricke kommen," *Der unverantwortliche Mißbrauch des heiligen Abendmahls*, TGP II.9:546.
62. *Der unverantwortliche Mißbrauch des heiligen Abendmahls*, TGP II.9:530, 538.
63. Francke, "Kurtzer und einfältiger Entwurf," 99. See also *Der unverantwortliche Mißbrauch des heiligen Abendmahls*, TGP II.9:522.
64. The following description of Francke's critique of the confessional practices of pastors is found in Francke, "Kurtzer und einfältiger Entwurf," 99–103. For a further perspective on Francke's teaching on the confessional offering, see Yoder, "The Economics of the Unconverted: Idolatry, Greed, and Theft in August Hermann Francke's Theology of Wealth," in *Pietismus*

und Ökonomie (1650–1750), ed. Alexander Schunka, Wolfgang Breul, and Benjamin Marschke (Göttingen: Vandenhoeck & Ruprecht, forthcoming).
65. *Der unverantwortliche Mißbrauch des heiligen Abendmahls*, TGP II.9:522.
66. Francke, "Kurtzer und einfältiger Entwurf," 102.
67. *Der unverantwortliche Mißbrauch des heiligen Abendmahls*, TGP II.9:550.
68. Ibid., 551. Francke warns of this divine punishment in *Collegium Pastorale*, 241.
69. Francke, *Collegium Pastorale*, 247.
70. Kramer, *Beiträge*, 175.
71. Spener, *Briefwechsel mit August Hermann Francke*, 435. See also *Der unverantwortliche Mißbrauch des heiligen Abendmahls*, TGP II.9:539–40.
72. Francke, *Ein Unterricht vom Kirchengehen*, 215–16.
73. Aland, "August Hermann Francke und die Privatbeichte," 273.

CHAPTER 7

1. Peschke mentions these six sermons in "Die Abendmahlsanschauung," 129. A good measure of Francke's continued vigilance is seen when in 1697 he remarks, "Denn das heilige Abendmahl wird von mir hochgeehrt, und würde es nicht von mir hochgeehrt, sondern hielt' ich es für eine geringe Sache, so würde ich solchen Ernst dabei nicht beweisen." Francke, *Am grünen Donnerstage*, 545. Elsewhere Francke made the hyperbolic claim that all of Christianity rests on the confessional and Eucharist: *Der unverantwortliche Mißbrauch des heiligen Abendmahls*, TGP II.9:517.
2. Francke, *Die nöthige Prüfung*, 10–14.
3. Francke claimed the *Endzweck* of the Eucharist should be the *Gedächtnis Christi*, which Peschke assumed to be the central theme of his Eucharist theology. Yet Francke also calls the theme of worthiness the *Hauptpunct*. In light of Francke's numerous references to the commemoration of Christ in the Supper and to the necessary worthiness of communicants it should be assumed that one idea served the other. The *Gedächtnis* is often associated with spiritual empowerment to live a life Francke considered worthy. See Peschke, "Die Abendmahlsanschauung," 131; Peschke, *Studien*, 1:111; Peschke, *Die frühen Katechismuspredigten Franckes*, 168–69; Francke, *Am grünen Donnerstage*, 556, Francke, "Die sechzehnte Predigt," 576.
4. *Der unverantwortliche Mißbrauch des heiligen Abendmahls*, TGP II.9:534.
5. Peschke, *Bekehrung und Reform*, 38.
6. Spankeren, "Das Ende des Pietismus in Halle," 607–10.
7. See Peschke, *Studien*, 1:111.
8. Francke paraphrases the text "Welcher unwürdig von diesem Brot esse und von dem Kelch des HERRN trinke, schuldig an dem Leibe und Blut des HErrn." Francke, *Der unverantwortliche Mißbrauch des heiligen Abendmahls*, TGP II.9:528.
9. Francke, *Am grünen Donnerstage*, 528–29, 553. Francke's recognition of Paul's connection between "Würdigkeit" and self-examination should not be seen as embodying Francke's own conception.
10. *Der unverantwortliche Mißbrauch des heiligen Abendmahls*, TGP II.9:529, 543.
11. *Book of Concord*, 473, 596. In the Lutheran confessions, the worthy manner of reception rested solely on approaching the altar with repentance and faith.
12. Francke, *Collegium Pastorale*, 432–34. Francke withholds Detharding's name and offers the abbreviated title *Kennzeichen der Wiedergebohrnen* for the twenty-four page tract. This is likely because Francke had some sense that the tract might lead opponents back to its author, Christian Hoburg. In a letter from Georg Friedrich Stieber to Francke (AFStH C817, Nr. 7), Stieber claims Detharding put to print what had been previously passed around in handwritten form, and apparently its printing caused a small stir. The tract is a replication of a portion of

Hoburg's *Der Sicherste Weg Zum Reich Gottes*, 93–111. The author is especially grateful to Jonathan Strom for insight and sources connecting the Hoburg and Detharding texts. Albrecht-Birkner has also noted Francke's propensity to exclude controversial author names and to abbreviate titles. See Albrecht-Birkner, "Franckes Krisen," 92. For information on Stieber, see Strom, *German Pietism*, 90–94. Interestingly, the Detharding booklet receives a positive review in Löscher's *Unschuldige Nachrichten*, 822–23. See Spehr, "Gelehrte Buchkritik," 276–79.

13. Francke, *Die nöthige Prüfung*, 124–26, 569–70. In this passage Francke applied both terms to circumcision and used the phrase *Gedächtnis-Zeichen* to refer to the aforementioned litany of God's signs of faithfulness. Peschke only notes Francke's connection of *Gedächtnis* to God's Old Testament expressions of faithfulness toward his chosen people and does not explore the role of signs. Peschke, "Die Abendmahlsanschauung," 132. Curiously, Lieburg notes, "In April 1702, [Theodorus à] Brakel wrote a letter to Francke in Halle. He praised Francke's efforts in the educational sphere and his conjoining of learning and piety, and noted his Calvinist leanings concerning the Lord's Supper." Lieburg "Dutch Factor in German Pietism," 73. It is worthy of note that Francke also referred to the Eucharist as *Gedächtnis* when he critiqued his congregation's neglect of Scripture. Since they had not made proper use of God's Word, the Lord provided a *Gedächtnis* in the Supper. Francke, *Ein Unterricht vom Kirchengehen*, 223–25.

14. Francke, "Die sechzehente Predigt," 568–70.

15. Ibid., 582.

16. *Der unverantwortliche Mißbrauch des heiligen Abendmahls*, TGP II.9:541.

17. Francke, *Die nöthige Prüfung*, 59. Francke acknowledged that since pastors relied upon outward signs of true repentance, parishioners could manipulate the situation. Francke, *Von den Thränenden Augen*, 448.

18. Francke, "Die sechzehente Predigt," 596. Francke complained that pastors granted their congregants absolution without allowing them to deal with the terms of their sins. See Francke, "Kurtzer und einfältiger Entwurf," 101.

19. Francke, *Am grünen Donnerstage*, 552.

20. *Die Wenigkeit der rechten Kinder GOttes*, TGP II.9:332; *Von dem Dienst untreuer Lehrer*, TGP II.9:414; *Das Geheimniß der Bosheit*, TGP II.9:503; *Vom Helden-Muth der Gläubigen*, TGP II.10:315.

21. Francke, *Am grünen Donnerstage*, 556–57; *Die gründliche und hertzliche Frömmigkeit*, TGP II.10:135–36; *Vom Helden-Muth der Gläubigen*, 318.

22. He called hypocrisy in relation to the Supper "all too common these days": *Das richtige Urtheil GOttes*, TGP II.10:480.

23. *Vom Helden-Muth der Gläubigen*, TGP II.10:312, 328; *Entdeckung der Boßheit*, TGP II.1:153; *Auffrichtige und gründliche Beantwortung*, TGP II.1:245; *Die höchstnöthige Kirchen- Hauß- und Hertzens-Reformations*, TGP II.9:293–94. Francke often used the terms *Schein*, *Mund*, and *Heuchel* to express this idea of superficial religion. See Francke, *Vom rechten Verhalten*, 434.

24. *Die Erlassung und Behaltung der Sünde*, TGP II.9:151, 301.

25. *Über das VII Gebot*, TGP II.10:559; *Von unserer täglichen Berufs Arbeit*, TGP II.10:519; *Die Gerechtigkeit und Stärke im* HERRN, TGP II.10:328.

26. *Das Geheimniß der Bosheit*, TGP II.9:506.

27. *Von den falschen Propheten*, TGP II.9:447, 450; *Das Geheimniß der Bosheit*, TGP II.9:492; *Der unverantwortliche Mißbrauch des heiligen Abendmahls*, TGP II.9:544.

28. Francke, "Die sechzehente Predigt," 595; *Der rechte Gebrauch des Wortes GOttes*, TGP II.9:356; *Die Verführung unter dem Namen GOttes*, TGP II.9:115; *Von dem Dienst untreuer Lehrer*, TGP II.9:403; *Von den falschen Propheten*, TGP II.9:450. For Francke's influence on Whitefield on this matter, see Hindmarsh, *Spirit of Early Evangelicalism*, 21–26.

29. *Das Aergerniß des Creutzes*, TGP II.9:569.

30. *Der unverantwortliche Mißbrauch des heiligen Abendmahls*, TGP II.9:544; Francke, *Am grünen Donnerstage*, 553.

31. Francke, *Am grünen Donnerstage*, 554; Francke, "Glauchisches Gedenck-Büchlein," 79–91.

32. *Der unverantwortliche Mißbrauch des heiligen Abendmahls*, TGP II.9:537; Francke, *Von den Thränenden Augen*, 365.

33. Francke, *Vom rechten Verhalten*, 414; see also Francke, *Anhang, Von drey unterschiedenen Stufen*, 647.

34. Francke, *Vom rechten Verhalten*, 414; see also Francke, "Die sechzehente Predigt," 577.

35. Francke, *Am grünen Donnerstage*, 553.

36. Francke often spoke of an empowerment in truly understanding the various doctrines attached to the Eucharist: Francke, "Die sechzehente Predigt," 576, 593.

37. Francke, *Am grünen Donnerstage*, 554.

38. Francke, *Franckes Tagebuch*, 14–15. The author is especially grateful to Christian Soboth for bringing this reference to his attention and to Anne Harnisch for providing the complete signature. Francke's categorization of worthy participation appears to touch on gender issues, but it is important to recognize that throughout his discussion he used both male and female titles (e.g., Magd/Knecht) and drew more directly from biblical language and mysticial uses of the terms.

39. Francke, *Anhang, Von drey unterschiedenen Stufen*, 643.

40. Francke, "Die sechzehente Predigt," 581.

41. Francke, *Anhang, Von drey unterschiedenen Stufen*, 643.

42. Francke, "Die sechzehente Predigt," 584–85.

43. Francke, *Anhang, Von drey unterschiedenen Stufen*, 644.

44. Francke, "Die sechzehente Predigt," 587; Francke, *Die nöthige Prüfung*, 35. See also Francke, *Das geschäffte des Hertzen*, 657.

45. Francke, *Von den Thränenden Augen*, 399. Francke writes, "So macht es auch GOtt der HErr, Er gehet auch als ein Bettler vor euch her, bittet und bettelt bey euch durch sein Wort." Francke, *Die Göttliche Rührung des Hertzens*, 39. Concerning identifying with Christ's humility, Francke claims, "so mercke nun wenn du zum heiligen Abendmahl gewesen bist, solstu dich fleißig erinnern solches heiligen Abendmahls, denn da durch gewinnt er neue Krafft, wenn ein gläubiger Christ zum heiligen Abendmahl gewesen, und ist daselbst fein gestärcket worden, so offt er nun daran gedencket, wie er nun da so Kräfftig sey gestärcket, hat er neue Krafft bekommen, wird sein Glaube stärcker, so wird seine liebe brünstiger gegen seinen Heyland, und wird gedulti[g]er in seinen Leyden, demühtiger gegen Gott und menschen, also sollest du dich deßen fleißig erinnern, was dir Gott der Herr vor Gnade darinnen erzeiget habe," Francke, *Vom rechten Verhalten*, 453.

46. Francke, "Die sechzehente Predigt," 591.

47. Francke, *Am grünen Donnerstage*, 562.

48. Arndt connects crying and tears to remorse over sin. Arndt, *Wahren Christenthum*, 1.8.16.

49. Francke, *Anhang, Von drey unterschiedenen Stufen*, 643.

50. Francke, *Vom rechten Verhalten*, 437–38.

51. Francke, *Von den Thränenden Augen*, 413–14.

52. Francke, *Die nöthige Prüfung*, 34. Though Francke recognized the possibility that someone might cry out of worldly sorrow, crying was one of the common signs he offered for worthy communicants.

53. Kramer, *Beiträge*, 170–71. For biographical material on Johann Jakob Spener, see Spener, *Briefwechsel mit August Hermann Francke*, 62n1; Whitmer, *Halle Orphanage*, 23.

54. Spener, *Briefwechsel mit August Hermann Francke*, 62.

55. Kramer, *Beiträge*, 171.

56. Francke, "Die sechzehente Predigt," 585.

57. Francke, *Anhang, Von drey unterschiedenen Stufen*, 644.

58. Ibid., 644–45.
59. Francke, "Die sechzehente Predigt," 582.
60. Kurten, *Umkehr zum lebendigen Gott*, 94; Peschke, *Studien*, 1:44.
61. Matthias, "Bekehrung und Wiedergeburt," 60–61; Peschke, *Studien*, 1:45.
62. *Von Kampff eines bußfertigen Sünders*, TGP II.10:31.
63. Francke, *Das Abendmahl des Lammes*, 27.
64. Francke, *Die nöthige Prüfung*, 3.
65. Francke, "Die sechzehente Predigt," 592.
66. Francke, *Am grünen Donnerstage*, 544.
67. Francke, *Die Göttliche Rührung des Hertzens*, 45–46.
68. Francke, *Anhang, Von drey unterschiedenen Stufen*, 645–46.
69. Francke, "Die sechzehente Predigt," 572.
70. *Die Wenigkeit der rechten Kinder GOttes*, TGP II.9:352. Francke exhorted his listeners elsewhere that there was no one that should avoid the Supper because it had lost its usefulness. According to him, there was no one that lacked the need to be a thousand times "stronger" or "closer" to Christ; Francke, "Die sechzehente Predigt," 590.
71. Francke, *Anhang, Von drey unterschiedenen Stufen*, 646.
72. *Anleitung zum rechten Gebrauch der an sich klaren Weissagung CHristi vom jüngsten Gerichte*, TGP II.10:263–64.
73. Francke, *Vom rechten Verhalten*, 453, 455; Francke, "Die sechzehente Predigt," 575.
74. Francke, *Die nöthige Prüfung*, 15, 103.
75. See Sattler, "August Hermann Francke and Mysticism," 3–17. Contrast Sattler to Peschke, "Die Bedeutung der Mystik," 294–316; Peschke, *Studien*, 2:219.
76. Peschke, *Bekehrung und Reform*, 38.
77. Francke, *Vom rechten Verhalten*, 447.
78. Francke, *Am grünen Donnerstage*, 550.
79. Peschke, "Die Abendmahlsanschauung," 138.

EPILOGUE

1. This should come as no surprise. As Lutheran theologian Jenson remarks, "We are called upon to interpret the Church by the sacraments that occur in her and the sacraments by the church in which they occur." Jenson, "Church and the Sacraments," 207.
2. Francke, "Von dem Eyffer um das Hauß Gottes," in *Buß-Predigten*, 1:239.
3. For a glimpse into developing conceptions of the church (especially regarding ecclesial law) in the early Enlightenment, see R. Lehmann, *Die Transformation des Kirchenbegriffs*, 185–338.
4. Francke remarks that Simeon serves as a good example for his church, "Denn bey Gott dem Herrn gilt kein Ausehen der Persohnen." Francke, *Ein Unterricht vom Kirchengehen*, 176–77. This sermon also appears in TGP II.9:602–30.
5. Francke, *Ein Unterricht vom Kirchengehen*, 205.
6. See H. Lehmann, "Sammlung der Frommen," 35, 43.
7. Francke, *Ein Unterricht vom Kirchengehen*, 206–7.
8. Ibid., 130, 209, 213.
9. Francke, "Von dem Eyffer um das Hauß Gottes," in *Buß-Predigten*, 1:247.
10. Francke, "Von der äusseren Kirche," in *Buß-Predigten*, 1:210–11.
11. *Nexus Legis et Evangelii*, TGP II.10:213.
12. Francke, *Ein Unterricht vom Kirchengehen*, 134–36. Francke attributes Pauline authorship to Hebrews in this portion of the sermon.
13. Ibid., 147–50.
14. Francke, *Von der Gesellschaft der Gläubigen*, 260–61.

15. Witte, *From Sacrament to Contract*, 49.
16. Francke, *Ein Unterricht vom Kirchengehen*, 225–27.
17. Shantz, "Christian Community in German Pietism," 214.
18. Francke, *Ein Unterricht vom Kirchengehen*, 228.
19. *Von der Gemeinschaft der Heiligen*, TGP II.10:358.
20. Francke, *Von der Gesellschaft der Gläubigen*, 206.
21. Ibid.; *Von der Gemeinschaft der Heiligen*, TGP II.10:358–59.
22. Francke, *Von der Gemeinschaft der Heiligen*, TGP II.10:360.
23. Ibid., 359–70. Elsewhere Francke claims these activities are found among those who "despise the worship of God." Francke, "Von der äusseren Kirche," in *Buß-Predigten*, 1:223.
24. Francke, *Ein Unterricht vom Kirchengehen*, 136.
25. *De Studio Renovationis*, TGP II.10:379–80.
26. Peschke, *Die frühen Katechismuspredigten Franckes*, 34–38.
27. Francke, "Die dritte Predigt," in *Catechismus-Predigten*, 85–87. See also *Book of Concord*, 352.
28. Francke, "Von der äusseren Kirche," in *Buß-Predigten*, 1:210.
29. Francke, "Die dritte Predigt," in *Catechismus-Predigten*, 88.
30. Ibid., 89–90.
33. Peschke, *Die frühen Katechismuspredigten Franckes*, 34.
34. Francke, "Die dritte Predigt," in *Catechismus-Predigten*, 102–3, 105.
35. Peschke, *Die frühen Katechismuspredigten Franckes*, 34.
36. Francke, "Von der äusseren Kirche," in *Buß-Predigten*, 1:211.
37. Francke, *Von der Gesellschaft der Gläubigen*, 248.
38. H. Schneider, "Understanding the Church," 15.
39. Sattler, *God's Glory, Neighbor's Good*, 102.
40. Bayer, *Martin Luther's Theology*, 262.
41. Worthen, *Apostles of Reason*, 128.
42. Granquist, "Between Pietism, Revivalism, and Modernity," 260–63. See also Granquist, *Lutherans in America*, 23; Kuenning, *Rise and Fall*, 67; Holifield, *Theology in America*, 399.
43. Gustafson, *Lutherans in Crisis*, 89. Gustafson's language "American religious scene" is quoted in Granquist, "Between Pietism, Revivalism, and Modernity," 267.
44. Nevin, *Mystical Presence*, 51–52. Though the Mercersburg theologian Nevin does not specifically mention his contemporary a little over forty miles east in Gettysburg, he mostly likely had Schmucker in mind when writing this critique of American Lutheran sacramental practices.

BIBLIOGRAPHY

PRIMARY MANUSCRIPT AND PRINTED SOURCES

Arndt, Johann. *Sechs Bücher vom Wahren Christenthum, Welche handeln Von heilsamer Busse herzlicher Reue und Leid über die Sünde und wahrem Glauben auch heiligem Leben und Wandel der rechten wahren Christen.* [...] *und nebst dem Paradies-Gärtlein* [...]. Schwabach: Johann Jacob Enderes, 1737.

Bayly, Lewis. *The Practice of Piety: Directing a Christian how to walk, that he may please God.* 71st ed. London, 1792.

———. *Praxis Pietatis: Das ist, Übung der Gottseligkeit* [...] *Anfänglich in Englischer Sprach beschrieben Durch Doct. Ludwig Bayli,* [...] *Hernacher auch in unsere Teutsche Sprach übersetzet* [...]. Basel: Verlag Emanuel und Joh. Georg Königen, 1692.

Böhme, Anton Wilhelm. "A short Account of Some Persons who have been Instrumental in promoting the most Substantial Points of Religion in some Parts of Germany." In August Hermann Francke, *Pietas Hallensis: Or, An Abstract of the Marvellous Footsteps of Divine Providence, Attending the Management and Improvement of the Orphan-House at Glaucha Near Hall; And of other Charitable Foundations relating to it,* edited by Anton Wilhelm Böhme, 5–28. London: John Downing, 1707.

The Book of Concord: The Confessions of the Evangelical Lutheran Church. Edited by Robert Kolb and Timothy J. Wengert. Minneapolis: Fortress Press, 2000.

Calvin, John. *Institutes of the Christian Religion.* Edited by John T. McNeill and Ford Lewis Battles. Philadelphia: Westminster Press, 1960.

Carpzov, Johann Benedict. "Vorrede." In *Doppelte Verthäidigung Des Eben-Bildes Der Pietisterey I. Wider einen Ungenandten Welcher unter dem Titul: Abgenöthigte Antwort auff die Charteqve, Eben-Bild der heutigen Pietismi solches als ein Paßquill beschuldigen wollen. II. Wider noch einen Anonymum, Der Imaginem Pietismi auch angefochten und solches mit einer Praefation Herrn D. Speners heraus gegeben. An statt einer anderen dieser des D. Speners Praefation, widerlegenden Vorrede ist einer Hochlöbl. Theologischen Facultät zu Leipzig unterthänigster Bericht an Churfürstl. Duchl. zu Sachsen auff M. Franckens dey dem Leipzigischen Protocol mit publicirten Defension-Schrifft aus denen unverfälschten Acten vorher gesetzet,* edited by Matthias Rothe, 3–60. Freyburg, 1692.

Chemnitz, Martin. *Eine Tauffpredigt geschehen bey der Tauff des Durchgeleuchtigen Hochgebornen Frewleins Annae Vrsulæ etc. in der Fürstlichen Capell zu Cella den 22. Aprilis. Anno 1572.* In *Drey Predigten: Die Erste, Von der Heiligen Tauffe. Die Ander, Von der Heiligen Absolution. Die Dritte, Von dem Heiligen Abendmal des HERn. Geschehen bey der Tauffe des Duchgeleuchtigen, Hochgebornen Frewleins, Frewlein AnnæVrsulæ, Hertzogin zu Braunschweig vnd Lüneberg. etc. in der Fürstlishen Schloß Kirchen zu Cella,* edited by Martin Chemnitz, Nicolaus Selnecker, and Chistophorus Vischer. Heinrichstadt, 1572.

Detharding, Georg. *Kennzeichen eines wiedergebohrnen Menschen.* Rostock, 1711.

Die Drey Confessiones, o. Glaubens=Bekaentnusse Welche in den Chur=Fuerstl. Branden. die Religion betreffenden Edictis zu beobachten befohlen werden: I. Johannis Sigißmundi Chur=Fuersten zu Brandenburg [...] *Glaubens=Bekaentnueß. II. Colloqvium Lipsiacum Anno 1631* [...]. *III.*

Thornische Declaratio, [...] Anno 1645 [...] *Hierbey auch Die Churfuerstl. Brandenburg. Edicta selbst nebst zweyen Declarationen.* Cölln/Spree, 1683.

Dyke, Jeremy. *Good Conscience or, a Treatise Shewing the Nature, Meanes, Markes, Benefit, and Necessitie thereof.* London: A. M. for Robert Milbourne, 1635.

Fox, George. *A Small Treatise concerning Swearing in the Old time of the Law, with its Use; And an End put to it in the Gospel by Jesus Christ, Who Forbiddeth all Swearing, and sets up Yea and Nay instead thereof.* London, 1675.

Francke, August Hermann. *Das Abendmahl des Lammes: In einer Predigt Uber das Evangelium Luc. XIV, vers. 16-24. Am 2. Sontage nach dem Feste der H. Drey-Einigkeit Anno 1697 in der Chur-Fürstlichen Schloß-Kirchen zu Lichtenburg in Sachsen vorgestellet.* Halle: Christian Henckel, 1697.

———. *Alles und in allen Christus.* In Francke, *Sonn-und Fest-Tages-Predigten*, 1164–83.

———. *Am grünen Donnerstage, vom Heiligen Abendmahle.* In *Predigten von August Herrmann Francke über evangelischen Advent und epistolische Texte, vom ersten Advent bis zum dritten Ostertage*, edited by Emil Francke, 542–66. Leipzig: Eduard Kummer, 1838.

———. *Anhang, Von drey unterschiedenen Stufen oder Classen derer, die würdig zum heiligen Abendmahl gehen.* In Francke, *Sonn-und Fest-Tages-Predigten*, 643–49.

———. "August Hermann Franckes Lebenslauf." In *Werke*, 4–29. pages?

———. *Buß-Predigten, darin aus verschiedenen Texten Heil. Schrift deutlich gezeiget wird* [...]. 1848. Reprint, Bielefeld: Missionsverlag der Evangelisch-Lutherischen Gebetsgemeinschaften, 1997.

———. *Catechismus-Predigten.* Halle: Verlegung des Wäysenhauses, 1726.

———. *Collegium Pastorale über D. Ioh. Ludouici Hartmanni Pastorale Euangelicum.* Halle: Verlegung des Wäysenhauses, 1741.

———. *Die Einladung zu dem grossen Abendmahl GOttes, Aus Luc. XIV, 16-24. Zu einer zu Halle in der Schulkirche Am II. Sonntag nach Trinit. Anno 1709.* Halle: Wäysenhauses, 1723.

———. *Franckes Tagesbuch.* AFStH A 171:1.

———. *Das geschäffte des Hertzen bey dem H. Abendmahl.* 1694. AFStH M 21b.

———. *Die Gnade GOttes In Christo JESu: Aus dem Evangelischen Text Luc. I, 57-80. Am Tage Johannis des Täuffers Ao. 1714. In einer auf Erfordern In der Stadt-Kirchen zu Gera im Vogt-Lande gehaltenen Predigt vorgestellet.* 2nd printing. Halle: WäysenHaus, 1723.

———. *Die Göttliche Rührung des Hertzens, Aus der Apostel-Geschicht II, 37. Da Sie das hörten, gings ihnen durchs Hertz, und sprachen zu Petro und zu den andern Aposteln: Ihr Männer, lieber Brüder, was sollen wir thun? Am Buß-Tag den 10. Jun. 1716. In der St. Ulrichs-Kirche in Halle, vorgestellt.* Halle: Wäysenhaus, 1723.

———. *Der Große Aufsatz.* In *August Hermann Franckes Schrift über eine Reform des Erziehungs- und Bildungswesens als Ausgangspunkt einer geistlichen und sozialen Neuordnung der Evangelischen Kirche des 18. Jahrhunderts, Der Grosse Aufsatz, mit einer quellenkundlichen Einführung*, edited by Otto Podczeck. Berlin: Akademie Verlag, 1962.

———. *Idea Studiosi Theologiæ, oder Abbildung eines der Theologie Beflissenen, Wie derselbe sich zum Gebrauch um Dienst des Herrn und zu allem gutem Werck gehöriger Maassen bereitet.* Halle: Wäysenhaus, 1713.

———. *JEsus CHristus als das Licht der Heyden Und der Preiß Israels Nach Anleitung des Evangelischen Textes Luc. II, 22-32. Am Tage der Reinigung Maria An.1714. Auf Veranlassung einer damals angestelleten Jüden=Tauffe, In der St. Georgen=Kirche zu Glaucha an Halle vergestellet.* Halle: Wäysenhauses, 1714.

———. "Kurtzer und einfältiger Entwurf von den Mißbräuchen des Beichtstuhls." In *Werke*, 92–107.

———. *Der Liebe Sohn des himmlischen VATERS an welchem er Wohlgefallen hat In einer Predigt über den Evangelischen Text Matth. III, v. 13-17. In der St. Georgen=Kirche zu Glaucha an Halle, Am I. Sonntage nach Epiph. 1715. Vorgestellet.* Halle: Wäysenhaus, 1715.

———. *Nicodemus, or, a treatise against the fear of man. Wherein the causes sad effects thereof are briefly describ'd. With some remedies against it Written in High Dutch by Augustus Frank* [...]. Translated by A. H. Boehm. London: Downing, 1707.

———. *Die nöthige Prüfung sein selbst vor dem Gebrauch des Heiligen Abendmahls Nach Anleitung der Epistol. Lection 1 Cor. XI, v. 23. u.f. An dem so genannten Grünen Donnerstage Anno 1712. In der St. Georgen-Kirche zu Glaucha an Halle vorgestellet, Und insonderheit mit zu einem Unterricht für diejenige, so sich aus mancherley Ursachen vom H. Abendmahl enthalten* [...] *Dabey ein Anhang von der unterschiedenen Beschaffenheit der würdigen Communicanten vom Autore zu Nürnberg vorgestellet den 6ten Mart. anno 1718*. 5th ed. Halle: Wäysenhaus, 1728 [In this edition, 1782 is erroneously printed on the title page.].

———. *Pädagogische Schriften*. Edited by Hermann Lorenzen. 2nd ed. Paderborn: Ferdinand Schöningh, 1964.

———. *Pietas Hallensis: Or, An Abstract of The Marvellous Footsteps of Divine Providence, Attending the Management and Improvement of the Orphan-House at Glaucha Near Hall; And of other Charitable Foundations Relating to It*. Edited by Anton Wilhelm Böhme. London: J. Downing, 1707.

———. *Predigten von August Herrmann Francke über evangelischen Advent und epistolische Texte*. Edited by Emil Francke. Leipzig: Eduard Kummer, 1838.

———. "Die sechzehente Predigt über die Lehre vom H. Abendmahl." In *Catechismus-Predigten*, 549–601.

———. *Segens-volle Fußstampfen des noch lebenden und waltenden liebreichen und getreuen GOttes, Zur Beschämung des Unglaubens und Stärckung des Glaubens, entdecket durch eine wahrhafte und umständliche Nachricht von dem Wäysen-Hause und übrigen Anstalten zu Glaucha vor Halle*. 3rd rev. ed. Halle: Verlegung des Wäysen-Hauses, 1709.

———. *Die Seligkeit Derer, Die zum grossen Abendmahl kommen, und das Brod essen im Reiche GOttes, Aus dem Evangelischen Text Luc. XIV, 16–24. Am II. Sonntag nach Trinit. M DCC XIV. In der St. Georgen-Kirche zu Glaucha an Halle*. Halle: Wäysenhaus, 1724.

———. *Sonn- Fest- und Apostel-Tags-Predigten. Theil 1–3*. Halle: Wäysenhaus, 1704.

———. *Sonn- und Fest-Tages-Predigten Welche Theils in Halle theils an verschiedenen auswärtigen Oertern von wichtigen und auserlesenen Materien gehalten worden. Nebst Vorbereitungen auf die hohen Feste und nutzlichen Registern*. 2nd printing. Halle: Wäysen-Haus, 1728.

———. *Die Unseligkeit Derer Die vergebens zu dem Abendmahl GOttes geladen sind Aus dem Evangelischen Text Luc. XIV, 16–24. Am II. Sonntag nach Trinit. 1715. In der S. Ulrichs-Kirche zu Halle*. Halle: Wäysen-Hauses, 1729.

———. *Ein Unterricht vom Kirchengehen*. AFStH M24.

———. *A Very Necessary Examination of a man's self, Whether he in faith, and if Christ dwelleth in him, drawn from the following Text 2 Corr: 13:5 With relation to a letter, formerly published on the foregoing Head, (viz; Christ for us)—By August Herman Francke S Theol Prof St. Ulrichs in Hall. 1716 Done from the German into English Feb: ye 10th 1716*. 1716. AFStH Stab/F 30/62.

———. *Vom rechten Verhalten vor, bei und nach dem Abendmahl*. 1694. AFStH M 27.

———. *Von den Thränenden Augen des Herrn Jesu*. 1694. AFStH L 5b.

———. *Von der Gesellschaft der Gläubigen untereinander in dieser Welt*. AFStH L 6a.

———. *Von der H. Tauffe: Nachmittags Predigt [Domin: III Adventag]*. 1694. AFStH M 21b.

———. *Von der Taufe Christi: Am 1. Sontag nach Epiph [Neu Jahres Tages]*. 1694. AFStH L 5a.

———. *Werke in Auswahl*. Edited by Erhard Peschke. Berlin: Luther-Verlag, 1969.

———. *Wie der Gemeinde und Schulen zu helfen*. 1701. AFStH I 12.

Gerhard, Johann. *Ausführliche Schrifftmässige Erkläring der beyden Artickel Von der heiligen Tauffe und Von dem heiligen Abendmahl Solcher massen angestellet daß jegliche Puncten derselben mit allen und jeden dahin gehörigen Zeugnüssen der heiligen Schrifft bewisen und die darwider streitend scheinende örter erkläret werden*. Frankfurt: Thomas Matthias Götzen, 1662.

Großgebauer, Theophil. *Treuer Unterricht Von der Widergeburt*. In Großgebauer, *Wächterstimme Auß dem verwüsteten Zion*, 1–108.

———. *Wächterstimme Auß dem verwüsteten Zion: Das ist Treühertzige und nothwendige Entdeckung.* [. . .] *Sambt einem treüen Unterricht Von der Widergeburt*. Frankfurt am Main: Joachim Wildens, 1661.

Hoburg, Christian. *Der Sicherste Weg Zum Reich Gottes, Und dessen würcklichen Erhöh- und Befestigung in dem Grund der Seelen, Krafft der wahren Wiedergeburt, Oder Erneuerung im Heil. Geist*. Frankfurt: J. Nicolaus Andreä, 1717.

Knapp, Johann Georg. "Des sel. Herrn Consistorialraths; D. Gotthilf August Franckens, Lebenslauf." In *Denkmal der schuldigen Hochachtung und Liebe gestiftet dem weiland Hochwürdigen und Hochgelarten Herrn D. Gotthilf August Francken, Königl. Preußl. Consistorialrath im Herzogtum Magdeburg, der Friedrichsuniversität, der Theologischen Facultät und des Stadt-Ministerii Senior und ersten Inspector im Saalkreis, wie auch des Pädagogii Regii und des Waisenhauses Director*, edited by Johann George Knapp, 1–60. Halle: Buchhandlung des Waisenhauses, 1770.

Lehmann, Georg. *Der Gefallene aber nicht weggeworffene Berechte Bey Christlicher und Volckreicher Leich-Bestattung Des Wohl-Ehrwürdigen Großachtbarn und Hochgelahrten Herrn Joachim Fellers*. Leipzig: Johann Christian Wohlfahrt, 1691.

Löscher, Valentin Ernst. *Unschuldige Nachrichten von alten und neuen theologischen Sachen, Büchern, Uhrkunden, Controversien, Veränderungen, Anmerckungen, Vorschläge u.d.g.* Leipzig: Johann Friedrich Braun, 1719.

Luther, Martin. *Luther's Works*. American ed. 55 vols. Philadelphia: Fortress; St. Louis: Concordia, 1955–86.

———. *Martin Luthers Werke: Kritische Gesamtausgabe*. [*Schriften*.]. 65 vols. Weimar: H. Böhlau, 1883–1993.

Molinos, Miguel de. *The Spiritual Guide*. Translated by Robert P. Baird. Mahwah, NJ: Paulist Press, 2010.

Neumann, Ernst. *Der Missionar am Volta. Der Sklavenbefreier. August Hermann Francke. Drei Erzählungen für jung und alt*. Haußschatz deutscher Erzählungen 857. Reutlingen: Enßlin und Laiblin, 1897.

Reichart, Jacob. *Davidischer Hertzen Beste Lust Bey der sehr traurigen und Volckreichen Sepultur* [. . .] *Herrn M. Joh. Heinrici Rumpelii, Wohlmeritirten Pfarrers und Superintendentens in Salzungen* [. . .]. Meiningen: Niclaus Hassert, 1699.

Sagittarius, Caspar. *Gründlicher Beweiß das seine Theologische Lehr-Sätze von dem Rechtmäßigem Pietismo noch fest stehen*. 1691.

———. *Theologische Lehr-Sätze von dem Rechtmäßigem Pietismo Zur Ehre GOTTes Beruhigung der Christl. Kirche und Fortpflantzung der wahren Gottseligkeit*. July, 1691.

———. *Untheologische und abgeschmackkte Lehr-Sätze vom Pietismo, Nicht zur Ehre GOttes sondern Verwirrung der Chrisl. Kirche und Hinderniß der wahren Gottseligkeit im Druck heraus gegeben und von einem der Warheit liebenden mit Gegen-Sätzen*. July, 1691.

Seckendorf, Veit Ludwig von. *Bericht und Erinnerung Auff eine neulich in Druck Lateinisch und Teutsch ausgestreuete Schrifft im Latein Imago Pietismi, zu Teutsch aber Ebenbild der Pietisterey genannt* [. . .]. 1692.

Spener, Philipp Jakob. *Briefwechsel mit August Hermann Francke 1689–1704*. Edited by Johannes Wallmann and Udo Sträter. Tübingen: Mohr Siebeck, 2006.

———. *Geminum de Athei conversione Judicum, quod diverso tempore rogatus dedit* [. . .]. Halle, 1703.

———. *Der hochwichtige Articul von der Wiedergeburt Dero Ursachen Mittel Art Pflichten Würden Kennzeichen und übrigen dahin gehörigen materin*. Frankfurt am Main: Johann David Zunners, 1696.

———. *Kurtze Catechismuspredigten*. Vol. 2.2 of *Schriften*, 1689. Reprint edited by Erich Beyreuther. Hildesheim: Georg Olms, 1982.

———. *Pia Desideria*. Translated by Theodore Tappert. Minneapolis: Fortress Press, 1964.
———. *Pia Desideria: Deutsch-Lateinische Studienausgabe*. Edited by Beate Köster. Giessen: Brunnen, 2005.
———. *Schriften: Drei Schriften Philipp Jakob Speners aus den Jahren 1693–1694*. Reprint edited by Erich Beyreuther. Hildesheim: Georg Olms, 1979–2005.
———. *Von der Bedeutung der Tauff nochmahl aus Rom. 6/4*. In Spener, *Kurtze Catechismuspredigten*, 534–42.
———. *Was die sacramenten seyen und was sie nutzen?* In Spener, *Kurtze Catechismuspredigten*, 448–54.
Stieber, Georg Friedrich. Brief von Georg Friedrich Stieber an August Hermann Francke. AFStH C817, Nr. 7.
Stürmer, Christian. Brief von Christian Stürmer an August Hermann Francke (1714). AFStH C599:4.
Walch, Johann Georg. *Philosophisches Lexicon, worinnen die in allen Theilen der Philosophie vorkommende Materien und Kunftwörter erkläret [. . .]*. Leipzig, 1775.
Zedler, Johann Heinrich. *Grosses Vollständiges Universal-Lexicon*. 64 vols. Reprint, Graz: Akademische Druck- u. Verlagsanstalt, 1961.

SECONDARY LITERATURE

Aland, Kurt. "August Hermann Francke und die Privatbeichte: Leonhard Fendt zum 75. Geburtstag." *Monatsschrift für Pastoraltheologie* 45 (1956): 272–85.
———. "Breithaupt: Joachim Justus." In *Neue Deutsche Biographie*, 2:576. 28 vols. Historische Kommission bei der Bayerischen Akademie der Wissenschaften. Berlin: Duncker & Humblot, 1953–2008.
———. "Der Pietismus und die soziale Frage." In *Pietismus und moderne Welt*, edited by Kurt Aland, 99–137. Witten: Luther-Verlag, 1974.
———. "Die Privatbeichte im Luthertum von ihren Anfängen bis zu ihrer Auflösung." In Aland, *Kirchengeschichtliche Entwürfe*, 452–519. Berlin: Gütersloher Verlagshaus Gerd Mohn, 1960.
Albrecht-Birkner, Veronika. *Francke in Glaucha, Kehrseiten eines Klischees*. Tübingen: Max Niemeyer Verlag, 2004.
———."Franckes Krisen." In *Die Welt verändern: August Hermann Francke—Ein Lebenswerk um 1700*, edited by Holger Zaunstöck, Thomas Müller-Bahlke, and Claus Veltmann, 81–97. Halle: Verlag des Franckeschen Stiftungen zu Halle, 2013.
———, ed. *Pfarrerbuch der Kirchenprovinz Sachsen. Vol. 5, Biogramme Kn-Ma*. Leipzig: Evangelische Verlaganstalt, 2007.
Albrecht-Birkner, Veronika, and Udo Sträter. "Die radikale Phase des frühen August Hermann Francke." In *Der radikale Pietismus: Perspektiven der Forschung*, edited by Wolfgang Breul, Marcus Meier, and Lothar Vogel, 57–84. Göttingen: Vandenhoeck & Ruprecht, 2010.
Althaus, Paul. *Theology of Martin Luther*. Translated by Robert C. Schultz. Philadelphia: Fortress Press, 1966.
Atwood, Craig D. *Community of the Cross: Moravian Piety in Colonial Bethlehem*. University Park: Pennsylvania State University Press, 2004.
Baird, Robert P. "Miguel de Molinos: Life and Controversy." In Molinos, *The Spiritual Guide*, 1–20.
Barth, Hans-Martin. *Atheismus und Orthodoxie: Analysen und Modelle christlicher Apologetik im 17. Jahrhundert*. Göttingen: Vandenhoeck & Ruprecht, 1971.
Barth, Karl. *Dogmatics in Outline*. New York: Harper & Row, 1959.
———. *Word of God and the Word of Man*. Gloucester, MA: Peter Smith, 1978.

Bartz, Ernst. *Die Wirtschaftsethik August Hermann Franckes*. Harburg-Wilhelmsburg: Verlag Wilhelm G. Frank, 1934.

Bayer, Oswald. "Lutherischer Pietismus: Oratio, Meditatio, Tentatio bei August Hermann Francke." In *Religiöse Erfahrung und wissenschaftliche Theologie: Festschrift für Ulrich Köpf zum 70. Geburtstag*, edited by Albrecht Beutel and Reinhold Rieger, 1–12. Tübingen: Mohr Siebeck, 2011.

———. *Martin Luther's Theology: A Contemporary Interpretation*. Grand Rapids, MI: Eerdmans, 2008.

Baylor, Michael G. *Action and Person: Conscience in Late Scholasticism and the Young Luther*. Leiden: Brill, 1997.

Becker, Judith. *Conversio im Wandel: Basler Missionare zwischen Europa und Südindien und die Ausbildung einer Kontaktreligiosität, 1834–1860*. Göttingen: Vandenhoeck & Ruprecht, 2015.

Beeke, Joel R., and Mark Jones. *A Puritan Theology*. Grand Rapids, MI: Reformation Heritage Books, 2012.

Benz, Ernst. "Ecumenical Relations Between Boston Puritanism and German Pietism: Cotton Mather and August Hermann Francke." *Harvard Theological Review* 54 (1961): 159–93.

———. "Pietist and Puritan Sources of Early Protestant World Missions (Cotton Mather and August Hermann Francke)." *Church History* 20 (1951): 28–55.

Berthold, Benjamin. "Kritik an der lutherischen Beichtpraxis in Gottfried Arnolds Unparteiischen *Kirchen- und Ketzerhistorie* am Beispiel (1699/1700) von Peter Moritz aus Halle." *PuN* 36 (2010): 11–48.

Beutel, Albrecht, and Martha Nooke, eds. *Religion und Aufklärung: Akten des Ersten Internationalen Kongresses zur Erforschung der Aufklärungstheologie (Münster, 30. März bis 2. April 2014)*. Colloquia historica et theologica 2. Tübingen: Mohr Siebeck, 2016.

Beyreuther, Erich. *August Hermann Francke, 1663–1727: Zeuge des lebendigen Gottes*. Marburg: Francke Buchhandlung, 1956.

———. *August Hermann Francke und die Anfänge der ökumenischen Bewegung*. Hamburg: Herbert Reich Evang. Verlag, 1957.

———. *Frömmigkeit und Theologie: Gesammelte Aufsätze*. Hildesheim: Georg Olms Verlag, 1980.

———. *Geschichte des Pietismus*. Stuttgart: J. F. Steinkopf, 1978.

———. "Der Ursprung des Pietismus und die Frage nach der Zeugenkraft der Kirche." *Evangelische Theologie* 11 (1951/1952): 137–44.

Bezzel, Ernst. "Beichte III." In Müller, *Theologische Realenzyklopädie*, 5:421–25.

Biereye, Johannes. "August Hermann Francke und Erfurt." *Zeitschrift des Vereins für Kirchengeschichte der Provinz Sachsen* 21 (1925): 31–56; 22 (1926): 26–51.

Bozeman, Theodore Dwight. *The Precisianist Strain: Disciplinary Religion and Antinomian Backlash in Puritanism to 1638*. Chapel Hill: University of North Carolina Press, 2004.

Bradley, James E., and Richard A. Muller. *Church History: An Introduction to Research Methods and Resources*. 2nd ed. Grand Rapids, MI: Eerdmans, 2016.

Brecht, Martin. "August Hermann Francke und der Hallische Pietismus." In *Geschichte des Pietismus*, vol. 1, *Der Pietismus von siebzehnten bis zum frühen achtzehnten Jahrhundert*, edited by Martin Brecht, 439–539. Göttingen: Vandenhoeck & Ruprecht, 1992.

———. *Ausgewählte Aufsätze*. Vol. 2, *Pietismus*. Stuttgart: Calwer, 1997.

———. "Die deutschen Spiritualisten des 17. Jahrhunderts." In *Geschichte des Pietismus*, vol. 1, *Der Pietismus von siebzehnten bis zum frühen achtzehnten Jahrhundert*, edited by Martin Brecht, 205–40. Göttingen: Vandenhoeck & Ruprecht, 1992.

———. "Luther's Reformation." In *Handbook of European History, 1400–1600: Late Middle Ages, Renaissance, and Reformation*, vol. 2, *Visions, Programs and Outcomes*, edited by Thomas A. Brady Jr., Heiko A. Oberman, and James D. Tracy, 129–59. Grand Rapids, MI: Eerdmans, 1995.

———. "Philipp Jakob Spener, sein Programm und dessen Auswirkungen." In *Geschichte des Pietismus*, vol. 1, *Der Pietismus von siebzehnten bis zum frühen achtzehnten Jahrhundert*, edited by Martin Brecht, 279–389. Göttingen: Vandenhoeck & Ruprecht, 1992.

———. "Pietismus." In Müller, *Theologische Realenzyklopädie*, 26:606–31.

Breul, Wolfgang. "'Hoffnung besserer Zeiten': Der Wandel der 'Endzeit' im Lutherischen Pietismus um 1700." In *Frühe Neue Zeiten: Zeitwissen zwischen Reformation und Revolution*, edited by Achim Landwehr, 261–82. Bielefeld: transcript, 2012.

———. "Theological Tenets and Motives of Mission: August Hermann Francke, Nikolaus Ludwig von Zinzendorf." In *Migration and Religion: Christian Transatlantic Missions, Islamic Migration to Germany*, edited by Barbara Becker-Cantarino, 41–60. New York: Rodopi, 2012.

Brown, Dale W. *Understanding Pietism*. Rev. ed. Nappanee, IN: Evangel, 1996.

Brown, Harold O. J. *Heresies: The Image of Christ in the Mirror of Heresy and Orthodoxy from the Apostles to the Present*. Garden City, NY: Doubleday, 1984.

Brown, Rezeau. *Memoirs of Augustus Hermann Francke*. Philadelphia: American Sunday School Union, 1830.

Brückner, Georg. *Neue Beiträge zur Geschichte deutschen Alterthums, zweite Lieferung*. Meiningen: F. W. Gadow & Son, 1863.

Brunner, Daniel L. *Halle Pietists in England: Anthony William Boehm and the Society for Promoting Christian Knowledge*. Göttingen: Vandenhoeck & Ruprecht, 1993.

Bunke, Ernst. *August Hermann Francke, der Mann des Glaubens und der Liebe*. Giessen: Brunnen, 1960.

Campbell, Ted A. *The Religion of the Heart: A Study of European Religious Life in the Seventeenth and Eighteenth Centuries*. Columbia: University of South Carolina Press, 1991.

Coalter, Milton J., Jr. "The Radical Pietism of Count Nicholas Zinzendorf as a Conservative Influence on the Awakener, Gilbert Tennent." *Church History* 49, no. 1 (March 1980): 35–46.

Collins-Winn, Christian T., Christopher Gehrz, G. William Carlson, and Eric Holst, eds. *The Pietist Impulse in Christianity*. Eugene, OR: Pickwick, 2011.

Dayton, Donald W. "The Pietist Theological Critique of Biblical Inerrancy." In *Evangelicals and Scripture: Tradition, Authority and Hermeneutics*, edited by Vincent Bacote, Laura C. Miguelez, and Dennis L. Okholm, 76–89. Downers Grove, IL: InterVarsity, 2004.

Deppermann, Andreas. *Johann Jakob Schütz und die Anfänge des Pietismus*. Tübingen: Mohr Siebeck, 2002.

Deppermann, Klaus. *Der hallesche Pietismus und der preußische Staat unter Friedrich III. (I.)*. Göttingen: Vandenhoeck & Ruprecht, 1961.

Dingel, Irene. *Geschichte der Reformation*. Göttingen: Vandenhoeck & Ruprecht, 2018.

Dörfler, Angelika. "Abendmahl und Aufklärung." In *Christentum im Übergang: Neue Studien zu Kirche und Religion in der Aufklärungszeit*, edited by Albrecht Beutel, Volker Leppin, and Udo Sträter, 185–204. Leipzig: Evangelische Verlagsanstalt, 2006.

Döring, Detlef. "Seckendorf, Veit Ludwig von." In *Neue Deutsche Biographie*, 24:117–18. 28 vols. Historische Kommission bei der Bayerischen Akademie der Wissenschaften. Berlin: Duncker & Humblot, 1953–2008.

Douglas, Mary. *Natural Symbols: Explorations in Cosmology*. New York: Pantheon Books, 1982.

Drese, Claudia. "Der Berliner Beichtstuhlstreit oder Philipp Jakob Spener zwischen allen Stühlen." *PuN* 31 (2005): 60–97.

Eire, Carlos. *Reformations: The Early Modern World, 1450–1650*. New Haven: Yale University Press, 2016.

Erb, Peter C. *Pietists, Protestants, and Mysticism: The Use of Late Medieval Spiritual Texts in the Work of Gottfried Arnold (1666–1714)*. Metuchen, NJ: Scarecrow Press, 1989.

———, ed. *Pietists: Selected Writings*. New York: Paulist, 1983.

Frantz, John B. "The Awakening of Religion Among the German Settlers in the Middle Colonies." *William and Mary Quarterly* 33, no. 2 (April 1976): 266–88.

Friedrich, Martin. "Philipp Jakob Spener und der Halberstädter Streit von 1678. Zugleich ein Beitrag zur Wiedergeburtslehre bei Spener." *PuN* 25 (1999): 31–42.

Gawthrop, Richard L. *Pietism and the Making of Eighteenth-Century Prussia*. New York: Cambridge University Press, 1993.

George, Timothy. *Theology of the Reformers*. Nashville, TN: Broadman & Holman, 1988.

Geyer, Hermann. *Verborgene Weisheit: Johann Arndts "Vier Bücher vom Wahren Christentum" als Programm einer spiritualistisch-hermetischen Theologie*. Berlin: Walter de Gruyter, 2001.

Goebel, Max. "Geschichte der wahren Inspirations-Gemeinden von 1688 bis 1850." *Zeitschrift für die historische Theologie* 24 (1854): 267–322, 377–438; 25 (1855): 94–160, 327–425.

Gordon, James R. "Theologies of the Sacraments in the Eighteenth to Twenty-First Centuries." In *Christian Theologies of the Sacraments: A Comparative Introduction*, edited by Justin S. Holcomb and David A. Johnson, 261–70. New York: New York University Press, 2017.

Granquist, Mark A. "Between Pietism, Revivalism, and Modernity: Samuel Simon Schmucker and American Lutheranism in the Early Nineteenth Century." In *Pietism, Revivalism, and Modernity, 1650–1850*, edited by Fred van Lieburg and Daniel Lindmark, 256–73. Newcastle upon Tyne: Cambridge Scholars, 2008.

———. *Lutherans in America: A New History*. Minneapolis: Fortress Press, 2015.

Gresch, Eberhard. *Die Hugenotten: Geschichte, Glaube und Wirkung*. Leipzig: Evangelische Verlagsanstalt, 2006.

Greschat, Martin, ed. *Zur Neueren Pietismusforschung*. Darmstadt: Wissenschaftliche Buchgesellschaft, 1977.

Gustafson, David A. *Lutherans in Crisis: The Question of Identity in the American Republic*. Minneapolis: Fortress Press, 1993.

Halfmann, Wilhelm. *Christian Kortholt: Ein Bild aus der Theologie und Frömmigkeit im Ausgang des orthodoxen Zeitalters*. Kiel: Walter G. Mühlau, 1930.

Heppe, Heinrich. *Geschichte des Pietismus und der Mystik in der reformierten Kirche, namentlich der Niederlande*. Leiden: Brill, 1879.

Hertzberg, Gustav Friedrich. *August Hermann Francke und sein Hallisches Waisenhaus*. Halle: Buchhandlung des Waisenhauses, 1898.

Herzog, Frederick. *European Pietism Reviewed*. San Jose, CA: Pickwick, 2003.

Hiestand, Gerald, and Todd Wilson, eds. *The Pastor Theologian: Resurrecting an Ancient Vision*. Grand Rapids, MI: Zondervan, 2015.

Hindmarsh, D. Bruce. *The Spirit of Early Evangelicalism: True Religion in a Modern World*. Oxford: Oxford University Press, 2018.

Hinrichs, Carl. *Preußentum und Pietismus: Der Pietismus in Brandenburg-Preußen als religiössoziale Reformbewegung*. Göttingen: Vandenhoeck & Ruprecht, 1971.

Hirsch, Emanuel. *Geschichte der neuern evangelischen Theologie im Zusammenhang mit den allgemeinen Bewegungen des europäischen Denkens*. Vols. 1 and 2. Gütersloh: Gütersloher Verlagshaus, 1960.

Holifield, E. Brooks. *Theology in America: Christian Thought from the Age of Puritans to the Civil War*. New Haven: Yale University Press, 2003.

Höltgen, Karl Josef. "Wer war Emanuel Sonthom?" *Wolfenbütteler Renaissance Mitteilungen* 7, no. 3 (1983): 154–56.

Hopf, Friedrich Wilhelm. "Anton, Paul." In *Neue Deutsche Biographie*, 1:319–20. 28 vols. Historische Kommission bei der Bayerischen Akademie der Wissenschaften. Berlin: Duncker & Humblot, 1953–2008.

Howard, Thomas Albert. *Protestant Theology and the Making of the Modern German University*. Oxford: Oxford University Press, 2006.

Ingle, H. Larry. *First Among Friends: George Fox and the Creation of Quakerism*. New York: Oxford University Press, 1994.

Jacobi, Juliane. "Das Bild vom Kind in der Pädagogik August Hermann Franckes." In *Schulen machen Geschichte: 300 Jahre Erziehung in den Franckeschen Stiftungen zu Halle*, edited by

Daniel Cyranka, Joachim Dimanski, and Paul Raabe, 29–40. Halle (Saale): Verlag der Franckesche Stiftungen, 1997.
Jenson, Robert W. "The Church and the Sacraments." In *The Cambridge Companion to Christian Doctrine*, edited by Colin E. Gunton, 207–25. Cambridge: Cambridge University Press, 1997.
Jetter, Werner. "Katechismuspredigt." In Müller, *Theologische Realenzyklopädie*, 17:744–86.
Jung, Martin H. "The Impact of Pietism on Culture and Society in Germany." In *Religion as an Agent of Change: Crusades—Reformation—Pietism*, edited by Per Ingesman, 211–30. Leiden: Brill, 2016.
Kamp, Jan van de. "Die Einführung der christlichen Disziplinierung des Alltags in die deutsche evangelische Erbauungsliteratur durch Lewis Baylys Praxis Pietatis (1628)." *PuN* 37 (2011): 11–19.
Kantzenbach, Friedrich Wilhelm. *Orthodoxie und Pietismus*. Gütersloh: Gerd Mahn, 1966.
Karant-Nunn, Susan C. *The Reformation of Feeling: Shaping the Religious Emotions of Early Modern Germany*. Oxford: Oxford University Press, 2010.
———. *The Reformation of Ritual*. New York: Routledge, 1997.
Kelter, Gert. "Der Taufexorzismus in der lutherischen Kirche." *Lutherische Beiträge* 1, no. 3 (1996): 137–48.
Kevorkian, Tanya. *Baroque Piety: Religion, Society, and Music in Leipzig, 1650–1750*. Burlington, VT: Ashgate, 2007.
Kingston-Siggins, Jan D. *Martin Luther's Doctrine of Christ*. New Haven: Yale University Press, 1970.
Koch, Ernst. "Generalsuperintendent Henrich Fergen und die Anfänge des Pietismus in Gotha." In *Rezeption und Reform: Festschrift für Hans Schneider zu seinem 60. Geburtstag*, edited by Wolfgang Breul-Kunkel and Lothar Vogel, 189–211. Darmstadt: Verlag der Hessischen Kirchengeschichtlichen Vereinigung, 2001.
———."Johann Benedikt Carpzov und Philipp Jakob Spener: Zur Geschichte einer erbitterten Gegnerschaft." In *Eruditio—Confessio—Pietas: Kontinuität und Wandel in der lutherischen Konfessionskultur am Ende des 17. Jahrhunderts; Das Beispiel Johann Benedikt Carpzovs (1639–1699)*, edited by Stefan Michel and Andres Straßberger, 161–82. Leipzig: Evangelische Verlagsanstalt, 2009.
Kolb, Robert. "Lutheran Theology in Seventeenth-Century Germany." *Lutheran Quarterly* 20 (2006): 429–56.
———. "Martin Luther." In *Christian Theologies of the Sacraments: A Comparative Introduction*, edited by Justin S. Holcomb and David A. Johnson, 132–51. New York: New York University Press, 2017.
Kramer, Gustav. *August Hermann Francke: Ein Lebensbild*. 2 vols. Halle: Buchhandlung des Waisenhauses, 1880–82.
———. *August Hermann Francke's Pädagogische Schriften: Nebst der Darstellung seines Lebens und seiner Stiftungen*. Langensalza: Verlag von Hermann Beyer & Söhne, 1885.
———. *Beiträge zur Geschichte August Hermann Franckes*. Halle: Buchhandlung des Waisenhauses, 1865.
———. *Neue Beiträge zur Geschichte August Hermann Franckes*. Halle: Buchhandlung des Waisenhauses, 1875.
Krispin, Gerald S. "Paul Gerhardt: Confessional Subscription and the Lord's Supper." *Logia: A Journal of Lutheran Theology* 4, no. 3 (1995): 25–38.
———. "Philip Jacob Spener and the Demise of the Practice of Holy Absolution in the Lutheran Church." *Logia: A Journal of Lutheran Theology* 8, no. 4 (1999): 9–18.
———. "*Propter absolutionem*: Holy Absolution in the Theology of Martin Luther and Philipp Jacob Spener; A Comparative Study." PhD diss., Concordia Seminary, 1992.
Krüger, Friedhelm. "Gewissen III." In Müller, *Theologische Realenzyklopädie*, 12:219–25.
Kuenning, Paul. *The Rise and Fall of American Lutheran Pietism*. Macon: Mercer University Press, 1988.

Kurten, Petra. *Umkehr zum lebendigen Gott: Die Bekehrungstheologie August Hermann Franckes als Beitrag zur Erneuerung des Glaubens*. Paderborn: Ferdinand Schöningh, 1985.

Lehmann, Hartmut. "Europäisches Christentum im Zeichen der Krise." In *Im Zeichen der Krise: Religiosität im Europa des 17. Jahrhunderts*, edited by Hartmut Lehmann and Anne-Charlott Trepp, 9–16. Göttingen: Vandenhoeck & Ruprecht, 1999.

———. "Four Competing Concepts for the Study of Religious Reform Movements, Including Pietism, in Early Modern Europe and North America." In Lieburg, *Confessionalism and Pietism*, 313–22.

———. "Pietism in the World of Transatlantic Religious Revivals." In *Pietism in Germany and North America, 1680–1820*, edited by Jonathan Strom, Hartmut Lehmann, and James Van Horn Melton, 13–21. Burlington, VT: Ashgate, 2009.

———. "Sammlung der Frommen: Formen religiöser Vergemeinschaftung im Pietismus." In *Religiöse Erweckung in gottferner Zeit: Studien zur Pietismusforschung*, edited by Hartmut Lehmann, 31–44. Göttingen: Wallstein, 2010.

———. *Das Zeitalter des Absolutismus: Gottesgnadentum und Kriegsnot*. Stuttgart: Kohlhammer, 1980.

Lehmann, Roland M. *Die Transformation des Kirchenbegriffs in der Frühaufklarung*. Tübingen: Mohr Siebeck, 2013.

Lieburg, Fred van. "The Dutch Factor in German Pietism." In Shantz, *Companion to German Pietism*, 50–80.

———, ed. *Confessionalism and Pietism: Religious Reform in Early Modern Europe*. Mainz: Philipp von Zabern, 2006.

Lindberg, Carter. *Love: A Brief History Through Western Christianity*. Malden, MA: Blackwell, 2008.

———, ed. *The Pietist Theologians*. Malden, MA: Blackwell, 2005.

———. *The Third Reformation? Charismatic Movements and the Lutheran Tradition*. Macon: Mercer University Press, 1983.

Lißmann, Katja. "'. . . der Herr wird seine Herrlichkeit an uns offenbahren . . .' Die Eheschließung Anna Magdalena von Wurms und August Hermann Francke (1694)." In *"Der Herr wird seine Herrlichkeit an uns offenbahren": Liebe, Ehe und Sexualität im Pietismus*, edited by Wolfgang Breul and Christian Soboth, 145–63. Halle: Harrassowitz, 2011.

Lovelace, Richard. *The American Pietism of Cotton Mather*. Grand Rapids, MI: Eerdmans, 1979.

Luebke, David M., Jared Poley, Daniel C. Ryan, and David Warren Sabean, eds. *Conversion and the Politics of Religion in Early Modern Germany*. New York: Berghahn Books, 2012.

Mader, Eric-Oliver. "Conversion Concepts in Early Modern Germany: Protestant and Catholic." In Luebke et al., *Conversion and the Politics of Religion*, 31–48.

Mahlmann-Bauer, Barbara. "Zeugnisse frühneuzeitlichen Konvertierten—Definitionen, Klassifikation und Textanalysen." In *The Myth of the Reformation*, edited by Peter Opitz, 92–123. Göttingen: Vandenhoeck & Ruprecht, 2013.

Marschke, Benjamin. *Absolutely Pietist: Patronage, Factionalism, and State-Building in the Early Eighteenth-Century Prussian Army Chaplaincy*. Tübingen: Max Niemeyer, 2005.

———. "Halle Pietism and the Prussian State: Infiltration, Dissent, and Subversion." In *Pietism in Germany and North America, 1680–1820*, edited by Jonathan Strom, Hartmut Lehmann, and James Van Horn Melton, 217–28. Burlington, VT: Ashgate, 2009.

———. "Lutheran Jesuits: Halle Pietist Communication Networks at the Court of Frederick William I of Prussia." *Covenant Quarterly* 65, no. 4 (November 2006): 19–38.

———. "Mish-Mash with the Enemy: Identity, Politics, Power, and the Threat of Forced Conversion in Frederick William I's Prussia." In Luebke et al., *Conversion and the Politics of Religion*, 119–34.

———. "'Wir Hallenser': The Understanding of Insiders and Outsiders Among Halle Pietists in Prussia Under King Frederick William (1713–1740)." In *Pietism and Community in Europe and North America, 1650–1850*, edited by Jonathan Strom, 81–94. Leiden: Brill, 2010.

Marsden, George M. *Jonathan Edwards: A Life*. New Haven: Yale University Press, 2003.
Martin, Lucinda. "More Than Piety: The Historiographic Neglect of Early Modern Lay Theology." *Church History and Religious Culture* 98 (2018): 2–29.
Matthias, Markus. "August Hermann Francke (1663–1727)." In Lindberg, *The Pietist Theologians*, 100–114.
———. "Bekehrung und Wiedergeburt." In *Geschichte des Pietismus*, vol. 4, *Glaubenswelt und Lebenswelten*, edited by Hartmut Lehmann, 49–101. Göttingen: Vandenhoeck & Ruprecht, 2004.
———. "Franckes Erweckungserlebnis und sein Erzählung." In *Die Welt verändern: August Hermann Francke—Ein Lebenswerk um 1700*, edited by Holger Zaunstöck, Thomas Müller-Bahlke, and Claus Veltmann, 69–79. Halle: Verlag des Franckeschen Stiftungen zu Halle, 2013.
———. "Gewissheit und Bekehrung: Die Bedeutung der Theologie des Johannes Musaeus für August Hermann Francke." *PuN* 41 (2015): 11–31.
———. "Die Grundlegung der pietistischen Hermeneutik bei August Hermann Francke." In *Hermeneutik, Methodenlehre, Exegese: Zur Theorie der Interpretation in der Frühen Neuzeit*, edited by Günter Frank and Stephan Meier-Oeser, 189–202. Stuttgart-Bad Cannstatt: Frommann-Holzboog, 2011.
———. *Lebensläufe August Hermann Franckes*. Leipzig: Evangelische Verlagsanstalt, 1999.
———. "Ordo salutis—zur Geschichte eines dogmatischen Begriffs." *Zeitschrift für Kirchengeschichte* 115 (2004): 318–46.
———. "Pietism and Protestant Orthodoxy." In Shantz, *Companion to German Pietism*, 17–49.
———. "Rechtfertigung und Routine: Zum Verständis der Rechtfertigungslehre im lutherischen Pietismus." In *Reformation und Generalreformation—Luther und der Pietismus*, edited by Christian Soboth and Thomas Müller-Bahlke, 1–20. Halle: Verlag der Franckeschen Stiftungen Halle, 2012.
McGinn, Bernard. *The Harvest of Mysticism in Medieval Germany*. New York: Herder & Herder, 2005.
———. "Miguel de Molinos and the *Spiritual Guide*: A Theological Reappraisal." In Molinos, *The Spiritual Guide*, 21–39.
McGrath, Alister E. *Reformation Thought: An Introduction*. 2nd ed. Oxford: Blackwell, 1993.
McIntosh, Terence. "August Hermann Franckes Behandlung des Themas Kirchenzucht in seinem Collegium Pastorale." In Zaunstöck et al., *Hallesches Waisenhaus und Berliner Hof*, 125–36.
———. "Pietists, Jurists, and the Early Enlightenment Critique of Private Confession in Lutheran Germany." *Modern Intellectual History* 12, no. 3 (2015): 627–56.
———. "Das 'Werck der Christlichen Disciplin' Herzog Ernsts des Frommen: Inspiration für die Glauchaer Kirchenzucht August Hermann Franckes?" In *Pietismus in Thüringen—Pietismus aus Thüringen: Religiöse Reform im Mitteldeutschland des 17. und 18. Jahrhunderts*, edited by Veronika Albrecht-Birkner and Alexander Schunka, 51–69. Stuttgart: Franz Steiner Verlag, 2018.
Mentzer, Raymond A., ed. *Sin and the Calvinists: Morals Control and the Consistory in Reformed Tradition*. Kirksville: Truman State University Press, 2006.
Mori, Ryoko. *Begeisterung und Ernüchterung in christlicher Vollkommenheit: Pietistische Selbst- und Weltwahrnehmungen im ausgehenden 17. Jahrhundert*. Tübingen: Max Niemeyer, 2004.
———. "The Conventicle Piety of the Radicals." In Shantz, *Companion to German Pietism*, 201–24.
Müller, Gerhard, ed. *Theologische Realenzyklopädie*. 36 vols. Berlin: Walter de Gruyter, 1977–2004.
Müller-Bahlke, Thomas. "The Mission in India and the Worldwide Communication Network of the Halle Orphan-House." In *Halle and the Beginning of Protestant Christianity in India*,

edited by Andreas Gross, Y. Vincent Kumaradoss, and Heike Liebau, 1:57–78. 2 vols. Halle: Franckesche Stiftungen, 2006.

Murray, Iain H. *Revival and Revivalism: The Making and Marring of American Evangelicalism, 1750–1858*. Carlisle, PA: Banner of Truth, 1994.

Nagel, William. "Exorzismus III." In Müller, *Theologische Realenzyklopädie*, 10:753–56.

Neuß, Erich. "Das Glauchaische Elend 1692." In *August Hermann Francke: Das humanistische Erbe des großen Erziehers*, edited by Franz Hofmann, 19–27. Halle: VEB Druckerei der Werktätigen, 1965.

Nevin, John W. *Mystical Presence*. 1846. Reprint, Hamden, CT: Archon Books, 1963.

Nischan, Bodo. "The Exorcism Controversy and Baptism in the Later Reformation." *Sixteenth Century Journal* 18, no. 1 (1987): 31–50.

Obst, Helmut. *August Hermann Francke und die Franckeschen Stiftungen in Halle*. Göttingen: Vanderhoeck & Ruprecht, 2002.

———. "August Hermann Francke und die ökumenischen Dimensionen des Halleschen Pietismus." In *500 Jahre Theologie in Wittenberg und Halle 1502 bis 2002: Beiträge aus der Theologischen Fakultät der Martin-Luther-Universität Halle-Wittenberg zum Universitätsjubiläum*, edited by Arno Sames, 79–92. Leipzig: Evangelische Verlagsanstalt, 2003.

———. *August Hermann Francke und sein Werk*. Halle: Verlag der Franckeschen Stiftungen zu Halle, 2014.

———. *Der Berliner Beichtstuhlstreit: Die Kritik des Pietismus an der Beichtpraxis der Lutherischen Orthodoxie*. Witten: Luther-Verlag, 1972.

———. "Elemente atheistischer Anfechtung im pietistischen Bekehrungsprozeß." *PuN* 2 (1975): 33–42.

Orsi, Robert A. *History and Presence*. Cambridge: Harvard University Press, 2016.

Packer, J. I. *The Quest for Godliness: The Puritan Vision of the Godly Life*. Wheaton, IL: Crossway, 1990.

Pelikan, Jaroslav. *The Christian Tradition: A History of the Development of Doctrine*. Vol. 4, *Reformation of Church and Dogma (1300–1700)*. Chicago: University of Chicago Press, 1984.

———. *Spirit Versus Structure: Luther and the Institutions of the Church*. London: Collins, 1968.

Peschke, Erhard. "Die Abendmahlsanschauung August Hermann Franckes." In *Kirche-Theologie-Frömmigkeit: Festgabe für Gottfried Holtz zum 65. Geburtstag*, edited by Heinrich Benckett, 128–39. Berlin: Evangelische Verlagsanstalt, 1965.

———. "A. H. Franckes Reform des theologischen Studiums." In *August Hermann Francke: Festreden und Kolloquium über den Bildungs- und Erziehungsgedanken bei August Hermann Francke aus Anlaß der 300. Wiederkehr seines Geburtstages 22. März 1963*, edited by Burchard Thaler, 88–115. Leipzig: B. G. Teubner, 1964.

———. "August Hermann Francke und die Bibel." In *Pietismus und Bibel*, edited by Kurt Aland, 59–88. Witten: Luther-Verlag, 1970.

———. *Bekehrung und Reform, Ansatz und Wurzeln der Theologie August Hermann Franckes*. Bielefeld: Luther-Verlag, 1977.

———. "Die Collegium Pastorale August Hermann Franckes 1713." In *Reformation und Neuzeit: 300 Jahre Theologie in Halle*, edited by Udo Schnelle, 157–94. Berlin: Walter de Gruyter, 1994.

———. *Die frühen Katechismuspredigten August Hermann Franckes, 1693–1695*. Göttingen: Vandenhoeck & Ruprecht, 1992.

———. *Katalog der in der Universitäts- und Landesbibliothek Sachsen-Anhalt zu Halle (Saale) vorhandenen handschriftlichen und gedruckten Predigten August Hermann Franckes*. Halle (Saale): Universitäts- und Landesbibliothek Sachsen-Anhalt, 1972.

———. "Die Reformideen des Comenius und ihr Verhältnis zu A. H. Franckes Plan einer realen Verbesserung in der ganzen Welt." In *Der Pietismus in Gestalten und Wirkungen:*

Martin Schmidt zum 65. Geburtstag, edited by Heinrich Bornkamm, Friedrich Heyer, and Alfred Schindler, 368–82. Bielefeld: Luther-Verlag, 1975.

———. "Speners Wiedergeburtslehre und ihr Verhältnis zu Franckes Lehre von der Bekehrung." In *Traditio-Krisis-Renovatio aus theologischer Sicht: Festschrift Winfried Zeller zum 65. Geburtstag*, edited by Bernd Jaspert and Rudolf Mohr, 206–24. Marburg: N. G. Elwert Verlag, 1976.

———. *Studien zur Theologie August Hermann Franckes*. 2 vols. Berlin: Evangelische Verlagsanstalt, 1964–66.

———. "Die Theologie August Hermann Franckes." In *August Hermann Francke: Wort und Tat: Ansprachen und Vorträge zur dreihundertsten Wiederkehr seines Geburtstages*, edited by Dietrich Jungklaus, 42–61. Berlin: Evangelische Verlagsanstalt, 1966.

———. "Die theologischen Voraussetzungen der universalen Reformpläne A. H. Franckes." In *Wort und Gemeinde: Festschrift für Erdmann Schott zum 65. Geburtstag*, edited by Heinrich Benckert, 97–111. Berlin: Evangelische Verlagsanstalt, 1967.

Pitkin, Barbara. *What Pure Eyes Could See: Calvin's Doctrine of Faith in Its Exegetical Context*. New York: Oxford University Press, 1999.

Pless, John T. "Liturgy and Pietism, Then and Now." *Logia: A Journal of Lutheran Theology* 8, no. 4 (1999): 19–27.

Pohl, Mirjam-Juliane. "Hallesche Wahrheitszeugen in Brecklings Gothaer Catalogus testium veritatis." In *Friedrich Breckling (1629–1711): Prediger, 'Wahrheitszeuge' und Vermittler des Pietismus im Niederländischen Exil*, edited by Brigitte Klosterberg and Guido Naschert, 41–48. Halle: Verlag der Franckeschen Stiftungen zu Halle, 2011.

Pollmann, Judith. "A Different Road to God: The Protestant Experience of Conversion in the Sixteenth Century." In *Conversion to Modernities: The Globalization of Christianity*, edited by Peter van der Veer, 47–64. New York: Routledge, 1996.

Preus, Robert D. *The Theology of Post-Reformation Lutheranism*. 2 vols. Saint Louis: Concordia, 1970/1972.

Prodi, Paolo. *Der Eid in der europäischen Verfassungsgeschichte*. Schriften des Historischen Kollegs, Vorträge 33, 5–35. Munich, 1992.

Ritschl, Albrecht. *Geschichte des Pietismus*. 3 vols. Bonn: Adolph Marchus, 1880–86.

———. *Three Essays*. Translated by Philip Hefner. Philadelphia: Fortress Press, 1972.

Rittgers, Ronald K. "Embracing the 'True Relic' of Christ: Suffering, Penance, and Private Confession in the Thought of Martin Luther." In *A New History of Penance*, edited by Abigail Firey, 377–93. Leiden: Brill, 2008.

Roeber, A. G. "The Waters of Rebirth: The Eighteenth Century and Transoceanic Protestant Christianity." *Church History* 79, no. 1 (March 2010): 40–76.

Roth, Alfred. *August Hermann Francke, einer, der Gott vertraute*. Neumünster: Christophorus, 1932.

Rublack, Hans-Christoph. "Lutherische Beichte und Sozialdisziplinierung." *Archiv für Reformationsgeschichte* 84 (1993): 127–55.

Rüttgardt, Jan Olaf. "Zur Entstehung und Bedeutung der Berliner Wiedergeburtspredigten Philipp Jakob Speners." In Philipp Jakob Spener, *Schriften*, edited by Erich Beyreuther, 7:1–112. Hildesheim: Georg Olms, 1994.

Ryken, Philip Graham. "Thomas Boston as Pastor Theologian." In *Becoming a Pastor Theologian: New Possibilities for Church Leadership*, edited by Todd Wilson and Gerald Hiestand, 93–107. Downers Grove, IL: InterVarsity Press, 2016.

Sames, Arno. *Anton Wilhelm Böhme (1673–1722): Studien zum ökumenischen Denken und Handeln eines halleschen Pietisten*. Göttingen: Vandenhoeck & Ruprecht, 1990.

Sattler, Gary R. "August Hermann Francke and Mysticism." *Covenant Quarterly* 38, no. 4 (1980): 3–17.

———. *God's Glory, Neighbor's Good: A Brief Introduction to the Life and Writings of August Hermann Francke*. Chicago: Covenant, 1982.

———. *Nobler Than the Angels, Lower Than a Worm: The Pietist View of the Individual in the Writings of Heinrich Müller and August Hermann Francke*. Lanham, MD: University Press of America, 1989.

Scaer, David P. "Johann Gerhard's Doctrine of the Sacraments." In *Protestant Scholasticism: Essays in Reassessment*, edited by R. Scott Clark and Carl R. Trueman, 289–306. Carlisle: Paternoster Press, 1999.

Schäufele, Wolf-Friedrich. "Taufe und Wiedergeburt bei Johann Konrad Dippel." In *Alter Adam und Neue Kreatur: Pietismus und Anthropologie*, edited by Udo Sträter, 219–28. Halle: Verlag der Franckeschen Stiftungen, 2009.

Schicketanz, Peter. *Der Briefwechsel Carl Hildebrand von Cansteins mit August Hermann Francke*. Berlin: Walter de Gruyter, 1972.

———. *Carl Hildebrand Freiherr von Canstein: Leben und Denken in Quellendarstellungen*. Tübingen: Max Niemeyer, 2002.

———. *Der Pietismus von 1675 bis 1800*. Leipzig: Evangelische Verlagsanstalt, 2001.

Schleiermacher, Friedrich. *The Christian Faith*. Edinburgh: T&T Clark, 1956.

Schmidt, Martin. "Atheismus." I/2. In Müller, *Theologische Realenzyklopädie*, 4:351–64.

———. "Biblizismus und natürliche Theologie in der Gewissenslehre des englischen Puritanismus, Zweiter Teil." *Archiv für Reformationsgeschichte* 43, no. 1 (1952): 70–87.

———. "Großgebauer, Theophil." In *Neue Deutsche Biographie*, 7:153. 28 vols. Historische Kommission bei der Bayerischen Akademie der Wissenschaften. Berlin: Duncker & Humblot, 1953–2008.

———. *Der Pietismus als Theologische Erscheinung*. Göttingen: Vandenhoeck & Ruprecht, 1984.

———. *Wiedergeburt und neuer Mensch*. Witten: Luther-Verlag, 1969.

Schmidt, Martin, and Wilhelm Jannasch, eds. *Das Zeitalter des Pietismus*. Bremen: Carl Schünemann, 1965.

Schneider, Hans. "Die evangelischen Kirchen." In *Ökumenische Kirchengeschichte*. Vol. 3, *Neuzeit*, edited by Raymund Kottje and Bernd Moeller, 46–99. Mainz: Kaiser-Grünewald, 1989.

———. *German Radical Pietism*. Translated by Gerald MacDonald. Lanham, MD: Scarecrow Press, 2007.

———. "Understanding the Church: Issues of Pietist Ecclesiology." In *Pietism and Community in Europe and North America, 1650–1850*, edited by Jonathan Strom, 15–36. Leiden: Brill, 2010.

Schneider, Max. "Die Lehrer des Gymnasium Illustre zu Gotha (1524–1859) (Ein biographisch-bibliographischer Beitrag zur Geschichte des Gymnasiums)." In *Gotha, Gymnasium, Schulprogramm*, 1–24. Gotha: Engelhard-Reyher, 1901. [Forschungsbibliothek Gotha signature: Goth. 4°. 56ª/2a]

———. "Neues zu August Hermann Franckes Schulleben auf dem Gymnasium Illustre zu Gotha 1677." *Mitteilungen der Gesellschaft für Erziehungs- und Schulgeschichte* 3 (1904): 238–41.

Schrenk, Gottlob. *Gottesreich und Bund im älteren Protestantismus vornehmlich bei Johannes Coccejus: Ein Beitrag zur Geschichte des Pietismus und der heilsgeschichtlichen Theologie*. Reprint, Giessen: Brunnen Verlag, 1985.

Schunka, Alexander. "Irenicism and the Challenges of Conversion in the Early Eighteenth Century." In Luebke et al., *Conversion and the Politics of Religion*, 101–18.

———. "Protestanten in Schlesien im 17. und 18. Jahrhundert." In *Geheimprotestantismus und evangelische Kirchen in der Habsburgermonarchie und im Erzstift Salzburg (17./18. Jahrhundert)*, edited by Rudolf Leeb, Martin Scheutz, and Dietmar Weikl, 271–97. Munich: Oldenbourg, 2009.

———. "Zwischen Kontingenz und Providenz: Frühe Englandkontakte der halleschen Pietisten und protestantische Irenik um 1700." *PuN* 34 (2008): 82–114.

Schuster, Susanne. "Johann Benedikt Carpzov und August Hermann Francke: 'Orthodoxe' und 'pietistische' Grenzziehungen im Zusammenhang der 'Leipziger Unruhen.'" In *Eruditio—Confessio—Pietas: Kontinuität und Wandel in der lutherischen Konfessionskultur am Ende des 17. Jahrhunderts; Das Beispiel Johann Benedikt Carpzovs (1639–1699)*, edited by Stefan Michel and Andres Straßberger, 183–202. Leipzig: Evangelische Verlagsanstalt, 2009.

Shantz, Douglas H. *Between Sardis and Philadelphia: The Life and World of Pietist Court Preacher Conrad Broske*. Leiden: Brill, 2008.

———. "Christian Community in German Pietism: Gottfried Arnold and Johanna Eleonora Petersen on the Church, with Special Attention to the Place of Women." In *Ecclesia semper reformanda est: A Festschrift on Ecclesiology in Honour of Stanley K. Fowler on His Seventieth Birthday*, edited by David G. Barker, Michael A. G. Haykin, and Barry H. Howson, 213–33. Kitchener, ON: Joshua Press, 2016.

———, ed. *A Companion to German Pietism, 1660–1800*. Leiden: Brill, 2015.

———. *Crautwald and Erasmus: A Study in Humanism and Radical Reform in Sixteenth Century Silesia*. Baden-Baden: Valentin Koerner, 1992.

———. *An Introduction to German Pietism: Protestant Renewal at the Dawn of Modern Europe*. Baltimore: Johns Hopkins University Press, 2013.

———. "The Origin of Pietist Notions of New Birth and the New Man: Alchemy and Alchemists in Gottfried Arnold and Johann Henrich Reitz." In Collins-Winn et al., *Pietist Impulse*, 29–41.

Spankeren, Malte van. "Das Ende des Pietismus in Halle." In Beutel and Nooke, *Religion und Aufklärung*, 605–21.

Spehr, Christopher. "Gelehrte Buchkritik: Der Beginn der theologischen Rezensionsjournale im 18. Jahrhundert." In Beutel and Nooke, *Religion und Aufklärung*, 269–84.

Spinks, Bryan. "Luther's Timely Theology of Unilateral Baptism." *Lutheran Quarterly* 9, no. 1 (Spring 1995): 23–45.

Stahl, Herbert. *August Hermann Francke, der Einfluss Luthers und Molinos auf Ihn*. Stuttgart: W. Kohlhammer, 1939.

Stein, Armin. *August Hermann Francke: Zeit- und Lebensbild aus der Periode des deutschen Pietismus*. Halle: Buchhandlung des Waisenhauses, 1885.

Stein, K. James. *Philip Jakob Spener: Pietist Patriarch*. Chicago: Covenant, 1986.

Stephens, W. P. *Zwingli: An Introduction to His Thought*. Oxford: Clarendon Press, 1992.

Stoeffler, F. Ernest, ed. *Continental Pietism and Early American Christianity*. Grand Rapids, MI: Eerdmans, 1976.

———. *German Pietism During the Eighteenth Century*. Leiden: E. J. Brill, 1973.

———. *The Rise of Evangelical Pietism*. Leiden: E. J. Brill, 1965.

Stolt, Birgit. *Martin Luthers Rhetorik des Herzens*. Tübingen: J. C. B. Mohr, 2000.

Sträter, Udo. "Aufklärung und Pietismus—das Beispiel Halle." In *Universitäten und Aufklärung*, edited by Notker Hammerstein, 49–61. Göttingen: Wallstein Verlag, 1995.

———. "August Hermann Francke und Martin Luther." *PuN* 34 (2008): 20–41.

———. "Gotthilf August Francke, der Sohn und Erbe: Annäherung an einen Unbekannten." In *Reformation und Neuzeit: 300 Jahre Theologie in Halle*, edited by Udo Schnelle, 211–34. Berlin: Walter de Gruyter, 1994.

———. *Meditation und Kirchenreform in der lutherischen Kirche des 17. Jahrhunderts*. Tübingen: Mohr Siebeck, 1995.

———. *Sonthom, Bayly, Dyke und Hall: Studien zur Rezeption der englischen Erbauungsliteratur in Deutschland im 17. Jahrhundert*. Tübingen: J. C. B. Mohr, 1987.

———. "Spener und August Hermann Francke." In *Philipp Jakob Spener—Leben, Werk, Bedeutung: Bilanz der Forschung nach 300 Jahren*, edited by Dorothea Wendebourg, 89–104. Halle: Verlag der Franckeschen Stiftungen, 2007.

Strom, Jonathan. "The Common Priesthood and the Pietist Challenge for Ministry and Laity." In Collins-Winn et al., *Pietist Impulse*, 42–58.
———. "Early Conventicles in Lübeck." *PuN* 27 (2001): 19–52.
———. *German Pietism and the Problem of Conversion*. University Park: Pennsylvania State University Press, 2017.
———. *Orthodoxy and Reform: The Clergy in Seventeenth Century Rostock*. Tübingen: Mohr Siebeck, 1999.
———. "Pietism." In Wengert, *Dictionary of Luther and the Lutheran Traditions*, 600–603.
———. "Pietism and Conversion in Dargun." *PuN* 39 (2013): 150–92.
———. "Pietism and Revival." In *Preaching, Sermon and Cultural Change in the Long Eighteenth Century*, edited by Joris van Eijnatten, 173–218. Leiden: Brill, 2009.
———. "Pietist Experiences and Narratives of Conversion." In Shantz, *Companion to German Pietism*, 293–318.
———."Problems and Promises of Pietism Research." *Church History* 71, no. 3 (September 2002): 536–54.
Strom, Jonathan, and Hartmut Lehmann. "Early Modern Pietism." In *The Oxford Handbook of Early Modern Theology, 1600–1800*, edited by Ulrich L. Lehner, Richard A. Muller, and A. G. Roeber, 402–35. New York: Oxford University Press, 2016.
Swain, Scott R. "Lutheran and Reformed Sacramental Theolology: Seventeenth–Nineteenth Centuries." In *The Oxford Handbook of Sacramental Theology*, edited by Hans Boersma and Matthew Levering, 366–79. Oxford: Oxford University Press, 2015.
Swensson, Eric Jonas. *Kinderbeten: The Origin, Unfolding, and Interpretations of the Silesian Children's Prayer Revival*. Eugene, OR: Wipf and Stock, 2009.
Taatz-Jacobi, Marianne. "Ein prekäres Beschäftigungsverhältnis—eine neue Sicht auf August Hermann Franckes Berufung und sein erstes Jahr in Halle 1691/92." In Zaunstöck et al., *Hallesches Waisenhaus und Berliner Hof*, 3–18.
Trueman, Carl. "Lewis Bayly (d. 1631) and Richard Baxter (1615–1691)." In Lindberg, *The Pietist Theologians*, 52–67.
Tuttle, Robert G., Jr. *John Wesley, His Life and Theology*. Grand Rapids, MI: Zondervan, 1978.
Untermöhlen, Gerda. "Die Rußlandthematik im Briefwechsel zwischen August Hermann Francke und Gottfried Wilhelm Leibnitz." In *Halle und Osteuropa: Zur europäischen Ausstrahlung des hallischen Pietismus*, edited by Johannes Wallmann and Udo Sträter, 109–28. Halle: Verlag der Franckeschen Stiftungen, 1998.
Vanhoozer, Kevin J., and Owen Strachan. *The Pastor as Public Theologian: Reclaiming a Lost Vision*. Grand Rapids, MI: Baker, 2015.
Venables, Mary Noll. "Pietist Fruits from Orthodox Seeds: The Case of Ernst the Pious of Saxe-Gotha-Altenburg." In Lieburg, *Confessionalism and Pietism*, 91–110.
Vogt, Peter. "In Search of the Invisible Church: The Role of Autobiographical Discourse in Eighteenth-Century German Pietism." In Lieburg, *Confessionalism and Pietism*, 293–312.
Wagenmann, Julius August. "Carpzov, Joh. Benedict II." In *Allgemeine deutsche Biographie*, 4:21–22. Historische Commission bei der Königl. Akademie der Wissenschaften. Berlin: Duncker & Humbolt, 1968.
Wagner, Falk. "Bekehrung II." In Müller, *Theologische Realenzyklopädie*, 5:459–63.
Wallmann, Johannes. "Die Anfänge des Pietismus." *PuN* 4 (1977/1978): 11–53.
———. "Eine alternative Geschichte des Pietismus: Zur gegenwärtigen Diskussion um den Pietismusbegriff." *PuN* 28 (2002): 30–71.
———. "Erfurt und der Pietismus im 17. Jahrhundert." In *Erfurt 742–1992: Stadtgeschichte—Universitätsgeschichte*, edited by Ulman Weiß, 403–22. Weimar: Verlag Hermann Blaus Nachfolger, 1992.
———. "Kirchlicher und radikaler Pietismus: Zu einer kirchengeschichtlichen Grunduterscheidung." In *Der radikale Pietismus: Perspektiven der Forschung*, edited by Wolfgang Breul, Marcus Meier, and Lothar Vogel, 19–43. Göttingen: Vandenhoeck & Ruprecht, 2010.

---. "Labadismus und Pietismus: Die Einflüsse des niederländischen Pietismus auf die Entstehung des Pietismus in Deutschland." In *Theologie und Frömmigkeit im Zeitalter des Barock: Gesammelte Aufsätze*, edited by Johannes Wallmann, 171–96. Tübingen: J. C. B. Mohr, 1995.

---. "Das Melanchthonbild im kirchlichen und im radikalen Pietismus." In *Pietismus-Studien: Gesammelte Aufsätze II*, 168–81. Tübingen: Mohr Siebeck, 2008.

---. "Die Nadere Reformatie und der deutsche Pietismus." In *Pietismus und Orthodoxie: Gesammelte Aufsätze III*, 406–26. Tübingen: Mohr Siebeck, 2010.

---. *Philipp Jakob Spener und die Anfänge des Pietismus*. Tübingen: J. C. B. Mohr, 1986.

---. *Der Pietismus*. Rev. ed. Göttingen: Vandenhoeck & Ruprecht, 2005.

---. "Pietismus und Orthodoxie: Überlegungen und Fragen zur Pietismusforschung." In Greschat, *Zur Neueren Pietismusforschung*, 53–81.

---. "Prolegomena zur Erforschung der Predigt im Zeitalter der lutherischen Orthodoxie." *Zeitschrift für Theologie und Kirche* 106, no. 3 (2009): 284–304.

---. "Was ist Pietismus?" *PuN* 20 (1994): 11–27.

---. "Wiedergeburt und Erneuerung bei Philipp Jakob Spener." *PuN* 3 (1977): 7–31.

Ward, W. R. *Early Evangelicalism: A Global Intellectual History, 1670–1789*. New York: Cambridge University Press, 2006.

---. "The Eighteenth-Century Church: A European View." In *The Church of England, c. 1689–c. 1833: From Toleration to Tractarianism*, edited by John Walsh, Colin Haydon, and Stephen Taylor, 285–98. Cambridge: Cambridge University Press, 1993.

---. "Evangelical Identity in the Eighteenth Century." In *Christianity Reborn: The Global Expansion of Evangelicalism in the Twentieth Century*, edited by Donald M. Lewis, 11–30. Grand Rapids, MI: Eerdmans, 2004.

---. *Protestant Evangelical Awakening*. New York: Cambridge University Press, 2002.

Weber, Max. *The Protestant Ethic and the Spirit of Capitalism*. New York: Charles Scribner's Sons, 1958.

Weigelt, Horst. *Pietismus-Studien*. Vol. 1, *Der spener-hallische Pietismus*. Stuttgart: Calwer, 1965.

Weiske, Karl. *August Hermann Francke als Philologe: Seine Führung durch die Philologie zur Theologie*. Halle: Buchhandlung des Waisenhauses, 1927.

---. *August Hermann Franckes Pädagogik*. Halle (Saale): Buchhandlung des Waisenhauses, 1927.

Wengert, Timothy J., ed. *Dictionary of Luther and the Lutheran Traditions*. Grand Rapids, MI: Baker, 2017.

Weyer, Adam. "Gewissen IV." In Müller, *Theologische Realenzyklopädie*, 12:225–34.

Whitmer, Kelly Joan. "Eclecticism and the Technologies of Discernment in Pietist Pedagogy." *Journal of the History of Ideas* 70, no. 4 (2009): 545–67.

---. *The Halle Orphanage as Scientific Community: Observation, Eclecticism, and Pietism in the Early Enlightenment*. Chicago: University of Chicago Press, 2015.

Wiggin, Bethany. "The Geography of Fashionability: Drinking Coffee in Eighteenth-Century Leipzig." *Seminar: A Journal of Germanic Studies* 46, no. 4 (2010): 315–29.

Wilken, Robert Louis. *The First Thousand Years: A Global History of Christianity*. New Haven: Yale University Press, 2012.

Willimon, William H. *Word, Water, Wine and Bread*. Valley Forge, PA: Judson Press, 1980.

Wilson, Renate. "Heinrich Wilhelm Ludolf, August Hermann Francke und der Eingang nach Rußland." In *Halle und Osteuropa: Zur europäischen Ausstrahlung des hallischen Pietismus*, edited by Johannes Wallmann and Udo Sträter, 83–108. Halle: Verlag der Franckeschen Stiftungen, 1998.

---. *Pious Traders in Medicine: A German Pharmaceutical Network in Eighteenth-Century North America*. University Park: Pennsylvania State University Press, 2000.

Winiarski, Douglas L. *Darkness Falls on the Land of Light: Experiencing Religious Awakenings in Eighteenth-Century New England*. Chapel Hill: University of North Carolina Press, 2017.

Witt, Ulrike. *Bekehrung, Bildung, und Biographie: Frauen im Umkreis des Halleschen Pietismus.* Halle: Verlag der Franckeschen Stiftungen, 1996.

Witte, John, Jr. *From Sacrament to Contract: Marriage, Religion, and Law in the Western Tradition.* Louisville, KY: Westminster John Knox, 1997.

Wood, Laurence W. "The Origin, Development, and Consistency of John Wesley's Theology of Holiness." *Wesleyan Theological Journal* 43, no. 2 (2008): 33–55.

Worthen, Molly. *Apostles of Reason: The Crisis of Authority in American Evangelicalism.* New York: Oxford University Press, 2014.

Wustmann, Claudia. *Die "begeisterten Mägde": Mitteldeutsche Prophetinnen im Radikalpietismus am Ende des 17. Jahrhunderts.* Leipzig: Kirchhof & Franke, 2008.

Yoder, Peter James. "The Economics of the Unconverted: Idolatry, Greed, and Theft in August Hermann Francke's Theology of Wealth." In *Pietismus und Ökonomie (1650–1750)*, edited by Alexander Schunka, Wolfgang Breul, and Benjamin Marschke. Göttingen: Vandenhoeck & Ruprecht, forthcoming.

———. "Francke, August Hermann." In Wengert, *Dictionary of Luther and the Lutheran Traditions*, 264–65.

———. "Francke, Gotthilf August." In Wengert, *Dictionary of Luther and the Lutheran Traditions*, 265–66.

———. "Hildebrand, Carl (Baron von Canstein)." In Wengert, *Dictionary of Luther and the Lutheran Traditions*, 326.

———. "'Königtum' und militärische Bilder in der Theologie August Hermann Franckes." In Zaunstöck et al., *Hallesches Waisenhaus und Berliner Hof*, 153–66.

———. "Pietas et Apologia: August Hermann Francke's 1689 *Defensions-Schrift* and the attack of Pietism." In *Verteidigung als Angriff: Apologie und* Vindicatio *als Möglichkeiten der Positionierung im gelehrten Diskurs*, edited by Michael Multhammer, 121–43. Berlin: De Gruyter, 2015.

———. "Rendered 'Odious' as Pietists: Anton Wilhelm Böhme's Conception of Pietism and the Possibilities of Prototype Theory." In Collins-Winn et al., *Pietist Impulse*, 17–26.

———. "'Temples in the Hearts of Heathens': Post-Contact Developments in August Hermann Francke's Theological Language." In *European Missions in Contact Zones: Transformation Through Interaction in a (Post-)Colonial World*, edited by Judith Becker, 179–94. Göttingen: Vandenhoeck & Ruprecht, 2015.

Zaunstöck, Holger, Brigitte Klosterberg, Christian Soboth, and Benjamin Marschke, eds. *Hallesches Waisenhaus und Berliner Hof: Beiträge zum Verhältnis von Pietismus und Preußen.* Halle: Verlag der Franckeschen Stiftungen, 2017.

INDEX

Endnotes are referenced with "n" followed by the endnote number.

Abraham, 87, 91, 98, 121, 170n12
absolution, 9, 32–33, 103, 105–17, 121
Adam
   baptism and the new, 78
   Christ as new or second, 76
   old, 78, 96
   sin of, 90, 127
adiaphora, 33, 99, 107
Aland, Kurt, 104
Albrecht-Birkner, Veronika, 2, 15–16, 31, 33, 109, 148
alchemy, 172n97
American Lutheranism. *See* Lutheranism
Anabaptist thought/Anabaptism, 25, 69, 99
Anfechtung. *See* trial(s), spiritual
Anton, Paul, 13, 17, 21, 41
Apostles, 77–78, 124
Apostles' Creed, 140
Arian heresy, 26
Aristotle, 53
Arndt, Johann, 4–6, 14, 46, 56, 90–91, 101, 133
Ascension. *See* Jesus Christ
Asia, east, 79
assurance of salvation. *See* salvation
atheism, 14, 53–57, 59, 63
atheist, 52, 58, 70, 122
Augsburg Confession, 2
Augustinerkirche
   in Erfurt, 22–24, 27
   in Gotha, 28
Awakening, Great, 148, 153n47
Awakening, Second Great, 147

Baier, Johann Wilhelm, 22
Balduinus, Friedrich, 61
baptism of the heart. *See* heart
Barfüßerkirche, 24
Basel, 67
Baxter, Richard, 61
Bayer, Oswald, 147
Bayly, Lewis, 61, 63, 66–69

begeisterte Mägde. *See* ecstatics, female
Beichtgeld. *See* offering, confessional
Bekehrung. *See* conversion
Berlin, 28, 35, 103, 107–9
Beyreuther, Eric, 2, 15, 23, 41, 57
Bible. *See* Scripture
biblicism of the heart. *See* heart
blessedness of God, 73, 93
Böhme, Anton Wilhelm, 21, 57, 79
Born, Martin, 18–19
breakthrough, 14, 16, 82
Breckling, Friedrich, 48
Breithaupt, Joachim Justus, 22–26, 29–30, 33–34, 49, 57
bride (as sign), 119, 127, 132–34
Buße. *See* repentance
Bußkampf (repentance struggle), 131–32
   conversion and, 44
   mysticism and, 134
   worship and, 143
   See also trial(s), spiritual
Bußtränen. *See* tears.

Calvin, John, 62
Calvinism (as theological system), 6, 61–62
   crypto-Calvinist, 100
   or Reformed theology, 2, 5, 41, 61–62, 98, 103, 108, 146, 148
Campbell, Ted, 7
Canstein, Carl Hildebrand von, 42
Canstein Bible Institute, 42, 81
Care, Andreas, 16, 55
Carpzov, Johann Benedict, 18–21, 25
catechism. *See* Small Catechism
   See also Large Catechism
catechization, 24, 27, 47, 125–26
Catholic(s), Catholicism, 5, 24, 26, 45, 68, 103–4
Chemnitz, Martin, 84–85
child(ren)
   baptismal covenant and, 82, 86, 89
   catechizing of (*see* catechization)

child(ren) *(continued)*
  confession and, 112
  the Eucharist and, 125
  Francke as, 23, 41
  Francke's instruction of, 15, 23–24, 42, 71, 139
  of God, 6–7, 41, 45, 73, 82, 84, 91, 94–95, 129, 143
  Pietist involvement of women and, 26–27
  renewal of the church and, 15, 71
  self-examination and, 113
  Timothy as biblical example, 38
  of the world, 41, 45, 95, 122
chiliasm, 4, 6–7, 30, 48
China, 79
Christenstaat, 22
church
  as body of Christ, 30, 147
  as bride, 41, 56
  as community of gifts, 139, 141
  as communion of saints, 140
  corporate worship of, 141–46
  as corpus permixtum, 145
  as decadent or corrupt, 4, 6, 39, 44, 47, 92, 97, 136–37
  discipline and *(see* discipline, church*)*
  early church, 26–27, 65, 106
  ecclesiola in ecclesia and *(see* conventicles*)*
  of the heart, 3, 9, 137–38, 140
  as hierarchical institution, 19–20, 48
  of the Holy Spirit, 137
  house churches, 139–40
  Lutheran *(see* Lutheranism*)*
  marks of, 147
  membership through baptism, 73, 96
  renewal and reform of, 9, 15, 18, 20, 22, 71, 106, 138, 145, 148
  the resurrection and, 77–78
  role of sacraments and, 3
  and suffering and tribulation, 77–78
  three estates doctrine and, 4
church discipline. *See* discipline, church
circumcision
  of the heart, 98
  Jewish practice of, 83, 86, 91, 98, 121
Coburg, 28
Coccejus, Johannes, 41
collegia pietatis. *See* conventicles
collegium exegeticum, 28
collegium philobiblicum, 13, 17, 107
Comenius, Johann Amos, 47
comfort, 9, 32, 45, 54, 56, 59, 79, 86–87, 89–92, 94
common priesthood. *See* priesthood of all believers

confession, auricular, 104
confessional formula(s). *See* formula(s), confessional
confessional offering. *See* offering, confessional
confessionalization, 99
conscience
  baptismal covenant and, 87, 90–91
  confession and, 104, 107–8
  the Eucharist and, 124, 127, 129–30
  the knowledge of God and, 59–63
consummation, 7, 77
conventicle(s), 15, 18–27, 30–32, 34, 42, 48, 49, 51, 69, 126–27, 139–40
  as characteristic of Pietism, 4–5
  ecclesiola in ecclesia, 5
  Schade and, 107
conversion
  baptism and, 98–99
  baptismal exorcism and *(see* exorcism, baptismal*)*
  chiliasm and, 7
  confessional formulas and, 111–12
  dating of, 129
  Francke's theology of, 42–45
  of Francke, Gotthilf August, 81–82, 101–2
  heart and *(see* heart*)*
  of Luther, 61
  Musaeus's theology of, 43
  rebirth and *(see* rebirth*)*
  signs of worthiness and, 119
  tears and, 129–30
  worship and, 137, 142–45
corpus permixtum. *See* church
covenant, baptismal, 66, 73
  and Gnadenbund, 84–85
  two sides of (bilateral), 83–86
creation, new. *See* rebirth
  cross (of Christ), 39–40, 76, 89, 94–95, 124, 130, 141
  baptism of, 77
  day of the, 144

Danckelmann, Eberhard von, 28
Denmark, 28
denominationalism, 9, 148
Deppermann, Andreas, 4
Detharding, Georg, 120
Devil. *See* Satan
devotional literature. *See* literature, devotional
discipleship, 131, 144
discipline, church
  the Eucharist and, 31–35
  confession and, 106–9, 113–14
Donatism, 19

doubt. *See* trial(s), spiritual
Dresden, 17, 19, 34, 107
drunkenness/drinking alcohol, 21, 31–33
Durchbruch. *See* breakthrough
Dyke, Daniel, 61
Dyke, Jeremy, 61

ecclesiola in ecclesia. *See* conventicle(s)
ecclesiology, 2–3, 145–47
ecstatics, female, 34
ecumenism, 79
education, 14, 19, 37, 38, 46–47, 68, 71, 79, 125
   See also catechization
Edwards, Jonathan, 153n47
Edzardus, Esdras, 12, 17, 21, 26
Eid. *See* oath
Elers, Heinrich Julius, 55
emotion, 18, 43, 128
   See also tears
England, 67, 69, 79
enlightenment, 41, 58
Enlightenment, the, 2
enthusiast, 25, 68
   See also Schwärmer.
Epicurean (as sign), 119, 122–26, 134
epistemology, 50, 52–54, 57–58
Erfurt, 12, 14, 22–29, 31, 42, 49, 50, 56
Erweckung. *See* revival
eschatology, 7, 48, 77
   See also chiliasm
eternal life. *See* salvation
Europe, eastern, 3, 79
evangelicalism, 3, 9, 139
ex opere operato. *See* sacraments
exegesis, biblical. *See* Scripture
exorcism, baptismal, 100
experimentalism, 6

faith
   at baptism, 100
   baptismal covenant and, 85, 88
   confessional and, 108, 111–12, 146
   conventicles and, 27
   conscience and, 58–60, 62
   the cross and, 33
   dead, 48
   delusional or historical, 95, 97
   education and, 37
   Francke's crisis of, 14, 54
   heart and (*see* heart)
   Musaeus and, 43
   justification by (*see* justification)
   living, 17, 21–22, 42, 141–42
   morality and, 18
   reason and, 54
   rebirth and, 94–95
   repentance and, 43–44, 143
   Scripture and, 38–40, 79–80
   Spener and, 4
   true, 23, 45, 57, 83, 136
   visible signs of, 121
   weak, 128
   worship and, 143–44
fallenness. *See* nature, fallen human
fasting, 20
Father, God the, 72–78, 84, 123, 128
fear
   Angst-Kampff, 131
   atheism and, 56
   confession and, 104–5, 111, 115
   conscience and, 59, 129
   of God, 25, 43, 133
   preaching of God's Word and, 142
   spiritual trials and, 91
formula(s), confessional, 103, 105, 107, 110–17
Foundations, Francke. *See* Franckesche Stiftungen
Fox, George, 69
Francke, August Hermann
   and atheism, 53–56
   conversion experience of, 14–15, 37, 41, 42–45
   as theologian of the heart, 99
Francke, Gotthilf August, 67, 81–82, 101
Franckesche Stiftungen, 3, 7, 24, 42, 48, 61, 78–79, 82, 115, 145
Frankfurt, 4, 5, 20, 22, 107
Freylinghausen, Johann Anastasius, 24, 100
Friedrich August I, Elector of Saxony, 13
Frömmigkeit. *See* godliness
fruit, spiritual. *See* godliness
Fuchs, Paul von, 28

Gedächtnis. *See* memorial
Gelassenheit, 134
Georgenkirche, St., 12, 28, 29, 31–32, 48, 49, 105
Gerhard, Johann, 65, 84–85
Gettysburg, 147
Glaucha, 28–35
Glauchasche Anstalten. *See* Franckesche Stiftungen
Gnadenbund. *See* covenant, baptismal
God the Father, 74–78, 84, 123, 128
godliness. *See* sanctification
Goodwin, Thomas, 61
Gordon, James R., 3
gospel, 4, 9, 38, 45, 47, 69, 77, 78, 85, 91, 93, 104, 114
   See also hermeneutic, law-gospel

Gotha, 22, 28, 29, 36, 42, 159n4
grace, 2, 14, 16, 23, 32, 35, 38, 39, 49, 51, 53, 56, 57, 60
grace, God's application of, 57
Greek, 11, 28, 36, 41, 99,
  Großgebauer, Theophil, 2, 8, 46, 56–57, 67, 98–101, 106–7, 117, 146

Hall, Joseph, 61
Halle (Saale), 3, 12, 14, 25, 28–35, 36, 38, 42, 48, 49, 50, 71, 81, 114, 129, 145
Hallesche Waisenhaus. *See* Franckesche Stiftungen
Hamburg, 12, 15–17, 20, 25–27
Hardt, Hermann von der, 11, 15
heart
  atheism and, 53–54
  baptism of the, 87, 98–99, 101
  baptismal covenant and, 86–89
  biblicism of the, 38–42, 46, 80, 137, 145
  bride-hearts, 133
  Bußkampf and (*see* Bußkampf)
  confession and, 105, 110–15, 117, 146
  conscience and, 62, 87
  conversion and, 37, 88, 94, 99, 143
  emotions and, 91, 124, 128
  empowerment and, 90, 93–95
  the Eucharist and, 134
  exorcism and (*see* exorcism, baptismal)
  faith and, 85, 94
  indwelling of God, 75, 88, 97, 138
  law and, 43, 58–59
  love and, 133
  mind (head) and, 18, 126, 136
  prayer and, 39
  rebirth and, 27, 94–96, 99, 119, 122, 141
  religion of the, 7
  repentance, 44
  ritual (practice) and, 91, 145
  self-examination of, 60, 91, 99, 125
  theology and, 36
  worship and, 142–43
Hebrew, 12–13, 15, 17, 28, 41, 54, 107
hermeneutic, law-gospel, 40, 43, 62, 93
Herzog, Frederick, 5
heterodox(y), 15, 17–18, 20–21, 23, 25, 27, 30, 32–34, 48
Hinrichs, Carl, 7
Hoburg, Christian, 120, 176n12
Hogel, Zacharias, 24
holiness. *See* sanctification
Holl, Karl, 61
Holy Spirit. *See* Spirit, God the Holy
hope for better times. *See* chiliasm

Horb, Johann Heinrich, 15
Howard, Thomas Albert, 37
Hütte Christi. *See* Jesus Christ
hypocrisy, 87–88, 110, 127, 141
hypocrite (as sign), 123–24

idolatry, 37, 52–53, 95
ignorance (as sign), 124–26
image of God, 89, 96, 130
Incarnation. *See* Jesus Christ
India, 79
  See also Tranquebar
indwelling of God. *See* heart
institutes, Francke's. *See* Franckesche Stiftungen
Israel/Israelites, 69, 74, 83, 86–87, 121, 137–38
  See also Jew/Jewish

James I, King of England, 67
Jena, 22, 24, 26, 29
Jerusalem, 129, 139
  heavenly, 78
  Stiftungen as New, 48
Jesus Christ
  Ascension and, 77–78
  as redemptive representative
  baptismal covenant and, 88–89
  as baptismal pattern of the church, 74–80
  body and/or blood of, 39, 56, 65–66, 75, 90, 119, 122, 132
  bride of (*see* church)
  church and (*see* church)
  cross of, 39, 76–77, 89, 94, 121, 144
  Crucifixion, 75–77, 129, 132
  the Eucharist and, 131–32, 134
  Great Commission of, 72
  Hütte Christi, 139
  Incarnation, 76
  indwelling of (*see* heart)
  Kampf and (*see* Kampf)
  as kernel of Scripture (*see* Scripture)
  merits of, 43–44, 73, 84, 88, 90
  mystical participation in, 41
  Old Testament as pattern of, 73
  rebirth and, 73, 96, 147
  Resurrection, 76, 78
  reign of, 77–78 (*see also* chiliasm)
  return of, 7
  as second Adam, 76, 78
  tears of, 129–30 (*see also* tears)
  union with, 56, 90, 140, 145
  worship and, 137–40, 142–44
Jew/Jewish, 7, 49, 54, 73, 86, 91, 123, 139, 142
  See also Israel/Israelite

John the Baptist, 72, 91, 143
judgment, divine, 7, 56, 59, 77, 87, 112, 118, 121–22, 124–26, 131, 134, 142
See also wrath, divine
justification by faith, 15, 16, 19, 26, 30, 39, 44, 83, 88–89, 90, 94–95, 97, 101, 155n28

Kampf (spiritual), 121, 131–32
See also Bußkampf
Karant-Nunn, Susan, 7, 104–5
Kiel, 22, 56–57
Knapp, Johann Georg, 82
Kolb, Robert, 9
Könnern, 81–82
Kortholt, Christian, 22, 56
Kramer, Gustav, 15, 29
Kraut, Christian Friedrich von, 28

Labadie, Jean de, 5, 14
Lange, Joachim, 15
Lange, Nicolaus, 15–16
Large Catechism, 120
Latin, 13, 17, 19, 50–51, 65, 66
Laud, William, 67
law, divine, 15–16, 24–26, 43, 58–60, 62, 69, 93, 138, 156n33, 168n13
See also hermeneutic, law-gospel
law-gospel hermeneutic. See hermeneutic, law-gospel
Lebenslauf, 36, 42–43, 54, 82, 86
legalism, 4, 18, 26
Lehmann, Georg, 25
Lehmann, Harmut, 5–7
Lehmann, Roland, 2
Leibniz, Gottfried Wilhelm, 3–4, 47
Leipzig, 1–4, 12–27, 29–31, 33–34, 42, 46, 48, 49–52, 55, 69, 101, 107, 129
Lindberg, Carter, 36, 41, 46, 47, 94, 96
literature, devotional, 5, 6, 8, 56, 58, 60–62, 67
London, 21, 57
love
of creatures (see idolatry)
God's, 58, 75, 121, 133, 145–46
gospel and, 43
Great Commandment, 16, 45
passionate love, 121, 127, 133–34
spiritual enlightenment and, 41
toward Christ, 39, 82, 124, 132–33, 142
toward neighbor, 16, 45–46, 141
works of, 132, 141–42
worldly, 95, 97
Ludolf, Heinrich Wilhelm, 79
Lüneburg, 11, 13–15, 23, 37, 41–43, 48, 53, 55, 67
Luther, Martin

baptismal covenant and, 83–84, 99
baptismal exorcism and, 99
baptismal waters and, 65
church and, 9, 147
conscience and, 61–62
confession and, 103–6, 117, 146
eschatology and, 77
Eucharist and, 118, 120
fallen human nature and, 52
Large Catechism and (see Large Catechism)
new Reformation and, 20
personal study of Scripture and, 48
polemics and, 12
priesthood of all believers and (see priesthood of all believers, doctrine of)
Small Catechism and (see Small Catechism)
systematizing the theology of, 36
Lutheranism
American 147–48
reforming, 5, 13–14, 46, 50, 100, 106–7
Lutheran Orthodoxy. See Orthodoxy, Lutheran
Lutheran Pietism. See Pietism

Mader, Eric-Oliver, 43
magic, 100
Maid (as sign), 127–30
Mary, Magdalene, 129–30
Matthias, Markus, 2, 37, 40, 42–44, 93
Mayer, Johann Friedrich, 25–26
meeting(s), private. See conventicle(s)
Meinders, Franz, 28
Melanchthon, Philip, 1, 44, 84, 85, 99
memorial, 121
memorialism, 66
Mencke, Otto, 13
Meuselwitz, 22
McIntosh, Terence, 109
missions, 1, 48, 79, 81
Molinos, Miguel de, 13–14, 20, 133–34
morality, doctrine of, 18
Mori, Ryoko, 2, 4
Müller-Bahlke, Thomas, 81
Musaeus, Johannes, 43–44, 54
mysticism, 9, 13, 20, 101, 133–34

Nachfolger. See discipleship
nature, fallen human, 46, 50, 52, 70, 163n15, 163n16
See also sinfulness; unbelief
Naumann, Elias, 31–33
Neukölln, 28
Nevin, John Williamson, 148
new birth. See rebirth
new creation. See rebirth

New Jerusalem. *See* Jerusalem
Nicodemus, 93

oath, sacramental, 8, 63, 65–70, 81, 85, 87, 100
obedience, 16, 48, 65, 118, 132, 138
offering, confessional, 31, 104, 106, 108, 115–17
Olearius, Johann Christian, 29–31, 33, 116
ordo salutis. *See* salvation
Orsi, Robert, 2
Orthodoxy, Lutheran, 6, 24

Parousia, 7
Passover, 121, 128
pastor theologian, definition of, 11
Paul, the Apostle, 1, 76, 119, 122, 139–40
Peace of Westphalia, 6
Peasants Revolt, 26
Pelikan, Jaroslav, 9
Pennsylvania, 147
Pentecost, 77
perfectionism, 15–16, 20, 24–26, 55, 134
Perkins, William, 61–62, 152n27
Peschke, Erhard, 2, 14, 40–41, 42, 80, 99, 118, 135
Peter, the Apostle, 129
Peter the Great, of Russia, 79
Pharisaism, 123, 127, 164n24
Pietism
  as Bible movement, 6, 7
    characteristics of German Lutheran, 4–7, 152n22, 152n27
  confessional, 5, 152n33
  churchly/ecclesial, 5
  Franckesche Stiftungen and, 3–4
    as preaching movement, 7
  radical, 5, 20
  Reformed, 148
  as renewal movement, 6–7
  Spener as father of, 4
plan(s), reform, 4–6, 8, 45
polemics, theological, 4, 11–12, 13, 22–25, 29–30, 48, 68, 99
prayer
  baptismal covenant and, 89
  books, 142
  confession and, 106, 115
  Eucharist and, 124, 133
  meetings (*see* conventicle[s])
  Scripture and, 39, 41
  worship and, 138–40
preaching
  on the catechism, 8, 50, 52, 63–65, 85, 92, 133, 142, 144
  Christocentric, 81
  conscience and 58
  critique of Lutheran, 4, 19
  emotion and, 18
  empowerment by, 144
  fides ex auditu and, 41
  as means of grace, 23
  movement (*see* Pietism)
  Old Testament and, 123
  participation in, 138
  repentance and, 142–43
  sermon manuscript and, 8
predestination, 46–47
Predigt. *See* preaching
Predigerkiche, 22
priesthood of all believers, doctrine of, 4–6, 39, 96–97, 101
Puritan/Puritanism, 11, 50, 58, 60–63, 66–68, 98

Quaker/Quakerism, 25–26, 48, 63, 68–69
Quedlinburg, 28
Quietist/Quietism, 13–14, 20

radical Pietism. *See* Pietism
Rappotsweiler, 67
rationalism, 100, 147
rebirth (regeneratio)
  baptismal regeneration, 8–9, 73, 81–83, 92–102
  as characteristic of Pietism, 4, 6–7
  confession and, 112, 116
  conscience and, 58
  conversion and, 3, 14, 16, 44–45
  definition of, 6–7, 93–97, 171n58
  education and, 47
  Eucharist and, 122
  new creation and, 9, 44, 82, 93, 96
  perfection and (*see* perfectionism)
  renewal in Christ's image, 96
  repentance and, 98
  Satan and, 93, 97, 99
  Scripture and, 41, 93
  second rebirth, 93
  signs of, 9, 120
  social reform and, 46, 96
  transformation and, 76, 116
  Temple of God and, 96–97, 101, 140–41
  Trinity and, 72–73
  worship and, 9, 136–37, 141, 145–47
redemption, 73, 75, 132–33
reform, social, 45–48
Reformation, new or second, 18, 20–21
Reformation, the, 2, 3, 5, 37, 47
Reformed theology. *See* Calvinism
Reformed Pietism. *See* Pietism

reforming Lutheran(s). *See* Lutheranism
reform plan(s). *See* plan(s), reform
regeneration. *See* rebirth
reign of Christ. *See* chiliasm
renewal
   baptismal covenant and, 85–88, 101
   church and (*see* church)
   Eucharist and, 130
   Pietism and (*see* Pietism)
   rebirth and (*see* rebirth)
   Spener and, 92
repentance
   atheism and, 56
   baptismal covenant and, 84–85, 87, 90–92
   baptismal exorcism and (*see* exorcism, baptismal)
   Eucharist and, 120–21, 127, 130
   confession and, 106–8, 111–12, 115
   conscience and, 58, 60, 62
   faith and (*see* faith)
   rebirth and (*see* rebirth)
   Scripture and, 38, 43
   tears of (*see* tears)
   worship and, 138, 142–44, 146
repentance struggle. *See* Bußkampf
revelation
   conscience and, 58–59
   divine, 37–39, 47, 58, 93, 120
   personal, 34, 165n56
   signs and, 120–21
revival/revivalism, 7, 153n47
   See also Awakening, Great; Awakening, Second Great
Roman, 65
Rostock, 2, 56–57, 120
Roth, Albrecht Christian, 29–30, 34
Rublack, Christoph, 105
Rührung. *See* stirring, spiritual
Rumpel, Johann Heinrich, 159n3
Russia, 79

Sabbath, 109, 121–22, 142, 144
Sacraments
   ex opera operato, 92, 143, 147
   Lutheran understanding of, 2
Sagittarius, Caspar, 22, 26–27
salvation
   assurance or certainty of, 9, 14, 16, 45, 58, 82, 91, 95, 105, 113, 145–46
   baptismal covenant and, 85, 87–88, 90
   confession and, 110–11
   eternal life and, 18, 38, 84, 86, 91, 95, 101
   heart and, 62
   order of (ordo salutis), 15–16, 92, 140

   as process, 57–58
   Scripture and (*see* Scripture)
   signs of (*see* signs)
   synergism and, 14, 138
   as universal call, 46–47
   worship and, 138
sanctification, 6, 16, 19–20, 27, 38, 62, 66, 78, 97, 132, 135, 136, 143
   as godliness, 16, 18, 19, 30, 38, 44, 56, 62, 76, 93, 101, 119, 123
   as holiness, 15, 51, 66, 88, 123, 134, 142, 144
   See also perfectionism
Sandhagen, Kaspar Hermann, 14, 41, 54
Satan
   baptismal covenant and, 84, 87–90, 92–93, 97, 99
   baptismal exorcism and (*see* exorcism, baptismal)
   Francke association with, 17, 21
   hypocrisy and, 123
   oath against, 66, 100–101
   rebirth and (*see* rebirth)
   reign of, 46
   struggle against, 66, 131–32, 143
   tears and (*see* tears)
   temptations of, 131
   confession and, 104, 105
   worship and, 144
Sattler, Gary, 146, 148
Scaer, David P., 65
Schabbel, Heinrich, 12
Schabbel scholarship, 12, 14, 53, 56
Schade, Johann Caspar, 55, 107–9
Scharff, Heinrich Wilhelm, 11
Schicketanz, Peter, 6
Schmidt, Johann, 18
Schmidt, Martin, 7, 60, 92
Schmucker, Samuel Simon, 147–48
Schneider, Hans, 2, 6
Schrader, Christoph, 34
Schütz, Johann Jacob, 5–6
Schwärmer, 48, 68
   Schwenckfelder, 25
Scripture
   atheism and, 54, 57
   biblicism of the heart (*see* heart)
   and conventicles, 48
   and the Eucharist, 121
   exegesis of, 20–21, 24, 36, 72, 76
   husk/kernel interpretation of, 40, 79
   inspiration of, 37–38
   law-gospel hermeneutic (*see* hermeneutic, law-gospel)
   lectiones of, 40

Scripture (continued)
    personal reading of, 4–5, 18, 23, 39, 48, 125
    and prayer, 41
    preaching of, 64–65
    signs and, 118, 121
    sola/tota Scriptura, 37
Seckendorf, Veit Ludwig von, 22
second Reformation. See Reformation, new or second
Segneri, Paola, 13
self-awareness, 45
self-denial, 39
self-examination, 88–89, 94, 111, 118, 119, 121, 127
separatist/separatism, 5, 14, 19, 68–70, 139–40
sermon. See preaching
signs, visible
    of worthiness at Eucharist, 118, 126–34
    of unworthiness at Eucharist, 122–26
    of conversion/rebirth, 9, 14, 97, 119–20, 124, 144, 146
Simeon, 137–38
sinfulness
    confession and, 105, 112
    conscience and, 59, 61
    Eucharist and, 33, 128, 130
    personal experience of, 55–56, 82
    See also nature, fallen human; unbelief
Small Catechism, 8, 49, 64, 72, 76, 113–14, 142
social reform. See reform, social
Society for Promoting Christian Knowledge, 3
Sonthom, Emanuel, 61
sorrow, 43, 127, 129, 131, 140
soteriology, 15, 43, 135
Spener, Johann Jakob, 129–30
Spener, Philipp Jakob
    atheism and, 54–55
    baptism and, 76
    baptismal covenant and, 85
    baptismal regeneration and, 92–93, 98
    baptismal exorcism (see exorcism, baptismal)
    Berlin network of, 28
    church discipline and, 33
    confession and, 107–9, 113–14
    conscience and, 60
    conventicle work of, 5
    as father or cofounder of Pietism, 4–7
    Francke's Dresden visit of, 17
    lay piety and, 15
    perfectionism and, 16
    polemics and, 26, 50
    reform plan of, 4, 46
    sacraments and, 64–66
    Scripture and, 41
    visit to Leipzig, 13, 41–42
    worship and, 137
Spinks, Bryan, 83–84
Spinoza, Baruch, 53
Spirit, God the Holy
    baptism and, 72–79, 98–99
    church of the, 137–38
    fruit of, 97
    gifts of, 141
    indwelling of, 41, 88, 97, 137, 140–41, 144
    prayer and, 138
    preparation for sacraments and, 64
    school of, 114
    Scripture and, 40–41
    self-examination and, 60
    spiritual empowerment and, 16, 41, 90, 93, 145
    work of, 32, 41, 91, 95, 132, 137–38, 140
    worship and, 138, 143–44
spiritual ignorance. See unbelief
spiritual trials. See trial(s), spiritual
Stephens, W. P., 67
Stieber, Georg Friedrich, 176n12
stirring, spiritual, 44, 60, 62, 132
Stolterfoth, Johannes, 61
Sträter, Udo, 2, 4, 16, 60
Strom, Jonathan, 5–7, 42, 148
Stürmer, Christian, 81–82
subjectivism, 10
Sweden, 28

Taatz-Jacobi, Marianne, 28
Talmud, 54
Taufbund. See covenant, baptismal
tears, 121, 127–30, 143
Temple in Jerusalem, 137, 139
tentatio. See trial(s), spiritual
Thirty Years' War, 6
Thomasius, Christian, 22, 30, 100
three estates doctrine, 4, 139
Tranquebar, 79, 81
transformation, spiritual. See rebirth
transubstantiation, 68
trial(s), spiritual (Anfechtung)
    atheism and, 54–56
    Arndt and, 91
    doubt and, 16, 54–56, 91, 131
    Molinos and, 14
    patterned by Christ's baptism, 79
    rebirth and, 94–95
    school of
        Scriptures and, 39
        as tentatio, 120
tribulation, 76–77, 90, 141, 144

Trinity, 71–74
Trueman, Carl, 67
Tschirnhaus, Ehrenfried Walther von, 47

Ulrichskirche, 30, 35, 81
unbelief, 52–53, 55, 87, 91, 110, 121–23, 140
  See also nature, fallen human; *also* sinfulness

virgin (as sign), 119, 127, 130–33, 146
visitation, pastoral, 34, 112–23, 117, 120, 134
Vogler, Jacob, 31–33

Wahnglaube. *See* faith
Walch, Johann Georg, 53
Wallmann, Johannes, 5, 6, 14, 37, 67, 92
Ward, W.R., 9, 21, 47, 101
Weimar, 28

Wesley, John, 15
Westphal, Heinrich, 55
Whitefield, George, 148
Whitmer, Kelly, 3, 45, 47, 68
Winckler, Johann, 15
Witt, Ulrike, 41
women, Pietist, 26–27, 30, 32, 34
Word of God. *See* Scripture
worldliness, 45, 51, 66, 98–100, 123, 132
wrath, divine, 43, 66, 109, 112, 118, 121–22, 125, 142
  See also judgment, divine

Zeichen. *See* signs, visible
Zeller, Eberhard, 15, 20
Zinzendorf, Nicholas Ludwig von, 168n20
Zwingli, Huldrych, 66–67